Searching for God
in the Sixties

Searching for God in the Sixties

David R. Williams

DELAWARE

Newark: University of Delaware Press

Associated University Presses
2010 Eastpark Boulevard
Cranbury, NJ 08512

The paper used in this publication meets the requirements of the American National Standard for Permanence of Paper for Printed Library Materials Z39.48-1984.

Library of Congress Cataloging-in-Publication Data

Williams, David R. (David Ross), 1949–
    Searching for God in the sixties / David R. Williams.
        p.   cm.
    Includes bibliographical references and index.
    ISBN 978-0-87413-083-6 (alk. paper)
        1. United States—Church history—20th century.   I. Title.
BR526.W537   2010
277.3'082—dc22   2009022317

The spiritual history of the Sixties has yet to be written.
—Camille Paglia, *Sex, Art, and American Culture*

*The decade, alternately violent and sentimental, seems to me
now a Protestant flowering. The famous activists of the 1960s
were secular Jews who heralded a Messianic future. But the
true fathers of Woodstock, of sit-ins and of rock pastoral, were
the dark-robed Puritan fathers.*
—Richard Rodriquez, *Days of Obligation*

*The first Bush had been shaped by World War II. The second
Bush was a product of the 1960s, at times more in sync with
the attitudes of sixties radical Jerry Rubin than with those of
Winston Churchill.*
—Thomas Ricks, *Fiasco*

*To everything there is a season, and a time to every purpose
under the heaven. A time to be born, and a time to die; a time
to plant and a time to pluck up that which is planted; a time
to break down, and a time to build up.*
—Ecclesiastes 3:1–3

Contents

Acknowledgments

Wɪᴛʜᴏᴜᴛ ᴛʜᴇ ᴘᴇʀsɪsᴛᴇɴᴛ sᴜᴘᴘᴏʀᴛ ᴏꜰ ᴅᴏɴᴀʟᴅ ᴍᴇʟʟ ᴀᴛ ᴛʜᴇ ᴜɴɪᴠᴇʀ-sity of Delaware Press, this book would never have seen print. To his belief that I might have something worth adding to our national debate, I owe everything. But I also could not have gotten this far without a little help from such friends and critics as Roger Lathbury, Mark A. Fletcher, Meg Seling, Bruce Levy, John Heck, John Tallmadge, Stephen Ronan, and many students over many years in my course on the Sixties too numerous to mention whose encouragement and opposition kept me going.

No institution, including the university at which I work, did anything to assist in the research, writing, or publication of this book. This comes from the wilderness outside the combine. Because of that, it is dedicated to my son Sam Williams, my brother Paul Williams, founder of *Crawdaddy*, and my friend, Wayne "Beats the woods" Rodgers who with many others like them have kept the faith and continued to try to live free.

I am especially grateful to Robert Crumb for permission to use the cartoons that grace the cover and occasional spots within the book. All are Copyright © Robert Crumb, 2009 Used by permission, Agence Lit-téraire Lora Fountain & Associates, Paris, France

Parts of this book appeared previously in a chapter titled "Back to the Garden: The Liberation of the ID in the Antinomian Sixties," part of a book titled *From Virgin Land to Disney World: Nature and its Discontents in the America of Yesterday and Today*, Bernd Herzogenrath, ed., Editions Rodopi, NY, 2001.

The section on Emily Dickinson and Bob Dylan, originally titled "Dylan and Dickinson: American Poets of the Broken Heart," appeared in *Crawdaddy*, new #19, Spring, 1998, Paul Williams ed. It is here reprinted with permission.

The Zippy cartoon is reproduced through the kind permission of the artist, Bill Griffith. The "May I see your ID" panels are from an underground comic titled *The Kingdom of Heaven is Within You Comix* (Spring, 1969, Print Mint, Berkeley) put together with the help of Allen Ginsberg by John Thompson who kindly allowed me to use the reproduction.

The Emily Dickinson poem, "Finding is the First Act," which is the structure and heart of the book, is reprinted by permission of the publishers and the Trustees of Amherst College from THE POEMS OF EMILY DICKINSON, Thomas H. Johnson, ed., Cambridge, MA: The Belknap Press of Harvard University Press, copyright © 1951, 1955, 1979, 1983 by the President and Fellows of Harvard College.

Searching for God
in the Sixties

Finding is the first Act
The second, loss,
Third, Expedition for
The "Golden Fleece"

Fourth, no Discovery—
Fifth, no Crew—
Finally, no Golden Fleece—
Jason—sham—too.

Emily Dickinson, "Finding is the First Act"

Introduction

I

"The Mind's True Liberation"

To head forth on a great quest only to have that quest and, finally, the questing self crumble in its own corruption; to discover not only that the world is corrupt but that the very "I" which would be the vehicle of revolution is itself caught up in the web of that corruption; to break out of Egypt only to be—like the Children of Israel—lost in the wilderness far from the Promised Land; in these the children of the Sixties repeated patterns established by their parents' parents and theirs before them. Even in our moment of liberation we were caught on the wheel.

Forty years later, the Sixties remain shrouded in myth, demonization, and nostalgia. To young Americans, that decade is a stumbling block; to Republican conservatives, foolishness; but to aging baby boomers who once felt themselves called to respond, that era still recalls something dimly remembered of wisdom, righteousness, and redemption. Something happened still not understood, something greater than the mere political events, more universal than one generation's memory of its youth. The story of the American Sixties is a chapter in the ancient and continuing story of the quest of consciousness to be free from itself.

Forty years later, we remain divided. The 2004 presidential elections proved, to much confusion, that the fault lines of our history remained rigidly in place. The 2008 election suggests a tectonic shift back to where we once belonged. We tried, but we cannot escape our selves— or our past. Nor can our past escape its past. What erupted in the Sixties was a challenge, not just to the particular moral values of the older generation, but a challenge to the very ideas of rationality and morality. And this challenge was but the reawakening of an ancient battle. The debate over "moral values" today is mistaken when it sticks to particulars like gay rights, feminism, racism, torture, or dirty words on television. These are the particulars, but the theme that binds them is the very necessity of moral values. Should we be bound or should we be free? How free can we afford to be? We Americans have always walked a tightrope try-

13

ing to balance both, as Daniel Webster said, "Liberty and Union, now and forever." We have imagined ourselves "E pluribus unum"—both a "pluribus," 300 million individuals all freely doing our different things, and a "unum," one nation indivisible under law. Even our national hymn, "America the Beautiful," proclaims paradoxically that our "liberty is law."

Just before his election to the papacy in April of 2005, Pope Benedict XVI identified this very theme as the debate of our time. Speaking for the Catholic Church, the very epitome throughout western history of tradition, stability, morality, and law, he identified his enemy as "the tyranny of relativism." Doing so, he echoed the words of Pope Leo X responding to Martin Luther at the dawn of the Reformation and the modern world. On one hand was the tyranny of structure married to the secular powers of the world, embedded in systems, but stable and safe. On the other hand, the freedom of the spirit, the wind that bloweth where it listeth, total freedom to do as the heart wants without the logical head, that eternal spoilsport, questioning why, or some moral tyrant shouting "Thou shalt not!"

In 1841, in "Self Reliance," Ralph Waldo Emerson, that great American romantic, that champion of the relativistic freedom of the spirit, asked himself the pope's question: suppose these whims you follow are from below and not from God? His answer: "They do not seem to me to be such, but if I am the devil's child, I will live then from the devil. No law can be sacred to me but that of my nature. Good and bad are but names very readily transferable to that or this; the only right is what is after my constitution; the only wrong what is against it." If good and bad are but names, then "morality" as such does not exist and we are free to follow our passions. We can ignore the historical structures of rules and regulations and as the Doors sang "break on through to the other side."

Thus, the legacy of the Sixties that continues to divide us today is not the issue of gay rights or abortion but the issue of freedom. What is it? What does it mean to be free? What are the benefits and what the dangers? Most commentators still speak of the Sixties as if the issue, then and now, were narrowly political, or maybe sexual, or irresponsibly personal. But what that decade exposed was a continuing rift in the American soul, a rift between those who retain some vision of what it might—with all the risks—mean to be free, and those who have, like the Children of Israel who revolted in the wilderness, fled back to the security of slavery in Egypt.

In this, Bill Clinton was the quintessential baby boomer, following his passions and ignoring his head. Even Boomer-in-Chief George W. Bush, who rejected established rules and went with his gut, was more in tune with the radical rhythms of the Sixties than is the more rational and cautious Barack Obama, despite what conventional wisdom asserts. Bush appeared at times to have been swept along in an emotional panic; with Obama, we return to rational, systematic self-control. Obama, on the surface, at a merely skin-deep level, looks to be the fulfillment of the Sixties; he may instead prove to be the opposite, more a return to the cautious rationalism of the Eisenhower and Stevenson model, our first post–baby boomer president.

In this, the Sixties repeated a pattern that is at the very heart of our culture, a pattern that repeats the story of what it means to be American—and what it means to be free. This book examines its particular expression both in the American Sixties and in the dominant myths of American history. But this is not a uniquely American pattern. This pattern can be found throughout human history and found, not just in cultures, but also in every human heart.

The larger pattern into which the experience of the Sixties fits is this: we humans swing back and forth, as individuals and as historic communities, between two extremes: between the security of structure and the exhilaration of freedom from structure, between our desire to be in control and our desire to let go and flow with the tides of the universe. On the side of security and control is our existence as particular rational identities in the world; on the other is the larger context in which our particular beings move and have life. These two needs stand at opposite extremes; the paradox is that we need both. We need the freedom to be ourselves, whatever that might mean, but we also need the security provided by the structures of community and morality. The romantic radical within us wants to be free of what Joan Didion calls "wagon train morality," all the inherited social codes of culture and religion. But the traditionalists like Didion are not wrong to point out the dangers inherent in such moral anarchy. We would be free of all the restricting grids; but we need them to survive. They arose for a reason; we should not abandon them lightly. Thus, unable to find that elusive place somewhere safely in the middle, we swing back and forth between freedom and structure.

The rational brain answers our need for structure, our need to control and to force reality into line, to create generalities that we can then call "truth." But the mind also longs to escape from those very structures, to break out of rationality's cages and let the emotions run free. Logic is the tool of structure; but emotions are the fire that deconstructs it. Morality is the word we use for the ultimate structures of belief; to be outside of structure is to be in a wilderness, that void outside the text, but a wilderness that, if we can survive the crossing, might lead us to Zion, the Promised Land of true vision. Through different myths and by different names, this duality has been with us always—from Apollo and Dionysus, to Egypt and Zion, the Classic and the Romantic, the establishment and the movement, the head and the heart, left-brain logic and right-brain intuition, social constructivism and essentialism, the arminian and the antinomian—and, in the Star Trek characters of Spock and McCoy, Data and Troy, this duality continues its voyage into the far and distant future. It also continues to command the very heart of our popular culture. "Egypt" is the Matrix. If we are to abandon illusion and seek Zion, we must each become a Neo and be prepared to "light out" for the wilderness.

Nor is this simply a right-wing/left-wing political distinction. The parties are coalitions of interest groups, not consistent philosophical schools. Even within the Republican Party, laissez-faire libertarians clash with those who would use government power to control individual behavior. Even among the Democrats, the desire to control "immoral" economic behavior sits in contrast to a desire to let individual liberty run free. Each party embodies this conflict within itself. The bold and, some say, reckless George Bush seems more a child of the antinomian Sixties than the rational and cautious Obama. Bush follows his heart and trusts his instincts; Obama, like Kerry before him, wants to rely on traditional structures of international stability. Which is the conservative? Which the radical?

An enduring characteristic of American history, this duality was there at the beginning; it is with us yet in repeated instances of generations awakening to the fact of their imprisonment in structure, then breaking free, and then ultimately carrying their freedom over the border into madness before pulling back. The Fifties present a classic example of a period of rational, conservative structure, the "time to build up" after the chaos of the Depression and the world war; the Sixties represent one of those moments of awakening and escape, the "need to break down" that which had become too structured and too oppressive. But this pattern has a long history that well predates the twentieth century. To understand it, and to put it in its proper context, we need to consider its origins, at least its origins in our American culture.

II

philosophy and logic which are of the devil

This duality was first powerfully expressed in our earliest crisis of cultural identity, in the Antinomian Crisis of 1636. In that episode, the Puritan patriarchs of Boston, accused of being logical, rational, unspiritual arminians, banished the mystic antinomian, the first American hippie,

1. *Zippy.* "The social constructed vs the essential self." Courtesy of Bill Griffith.

Anne Hutchinson, into the wilderness. They had come to America to build a spiritual community that adhered to the moral laws of scripture as they interpreted them. Hutchinson, instead, followed the freedom of the spirit as she felt it in her heart and refused to follow external laws laid down by those not touched by the spirit. The patriarchs feared that such rebelliousness, based on her subjective perception of truth, would, if it spread, destroy their infant community. They had come to the New World seeking freedom from persecution themselves. They were, they imagined, the high tide of a worldwide movement of rebels trying to break out of the repressive structures of the past. But from the very start, they were painfully aware that while stepping outside of structure held the promise of liberation, going too far too fast also posed the threat of annihilation. They wanted freedom, but they feared anarchy. They wanted to become their own true selves, but they also feared that the true self, once revealed, might be Satan and not Christ. They were willing to open up slowly to the spirit within, but they did so in fear and trembling. Afraid on one side of their emotions, they also feared falling once again into false belief—or returning to Egypt and mistaking it for Zion. As one New England preacher, Jonathan Mitchell, lamented, "I shall never know God for mine in truth, but live and die in an unsound and self-deceiving way: that I should have many fears and prayers, and good affections, and duties and hopes and ordinances and seemings, but . . . never have God's special love revealed and assured to me! Lord, Keep this fear alive in my heart!" As much as they wanted salvation, they feared even more that salvation would cause them to embrace "seemings," another illusion created by the "Old Deluder" to deceive them.

They thus recoiled from the mystic's unrestrained plunge into the emotional waves. These uptight English white males wanted love, but they were afraid of their own emotions. Their arminian heads distrusted their antinomian hearts. But they also knew how destructive reliance upon mere works could be. While the Puritan fathers accused Hutchinson of being an ecstatic antinomian, someone who lived outside all law, she accused them of being rigidly logical arminians who still followed a popish covenant of works. Both sides had a point.

The word "arminian" derives from a Dutch theologian named Jacob Arminius, who argued—against the more radical theologians of the early 1600s—that the Bible was most importantly a guide to morality, that salvation was a reward for good behavior, that externals count, that human beings could control themselves—a position sometimes referred to as moralism. Arminian thinking stems from a need for order, from the struggle for survival in a hostile world. It assumes that we humans can know the truth through the rigorous use of intellect and thereby act as the Universe wishes. The analytical mind is a tool for arminian control. It imposes structures of meaning on both the external world and the unruly self. It breaks and domesticates the wild broncos of the soul. The rational head in control of the lesser members of the passionate body is an aristocratic imposition of structure from the top down in an attempt to control its lesser members. In psychological terms, it is anality. In theoretical terms, it is what once was called "rationalism" but today we call "modernism."

In its normal occurrences, arminian rationalism is a necessary tool of human survival. In normal human development, a necessary process that Freud called repression allows the rational mind to restrain the irrational impulses of the body. But carried to its most extreme, arminian rationalism becomes anal-compulsive and totalitarian. Hitler's propaganda movie "Triumph of the Will," a good example of the affinity between order and will power, expressed the belief that the rational will must control the irrational. The Nazis saw all the mysteries of Jerusalem, of the Old Testament, and the Torah as symbols of this irrationality. Marxist societies, with their emphasis on central control, obedience, and conformity are also rigidly arminian. The Victorians had nothing on the sexual repression of Chinese Communist society. Joseph Campbell, the scholar of human mythology, told us that Darth Vader, the Lord of the Dark Side, is a symbol of the "intellectual side" attempting to control the free flow of life.

G. Gordon Liddy, whose politics come as close as those of any modern American to being fascist, once held his hand over a flame to demonstrate how much self-control he had. His autobiography, *Will*, shares with Hitler's propaganda an admiration for the rational mind's ability to control the body. The military, too, exemplifies these arminian traits. Trained to be defensive, soldiers are necessarily watchful, alert, suspicious, expected to stay mentally sharp, to obey quickly, to respect authority, to stay clean, and to be in complete control. Arminians tend to follow and defend the given constructions of society, politics, and mind. They do not trust their emotions, but depend upon their intellects. They believe in control. They defend law and order. They help us survive.

The term "antinomian," at the other extreme, literally means "against or beyond the law." It is thus against moralism and opposed to any obedience to legal codes of external morality, codes that antinomians dismiss as mere "works," that they condemn as insincere rituals, utterly meaningless and utterly phony. Salvation, said the Protestant reformers, is not by works but by faith, not by ritual behavior but by the true spirit within. Those who have the spirit do not need the law. Antinomianism is the theology of people who believe that, since they somehow feel God within, they are truly sincere and do not need the discipline of external codes of behavior. Unlike the anxious, repressed arminians, antinomians are filled with self-confidence, with hope, with joy. They reject the logic-chopping brain and let their feelings flow. They do not try to exercise control, but imagine that life controls them. Believing that their unre-pressed emotions come from whatever righteous force it is that runs the universe, they believe the impulses of the self can be entirely trusted. Like Luke Skywalker removing his helmet and trusting "the force," they let rational self-control go and abandon themselves to the flow of their feelings. They go beyond social rules and what they perceive as the arti-ficial constructions of the world. They reject intellectual formulations that assume to know truth and instead let themselves be led by what they imagine as some mystic force that they feel within their own con-sciousness. When God himself is the source of one's desires, then any self-control is an affront to God, and rational codes of morality are the anti-Christ, or Devil. Cotton Mather colorfully quotes an antinomian Quaker who attacked logical Puritans like himself, the Quaker shouting: *"Thou hedge hog and grinning dog; thou bastard that tumbled out of the mouth of the babilonish baw; thou mole; thou tinker; thou lizard; thou bell of no metal but the tone of a kettle; thou wheelbarrow; thou whirlpool; thou whirlegig. O thou firebrand, thou adder and scorpion; thou louse; thou cow-dung; thou moon-calf; thou ragged tatterdemalion; thou Judas; thou livest in philosophy and logick which are of the devil."*

Antinomians like this wild-eyed Quaker are libertine hippies, beyond order, beyond structure, beyond control, whose desire is to let the spirit within hang out, and to hell with "logick"! When in 1636 the arminian-leaning magistrates of Boston tried to reason with Anne Hutchinson and convince her that her truth was a deception from the Devil, not in ac-cord with Scripture and Calvinist dogma, she replied, "I seek not for graces but for Christ, I seek not for promises but for Christ, I seek not for sanctification but for Christ, Tell me not of meditation and duties but tell me of Christ." I don't want definitions of love, or signs of love, or promises of love, she emotes, I want not words but the real thing. No more the repression, no more the pretending, no more the lies of armin-ian rationalization, I want love.

The arminian need to keep it all tucked in and under control, on the other hand, is reflected in a string of corresponding characteristics: ra-tionality, cleanliness, fear, hierarchy, and conservative politics. It is often thought of as the defining characteristic of maleness. Where arminians are tight-assed, antinomians are loose as the proverbial goose. Where arminian cleanliness is a sign of order, antinomians let the dirt fall where it may. Where arminians are rational, wordy, and exercise masculine control, antinomians are emotional, living on feeling—hence romantic, long haired, flower-bedecked, and associated with the feminine.

Thus, our arminian brains try to seize and keep control. They put experience into words, as if that somehow gives us control, as if knowing the name of a flower tells us any more about it than we know by sight and smell. It doesn't. But words give us the power of naming and help us feel as if we are in control. And so our brains classify and generalize until we have surrounded ourselves with a model of experience, a cage made out of words in which we feel secure and in charge. Our arminian need to generalize is, in Freudian terms, anal-compulsive. It is rationality attempting to protect us from a hostile environment. Like social, political, and architectural structures, these structures of the mind help our weak bodies survive. We view reality from within these structures. And what we see and call real are in fact projections of the beliefs of these constructions. The arminian male, no matter how lost, refuses to ask directions because he needs to believe he is in control. As the Sixties philosopher Norman O. Brown said, "The world is the veil we spin to hide the void."

Meanwhile, our antinomian hearts burst with a desire not to control but to break out of the arminian cage and flow with the deep turbulent flood, to become one with experience, to escape from these complex superstructures of rationality, to return to the sea's wet embrace. When we sense the falsehood of our supposed beliefs, we long to return to that which feels real and true within us. We want not more rationalizing but the experience of the true ground of our being, the essential force we feel must underlie our constructions. This is the romantic, the Dionysian, the mystic, the antinomian, the longing for love. In today's jargon, social constructionists represent arminian belief in the inevitability of structure; there is, they say, nothing outside the text. Essentialists disagree. Both are right.

In a cultural context, these two extremes reflect a world of distinctions found in politics, literature, religion, gender stereotyping, and human personality. Our history is a pendulum that swings from periods of arminian control to antinomian excess and back again, from structure to rebellion back to structure again. The transition from the Fifties to the Sixties therefore fits a pattern that is at once both profoundly personal and richly historic.

Why, then, if the Sixties were a repetition of an enduring pattern within American culture, did that moment pass away so quickly? Why did it begin? Why did it happen? Why did it end? Why did it fail?

Our personalities are not born fully realized within us but are shaped by the circumstances of the environments in which we are raised. Therefore we all unavoidably inherit the prejudices and the promises of our families and our cultures. This is a truism restated in different ways in every generation. That we are shaped by the contingencies of our total environment, that we are so precisely the products of time and place and gender and all the rest, means that we are, as Shakespeare said, each an actor on the stage, each playing a role. That there is a "we," a central perceiving consciousness, inside each person means that "we" are trapped in cultural cages that, from moment to moment, we cannot even see, much less see out of. It is as if after we were born, we were given virtual-reality helmets already programmed for us. It is as if the reality we think we inhabit were the product of this preset program. To escape from the social programming of the virtual-reality dream; to awake out of the "matrix" and be for the first time truly free of all the shams and lies: that is the goal of the expedition of consciousness.

One of the purposes of humanistic studies is to help us know ourselves. Our individual personalities are the creation of all of the many influences, from the biological to the environmental, that shape our development. Taken together, all of these influences make up what we call culture. Because literature reflects the cultures of our pasts and serves as a window on those pasts, the analysis of literature, or what is called literary criticism, provides one means by which we can examine the subtle processes of our enculturation. History likes to think itself a science, but in many ways it is also a branch of literature, an art as much as a discipline, made up of stories and hopes and dreams as much as facts.

These songs, poems, and histories, all of the stories of our past, are more than mere historical curiosities; they also shaped our grandparents and our parents and, through them, us. Our texts are, therefore, both evidence of our cultural constructions *and* the system through which those constructions have been transferred to—and reinforced in—each new generation. We analyze these texts to reveal the many aspects of the cultural roles, the cages in which we are trapped. We can see in our culture's ancient texts the origins of the programming of our virtual-reality helmets. By studying the past, we learn part of the process that made us who we are.

But we must remember, as we do so, that each analysis learned is but another subjective, constructed dream. The mindsets with which we deconstruct our dreams are also dreams, themselves in need of deconstructing. When we try to look ourselves in the eye or the "I," we are always caught in the infinite regression of trying to step outside of ourselves but taking some part of ourselves with us at every step. Each lifting of the virtual-reality helmet reveals another underneath through which we perceive the lifting of the first. We cannot step outside ourselves and objectively behold the "I" that is at the core of our consciousness; we cannot watch ourselves watching ourselves, for there is always another step backward needed in order to watch the watcher. At best, we chase our tails like the squirrel on the wheel in a cage. We can only escape from smaller cages into larger ones. Yet we dare not rest even there. As Scripture warns, "Woe to them that are at ease in Zion" (Amos 6:1).

III

"You never know what vision has been humping you through the night."

The Fifties were just such complacent years, at ease in the Zion of their defensive security; the Sixties were one of those periodic attempts to escape from the cage. But if the Fifties were a decade of security and control and the Sixties a period of liberation from that control, even that liberation was only relative. At best, it was a change from a more restrictive to a less restrictive cage. At the time, it was not evident; but looking back at the era, we can now begin to see the larger patterns that controlled us. We can begin to see how the rebellion against structure itself followed an historically structured if less visible pattern. For one of the most enduring legacies of American history and our religious past is a model of transformation that allows us to change and grow, a model that acknowledges the cage but provides a means to break out of it.

The literature we value most from any era is that in which we see the efforts of a very few writers who struggle against this encagement, who try to free themselves from all their cages and look with clear eyes at our condition and our conditioning, at the deep myths that control us. James Baldwin said it best: the role of the writer, the truly great writer, is to "help to excavate the buried consciousness of this country." Because, as his friend Norman Mailer put it, "You never know what vision has been humping you through the night."

However, what humps you may not be what humps me. In this book I will build a model of meaning for the Sixties in order to understand the events of that decade within a pattern that is coherent, if not for everyone then at least for me. I confess it. To claim that my interpretation is anything more than my own interpretation would be to say more than any one of us can honestly say. But we do not have to pretend to believe that we are objective. We can say, "This is what I see; this is what the world looks like from my particular perspective." Not that it is "True" in some absolute, arminian sense, but that it is what I or we have been programmed to believe and is the deepest layer of programmed belief I can get to. Nor is there anything new in this. Generations East and West have repeated the tale of the blind men, each of whom had hold of a different part of the elephant. One holding the tail claimed that an elephant is like a rope; one touching the ear said it is more like a huge leaf; a third at the trunk said it is a kind of snake; a fourth, grabbing a foot, said no, it is really like the trunk of a tree. Each was wholly blind and only partly right, but their combined false perceptions got closer to the truth of the elephant than did any one of them alone. Any of us blind men who thinks that what we feel is the total truth needs to have his constructions deconstructed. But once we have accepted our mutual contingency, we can at least report on what we seem to see, as long as we remember that it is only "seeming."

Academic discourse is presently dominated by the realization that human beings inhabit separate loci of experience and have different perceptions of reality, and that these perceptions are shaped by contingencies like race, class, and gender. Every interpretation, even this one, serves someone's self-interest. Thus, any attempt to generalize about the part of the elephant we hold is seen as an attempt to order the world according to the language and contingencies of personal conditioning, and little more. Generalizations are by their very nature false and tend to serve the self-interest of whoever is creating the generalization. History, as feminists like to say, is only "his story." Yet such stories, someone's stories, are also unavoidable and necessary. Hence the paradox: all generalizations are false, even this one. To spread a cloak of meaning over the Sixties is to generalize, to force a personal construct, a self-serving sense of order, upon the decade. All generalizations and constructs are arminian lies, yet we need those lies; we cannot live without them. As Kurt Vonnegut says in *Cat's Cradle*, "Anyone who does not understand how a useful religion can be founded on lies will not understand this book either."

Just as we need the grid, or the structures like our bodies that sustain us, we cannot understand the past unless we understand its lies. It is when we discover that our own beliefs are also lies that we yearn to escape again from the cage. Once we realize that what we thought was real is only the programming of our virtual-reality helmets, then we can no longer bear to wear them. And yet we always view the world through virtual lenses of some sort. We are thus torn between the intolerable necessity of structure and a doomed rebellion against it. Like Huck Finn, we can stand neither the corruption of human culture on the shore nor the lonesomeness on the flowing river, and so we beat back and forth between the two extremes trying to find a home we can be at truth in.

From the greatest imaginable perspective, all of the beliefs of the world are false, all social constructions self-serving illusions, all dogmatic statements of belief lies, all pride in human achievements idolatry:

"vanity, vanity, all is vanity." Yet we humans do not live in anything even close to that highest imaginable perspective. We live in the fallen world of lies and illusion and vanity—as the movie called it, a "matrix" in which we innocently believe our own beliefs. Whether capitalist, communist, Christian, Muslim, Buddhist, deconstructionist, nihilist, or essentialist, we each have our particular security blanket of words and feelings. We need beliefs even to get up and get dressed in the morning. We live in the particularity of the fallen world even in those rare moments when we are aware of the universality of the absolute perspective that stands in condemnation of our illusions. The relativism that has dominated intellectual life in America since the Sixties has valid origins. No one knows what is really going on.

Unable to browse contentedly like India's holy cows, we humans strive for knowledge and control and generalities that unify, which then become the truths that become our cages. In this way, we have created the cultural cages of the fallen world. This urge to generalize is as natural as breathing, as unavoidable as sin. Perhaps in our paleolithic past, survival depended on the ability to generalize; perhaps the need to huddle together under a cloak of meaning is an evolutionary conservative urge rooted in the fear of the unknown corners of the cave.

We thus have two poles of consciousness in our bipolar brains, in our gender conditioning, and in our cultural works. The arminian need for order and structure may be anal-compulsive, macho, and conservative, but it is still a necessary part of life. To be clear, to be clean, to be in control, to know, are all aspects of it. But the antinomian urge to free ourselves from structure, the desire to turn off the brain's controls and let the waters of the soul break through the dam and drown rationality in sensual experience is what liberates us. In the baptism of the breaking of those waters, we would be born again.

These two extremes compete within us like the Ishmaels and Ahabs of our souls. We desire neither surrender nor complete command, neither anarchy nor totalitarianism, but both, in some degree of freedom and control, liberty and union. We need both the security of traditional community and the freedom of our millions of separate selves; we need both "unum" and "pluribus." We need to generalize so that the rational mind can build defenses for the self; but we also need to break free from the cage of cultural conditioning so that we can see ourselves behaving and force ourselves to change.

Arminian control is eventually overthrown by an antinomian revolution, but antinomian excess eventually forces a return to arminian control. When structure becomes oppressive, we must question everything, or as the postmodernists like to say, "problematize" it. But when we pass out of sight of land and leave the literal behind, we approach the nihilism of madness. If the text is all we know, then to deconstruct the text too deeply is to back out of rationality into the void. If everything is relative, then there is no truth, no values, no good, no bad; and thus, as Melville said, we lose our identity, and "over Descartian vortices" we hover. So we swing back and forth between the two poles, order and freedom, the literal and the abstract, propelled forward by the pulsating energy thus generated. Like a sailboat heading into the wind, we advance not by tying down the helm but by tacking back and forth between port and starboard. Having sailed as close to the antinomian rocks as I dare, I have chosen to tack to port. And in the wake of the terrorist attacks of 9/11, I am not alone.

This book, then, will not be an effort to break down and deconstruct but to build up, to reconstruct, to impose a structure of significance, if only my own, a meaning for the Sixties—and then fit that structure into the larger patterns and structures of the American experience itself. That such presumptuousness ultimately must be undone is a given. This too shall pass, and a time to break down shall come again. That there are dangers in any attempt to generalize, I would be the last to deny. Ultimately, both sides of the spectrum are false, each only a partial truth. All discourses are, as the postmodernists say, just discourses, equally without foundation. Some dislike the older discourse of Christianity and prefer a Marxist or post-modern jargon instead. For them, to paraphrase George Orwell on Marxist hypocrisy, all discourses are equal, but some discourses are more equal than others. I make no apology for the discourse I use; it too is part of the diversity of the American experience.

This then is what the Sixties look like to me. If my generalities harm anyone, I am sorry, but I have no choice. Between sin and silence, I will follow Martin Luther's advice and "Sin boldly!"

IV

These disturbances that have come among the Germans have been all grounded on revelations, and so they that have vented them have stirred up their hearers to cut the throats one of another, and these have been the fruits of them, and whether the devil may inspire the same into their hearts I know not. For I am fully persuaded that Mrs. Hutchinson is deluded by the devil.

—Gov'r John Winthrop

This interpretation of the American Sixties must begin with Luther, for Luther's religious Reformation in the sixteenth century set the dominant pattern in motion. The line from Martin Luther to Martin Luther King Jr. is direct and clear and not just a coincidence of name. For it was Martin Luther, and the Protestant Reformation, that first began to define the metaphor of transformation that inspired Martin Luther King and made the entire Sixties experience possible. The political, social, and intellectual movements of the Sixties arose from the minds of people already shaped by the forces of their very peculiar cultures. Although the expectations of the new generation clashed with the institutions of the older generations, both were products of an American historical and cultural context. Both were shaped within a similar American mold. To understand the full picture of the Sixties requires a larger understanding of that mold and the forces that created it.

However unjustly, the WASP tradition has continued to dominate the national discourse. As the existence of an anachronism such as the academic field of "ethnic studies" shows, Americans of any ethnic background still tend to think of Anglos, or WASPs, as "Americans" and others as "ethnics." The language and values of that Anglo mainstream are still our dominant form of discourse. This is not to say that they should be, but that they are. If we are to free ourselves from the past, we have to understand that past, what it is in us, how it got in us, how it controls us, and why it arose in the first place. Centuries of cultural evolution are embedded in us. However much we might want to, we cannot turn and pretend they are not there. Like it or not, we in the United States need to study the implicit "civil religion" that is a product of this WASP mainstream.

The founding of the English colonies in North America was a result of the European Reformation, a movement begun in the 1500s and led by men like Martin Luther and John Calvin who wanted to create the foundations for a freer and better world by replacing the feudal collectivisms of Europe with an individualistic polity. In the early 1600s, the highest tide of this movement swelled across the Atlantic and washed up onto the shores of the New World. This Reformation was but one in a long line of awakenings that attempted to tear down the old ideological structures and to rebuild the world from scratch. The language and the metaphors these reformers used spoke not just of reform but of radical change, and the institutional constructs that arose from their efforts contained the seeds of a culture with an identifiable strain committed to radical transformation. For this reason, Michael Walzer wrote in *The Revolution of the Saints* that these men were the predecessors of Lenin.

The theologians of the Reformation, like today's social constructionists, also believed that worldly personalities were constructions and not essential. Their word for the falseness of the human texts, or paradigms, or virtual-reality illusions we each inhabit, was "worldliness." When they used this term, they meant that all of the things of worldly reality, politics, culture, family, even the very self, are illusory constructs, contingent upon the accidental circumstances of worldly events. Because our beliefs are based upon the accidents of birth and circumstance, at bottom we cannot justify them. Because our personalities, our identities, are made up of contingent beliefs we have no real foundation under our feet. To express the idea that there was no essential grounding in which they could trust, the theologians said, "We cannot be justified in ourselves." Their understanding of the way in which personality and consciousness are shaped by contingencies was expressed in the language of predestination. Human constructs, they said, are an illusion: all is but a text. "All we conceive concerning God in our own minds is an insipid fiction," said Calvin. People who think they are worshipping God "are worshipping not God but a figment and a dream of their own heart," for "the human mind," he explained, "is a perpetual factory of idols," nothing more.

Unlike the current postmodern theorists, however, these theologians never proclaimed that nothing existed outside that text. They believed in a truth, an ultimate reality, but they believed it was unknowable, beyond human comprehension. They called this unknown but ultimate reality "God," and they knew Him not as an answer, but as a mystery. They knew him not as a comforting presence but as a profound absence experienced only in those terrifying moments in which they managed to escape the cages of worldliness and to stare into the void that exists beyond our human texts. They named this terror the "Fear of God," and they sought to lose themselves to it. Out of this crucifixion of worldly illusion, they hoped they might receive a new perception, a new sense of essential truth, a rock upon which they could build new and better constructs. Trusting neither the head nor the heart, they went into the spiritual wilderness and waited for the revelation of a new truth, a new perception of reality, which they called "Christ."

Their greatest fear was that they would accept one of the many temptations of the "old deluder," their name for Satan, and fall to some variation of the matrix and forget that it is but a virtual and not the ultimate reality. This is why Cotton Mather, in his *Magnalia*, quotes approvingly Jonathan Mitchell's prayer that "I shall never know God for mine in truth, but live and die in an unsound and self-deceiving way: that I should have many fears and prayers, and good affections, and duties, and hopes, and ordinances, and seemings." Wanting truth, true love, but fearing the wiles of the old deluder, they preferred to be left in the howling wilderness of terror rather than tricked into mistaking some pleasant oasis for what Calvin had called the "Kingdom of Freedom."

What these reformers wanted was nothing less than a change in human nature and human culture from the old false constructions to some new way founded upon essential and authentic truth, reality! They wanted to see human nature transformed so that greed and selfishness and brutality could be eliminated and a utopia of righteousness prevail. They had no illusions that rational argument could do any more than produce superficial, temporary adjustments in behavior. Logic was at best a useful expedient for getting along within the old matrix. Nor did they imagine that simply changing the external social environment would make saints out of sinners and bring truth out of falsehood. For true social change to occur, it had to come from the bottom up, it had to come from the people—not the elite. And for people to change, the radical restructuring of the human individual also had to come from the bottom up, from the heart, not the elitist head. The pattern they embraced for achieving such personal and historical change eventually became the pattern that shaped and defined the events of the Sixties.

Before Martin Luther, the prevailing philosophy ruling Europe had been that of a rigid hierarchy of conservative stability. At the time of the Reformation, Catholic Europe was arminian to the core. From the feudal manor, where the authority of the local lord was largely unquestioned, to the emerging nation-state backed by the authority of the Roman Catholic Church, the ruling paradigm was Thomas Aquinas's Great Chain of Being. This static universe imagined God at the top and authority coming from Him down through the church, from the church through secular authority, from the local authorities to the peasantry. Each person looked not to himself or herself, or even to the community, but to the person directly above in the chain. The international elite even read and spoke to each other in a separate language, Latin, while the peasants communicated in the vulgar languages of their separate regions. This was a reflection of the rigidity of the social hierarchy. Neither owning property nor able to read, conceived of as barely able to think, those peasants on the bottom were passive recipients of orders from above. They were isolated from the sources of authority and taught to believe that the gentry and clergy were superior beings, that they themselves were as inferior to those beings as their dogs and cattle were to them. It was a static world in which an absolute God ruled through fixed temporal authorities, in which ordinary people were too weak and sinful to even speak up, and in which change was inconceivable.

Luther brought to this rigidly ordered world one great revolutionary insight: that authority comes not from the top down, but from the bottom up, socially and personally; not from the pope or king but from the people; and not from the head but from the heart. In politics and church government, the implications were obvious. The medieval hierarchy was directly threatened by a movement that challenged its right to rule. Denouncing Luther, Holy Roman Emperor Charles V declared, *"This devil in the habit of a monk has brought together ancient errors into one stinking puddle, and has invented new ones. He denies the power of the keys, and encourages the laity to wash their hands in the blood of the clergy. His teaching makes for rebellion, division, war, murder, robbery, arson, and the collapse of Christendom. He lives the life of a beast."*

The pope as head of the church, and the king as head of the state, each had reason to fear the idea that authority did not really flow from the top down. No sooner had Luther preached that faith alone justified them, then peasants, seizing on these ideas, proclaimed themselves touched by the spirit of faith and justified in rebellion. The revolutionary anarchy of the peasant revolts that broke out at the start of the Reformation were clear evidence that Luther's ideas were dangerous to the state.

Moreover, the Reformation's challenge to the authority of the head was not just a political or ecclesiastical challenge to the rational structures of the state and society; it also challenged rationality itself. "Sola fides," "Faith alone," was the slogan of the Reformation. Luther translated the Bible into German so that ordinary people could be touched directly by God's word and experience this faith that was, in Luther's formulation, a mystic state far superior to the political one. It existed in the hearts of the believers. The logical constructions of the scholastics, which had for centuries buttressed the structures of authority, were challenged not by a new logic or more rational argument, not by a better reading of the Bible, but by a mysticism said to flow through Scripture. And because it was mystical experience and not rational knowledge, this faith did not require that its recipients know Latin or even be able to read. It did not require that they be members of the gentry; any person could be chosen. Within society, the lower orders no longer had to defer automatically to their superiors. And within each convert, if ideas of the head argued with feelings of the heart, then the heart no longer had to defer to the head. "Sola fides" brought to the fore in Christianity the idea that the human heart could be the means through which the individual could be in direct communication with God. On this foundation, Luther proclaimed the possibility of a priesthood of all believers.

Taking Luther's ideas further than Luther imagined, John of Leyden spread the word that the coming of Christ's grace into the hearts of believers freed those believers from the rule of law. He passed beyond abstract virtual possibility, beyond theory and theology, and proclaimed that the coming of the Lord was a physical reality. At the city of Muenster in 1535, eighteen years after Luther had nailed his ninety-five theses to the church door at Wittenburg, John of Leyden declared all worldly institutions, including marriage, abolished by the coming of the Holy Spirit. His followers believed they had access to a truth, a spirit that needed no human law, a love that would create utopia now, here, not in some distant ethereal realm. They established what they imagined was the Kingdom of God on earth, a perfect utopian communism, run by a committee of public safety called "the elders of the twelve tribes of Israel," with John of Leyden as the "King of Israel."

Nor was this a solitary example. Radicals like John of Leyden presided over an outbreak of antinomian anarchy that terrified a Europe not ready for such radical individualism. The peasant rebellions had their origins in economic and political grievances that began long before the Reformation. But, as one historian put it, Luther's "gospel of Christian liberty proved a mighty solvent. For the spiritual freedom which he taught, multitudes substituted freedom from political oppression, from social injustice and from economic burdens. Like heady wine, the reading of the Bible exalted and intoxicated them, leading not to revolution but to absolute anarchy."

Luther himself was appalled by what he considered too literal a reading of the spiritual text. He denounced the peasants' translation of the spiritual freedom he imagined into a worldly political freedom. Such a reading, he thundered, "would make all men equal, and turn the spiritual kingdom of Christ into a worldly, external kingdom, and that is impossible." The love-in ended only after the local princes, with Luther's blessing, sent in their soldiers and slaughtered the inhabitants. The rebellious peasants of Muenster were classic antinomians rejecting traditional rules and structures to follow the Reformation's belief in faith alone. In this, and in their bloody end, they foreshadowed Charlie Manson's family. Like the participants of so many awakenings to follow, including that of the Sixties, they rejected established tradition to follow the new faith of their romantic hearts. They elected to believe that the spiritual promise could be made real, here, in this world, in this flesh, that the theoretical abstractions of the intellectuals could be realized in the flesh and that the promptings of their hearts, not the rationalizations of their heads, could lead them back to Eden.

To define such a faith would itself be an act of intellect and thus counterrevolutionary. It would be the head trying to impose a structure of meaning on the heart. Any rational attempt by the head to create meaning threatens to wrest authority from the heart. This book, in its attempt to create a structure of meaning with which to understand the Sixties, is thus a counterrevolutionary book—I confess it. But rather than defining this faith, it is more important to try to understand the process by which it was thought to come into the hearts of believers.

To the English Protestants who first settled New England, and who set in motion many of the patterns from which our present culture derives, desire for this transformation was the central experience of existence. To be converted on the cross, to traverse the wilderness and enter Canaan, was to undergo a profound emotional experience in which the old arminian structures of rationality and authority were destroyed and a new and authentic spirit flooded into the heart.

Those old Calvinists preached their hellfire and damnation sermons not to scare people into obedience, not in the service of the conservative structures of the church and the state, but in order to drive people out of rationality, out of their minds, into the mental wilderness beyond the borders, beyond limits, in the hope that out of the destruction of the old structures, the free spirit of God's grace would flood into their empty hearts.

John Winthrop, the leader of the first expedition of English Puritans to settle in Boston, spoke to his people before his ship even landed in the New World. Knowing the history of the Reformation, he feared that their attempt to create a Protestant society of free individuals would become another Muenster and disintegrate into anarchy and chaos. In an experiment to try to create a new society without the structures that held the old together, how could society survive? Without the authority of king and church and history, without armies and aristocrats and mounted knights, what force would hold these people in community? What would prevent each one from following his or her own spirit in the heart separate from the others? They were, like the Children of Israel, leaving the structures of Egypt and entering the wilderness. What worldly authority could they appeal to?

"So the way to draw men to works of mercy," preached Winthrop, "is not by force of argument by the goodness or necessity of the work; for though this course may enforce a rational mind to some present act of mercy . . . , yet it cannot work such a habit in the soul, as shall make it prompt upon all occasions to produce the same effect, but by framing these affections of love in the heart which will as natively bring forth the other, as any cause doth produce effect."

Not by rational argument are people to be led to Zion. The authority of the head is here in typical Reformation fashion discarded. It is by love, only by love. Unless love lives in the social body, then the ligaments cannot hold that body together and the body cannot live. The new Kingdom of God, what John Calvin called the "Kingdom of Freedom," cannot exist unless love flows in the hearts of the people. Freedom cannot exist unless the members of the society love each other and do not rob and cheat and exploit and hate each other. The Kingdom of Freedom is the kingdom of love or it is nothing.

But, wrote Winthrop, the "next consideration is how this love comes to be wrought." And his answer to the question "How?" is the "new birth" in which "Christ comes and takes possession of the soul and in-

fuseth another principle, love to God and our brother." This new birth
is the experience of crucifixion and resurrection, the conversion experience, the terror of the wilderness and the passage into Canaan. It is the
death of the old Adam on the cross and the three days in hell and the
resurrection. It is the passage from Apollonian structure to Dionysian
freedom, from the authority of the head to the freedom of the heart. It
is the sojourn from the lies and idols of social constructions, across the
wilderness of absence, to a new essential perception from which a new
construction may be born.

In this way, with the mythos repeated and retold endlessly for generations, the need to pass from structure through chaos to freedom became
one of the leading metaphors of American culture, with Christ as the
leading symbol of this "regeneration through violence" for most Americans even well into the twentieth century, certainly to the Sixties and
even today. The literal wilderness became the symbolic scene of the entrance into the spiritual wilderness, in Mary Rowlandson's captivity narrative, in Daniel Boone's crossing of the frontier, even in the escape
from structure of Thelma and Louise to find spiritual freedom in the
desert wilderness. And if to rational Greeks this appeared like a kind
of foolishness, even madness, then—make the most of it. This is what
Americans were called to.

The 1630s had thus been a period of mystic enthusiasm. The original
Europeanizing of New England had been carried forward on a surge of
piety. The most extreme mystics, antinomians like John of Leyden and
Anne Hutchinson, who had stood against the law and threatened the
very survival of the infant community, had been expelled. Winthrop, despite his call for Christian love, had felt he knew when love itself threatened to degenerate into anarchy and disruption, when it had become
not true Christian love but an artificial imitation of it, a magnification of
self rather than true selflessness. The very term "antinomian" signified
those, like the enthusiasts of Muenster, who mistook the lusts of their
hearts for true Christian faith, who followed their hearts to damnation
instead of liberty. And as the century aged, piety cooled and Puritanism
became another structure, another church-state, another fearful head
suspicious of the heart.

So the pattern repeated itself. By the 1690s, reason had reestablished
its kingdom and proclaimed the borders of that kingdom to be uncross-
able. Sinful man had to suffer and submit, to defer to power both temporal and divine. Witches had to be put to death and Quakers whipped.
The structures built by the fathers had to be defended. But in time the
spirit in the heart once again rebelled, shouting its defiance, once again
attacking Pharaoh and fleeing Egypt. Once again, a mystic awakening

against the coldness of structure proclaimed the possibility of a new birth of freedom, the coming of God's kingdom on Earth.

In the 1740s, riding this new wave of piety and hellfire preaching, Jonathan Edwards led a revolt against the rigid Puritanism he had inherited. The Great Awakening, as it came to be known, was a passionate rejection of the worldly authority of church and state, a rejection of the structures of the head in favor of the longings of the heart. There are two ways, wrote Edwards, in which the mind comprehends reality. The first is arminian in nature; it is *"merely speculative and notional, as when a person only speculatively judges."* The other way he called "the sense of the heart." There is a difference, he wrote, *"between having an opinion that God is holy and gracious, and having a sense of the loveliness and beauty of that holiness and grace. There is a difference between having a rational judgment that honey is sweet, and having a sense of its sweetness."* One side of the mind is merely speculative; the other side actually experiences. One side is arminian formality; the other side is grace and life. One side knows only that honey is sweet; the other actually experiences the sweetness of the taste of honey. The letter killeth, but the spirit giveth life.

Edwards believed the human mind to be capable of both rational ordering of experience—a form of distancing and control—and an emotional apprehension of experience, a "sense of the heart." On the orderly, rational side of this divide stands the security of the familiar ideology, of worldliness; one can get to the emotional side only by crossing the terror of the void. To let go of the web that holds one over the pit of that hell takes an act of faith or a terrifying shaking of the web. But if ideology and worldliness are false constructions, then that terror is the only available truth. That terror is the fear of God that had to be faced. When Edwards looked into his own consciousness and tried to find some sure unmediated absolute presence, he found only layers below layers below layers in an infinite regression, and so he went about the streets muttering "infinite upon infinite, infinite upon infinite." He knew that he walked "over the pit of hell as on a rotten covering," and he felt like a spider dangled on a thread over that infinite pit. But that pit and the fear of it became themselves the only certain absolute. Facing absence meant facing Truth, and through the terrible crucifixion of the soul in that experience alone might true resurrection be possible.

Thus, in the name of the true sense of the heart, the Great Awakening denounced Harvard and made fun of Yale for knowing only the rationalizations of the mind and not the terrors and rebirthings of the spirit. In this multicolony revolt, the younger generation, so Edwards confirmed, shook off the complacency of its elders and went in search of liberty in the wilderness. The Great Awakening of the 1740s was a generational revolt against an entrenched establishment well fortified by the rationalists of Harvard. It was explicitly a revolt of the heart against the head, of the spirit against structure, of life against institutions. John Davenport attacked the Harvard faculty for being unconverted. Edwards's son-in-law, David Brainerd, in an act foreshadowing the Sixties, was thrown out of Yale for saying that his tutor had "no more grace than a chair." Then he went to live among the Indians.

Out of this explosion came the splintering of Puritanism. The initial terror of awakening turned to joy as sinners, dead to their old selves, felt their hearts profoundly stirred. Out of this rebirth came the flowering of American denominationalism. But out of it also came an excess of enthusiasm that bordered on madness. Edwards, appalled by the antics of the most bizarre enthusiasts, wrote *Religious Affections* to try to distinguish true religious affections from false. But the general reaction soon set in, and in time, this new spirit also cooled. The new light became new structures. Even Edwards was expelled by a congregation eager, if not to return to the leeks and onions of Egypt, then at least fearful of heading any further into the wilderness. The new congregations became new orthodoxies, new dogmas, new structures, new Egypts awaiting another rebirth of spirit sometime in the future.

The arminian rationalists recoiled from the enthusiasms of the Great Awakening, retreating in horror from the chaos. Their favorite word was "order." It is, said the cold arminian preacher Charles Chauncy, "a dignified order that characterizes true Christian faith." An orderly body in an orderly society in an orderly world was their ideal. He complained that youth, women, and even Negroes were allowed to speak in the churches of the Awakening. The arminian Chauncy insisted on a return to control. But the social order was shattered nonetheless by a generation freed from the perception that power flows from the top down, by a generation determined to leave Egypt and create on earth that which they had seen in heaven. This was, as Harriet Beecher Stowe confirmed, the generation that provided the fire of the American Revolution thirty years later.

Sam Adams, the great Boston revolutionary, was converted in the Great Awakening of 1741 and never lost his enthusiasm for the creation of what he called "a Christian Sparta." More enlightened gentlemen like Franklin and Jefferson have been given much of the credit for the Revolution. Their leadership did come from the head, but most of the soldiers fought from the heart. One needs to look not to the politicians who crafted policy in the State House in Boston but to the farmers and mechanics who fought so stubbornly at Bunker Hill. They believed that they were building the New Jerusalem, not the new Athens. After the Revolution, Jefferson, the rationalist, thought that Kentucky was going to be the new center of enlightened rationality, a new Greece; instead he got the enthusiastic religious revivals of Cane Ridge.

After the Revolution, instead of a sober community bound by law and tradition, the confederation unleashed an individualism that verged on anarchy. The Constitutional Convention of 1787 was the product of a conservative reaction to the antinomian excesses of the confederation. Too much individualism had threatened the structures of society. The gentlemen who met in Philadelphia felt, as Winthrop once had, that Muenster was around the corner and that there was a need to reassert central control. They got their arminian Constitution but only after the libertarian radicals had forced them to guarantee the freedom of the individual with the Bill of Rights. And so structure returned, but the antinomian spirit became embedded in the heart of even the American Constitution. This conflict is thus embodied within our most important political document.

After the Revolution, and one hundred years after the Great Awakening, after the enthusiasm had once again cooled into structure, and after a rational Unitarianism had taken over the pulpits of greater Boston, another generation again revolted in the name of intuition and spirit against the tyranny of the head. The Transcendentalists of Concord also believed they were the channels of a mystic spirit that could change the world. The Concord philosopher Ralph Waldo Emerson called for an individualistic self-reliance that assumed the impulses of the heart were "part and parcel of God." And as in previous periods of awakening, the new vision required new forms. The 1840s were a period of deep social reform, of abolitionism, of women's rights, of temperance and a host of other movements that promised to change the world from the bottom up. Brook Farm and Fruitlands were only two of the more famous of the utopian communes. Every enthusiasm that came along was embraced in the name of the new world being born. Emerson, Thoreau, and Whitman are the most famous of the names associated with this awakening of romantic, antinomian spirit, but there were thousands of others who broke from a paralyzing orthodoxy to build a new heaven and a new Earth in the wilderness.

Emerson rejected what he called his ancestors' "Hebraic mythology" and instead turned to Europe, to the literary language of Romanticism, for an idiom within which to express this latest revolt of antinomian spirit against arminian structure. But the spirit was the same even if the words were different. Frothingham was right: "Transcendentalism simply claimed for all men what Protestant Christianity claimed for its own elect." And so Emerson led a new revolt of the sense of the heart against the rationalizations of the head, of mystic feeling against anal-compulsive logic. And as in the first Great Awakening one hundred years before, the revolution of the spirit was accompanied by political and social revolts well beyond the borders of the subjective self.

It was in reaction against the rationalism of Harvard that Emerson declared the uncontested rule of primal instinct. Trust your heart and not your head; trust yourself and not your learning; do not test every emotional impulse against your beliefs but let them speak. *"Suppose you should contradict yourself? What then? . . . In your metaphysics you have denied personality to the Deity, yet when the devout motions of the soul come, yield to them heart and life, though they should clothe God with shape and color. Leave your theory, as Joseph his coat in the hand of the harlot, and flee. A foolish consistency is the hobgoblin of little minds, adored by little statesmen and philosophers and divines."*

Do not follow orders, do not follow tradition, but, said Emerson, do your own thing. The Transcendentalists declared the human will not only free but holy, the individual not only empowered but all-powerful: "Aye," wrote Henry David Thoreau, "if one HONEST man, in this state of Massachusetts, ceasing to hold slaves, were actually to withdraw from this copartnership, and be locked up in the county jail therefore, it would be the abolition of slavery in America. For it matters not how small the beginning may seem to be: what is once well done is done forever." The individual who has the truth in his heart can change the world.

In one crucial difference, however, from Edwards and the followers of the first Great Awakening, the romantic Transcendentalists of Concord no longer believed that they had to pass through fear in order to get from the old structures into the new. They had a faith in presence and believed that they could find within themselves what Thoreau called "a hard bottom and rocks in place, which we can call reality" without having first to spend three days in hell or forty years in the wilderness. They were trying to go from Egypt to the Promised Land without having to cross the wilderness. Theirs was a naive romanticism that inherited only part of the faith once carried to the saints.

But even in Massachusetts, in the home of the Romantics' revolution against what Emerson called a "corpse cold" Christianity, a few remembered the old mythology. In Amherst, in the 1860s, Emily Dickinson experienced a breakdown of the structures of the rational mind. For a time she descended into a freedom beyond the borders of rationality and named it "madness." But as a child of a Calvinist culture, she interpreted her experience within the old categories, not as disease but as crucifixion: "Much madness is divinest sense." Her sojourn in the wilderness waiting for the dawn of Christic vision is the subject of the bulk of her poetry. But even she recognized that the story of the sojourn from structure to wilderness has many forms and has been expressed through many mythologies. As with Emerson, the language is less important than the pattern. But the pattern was the ancient one that drove her ancestors into the American wilderness in the first place.

Finding is the first Act

The first act of Jason's voyage is "finding." Here is the moment of awakening when the sleeping sinner suddenly awakens to the possibility of new vision, when the Children of Israel realize that they are still the Children of Israel but enslaved in Egypt.

The second, loss,

The second act is the sense of loss when the vision is not realized, when they realize how terribly they are still enslaved and that Pharaoh's heart will not be moved.

Third, Expedition for
The "Golden Fleece"

And so, in the third, they set out from Egypt to find the Promised Land, the Golden Fleece.

Fourth, no Discovery—
Fifth, no Crew—
Finally, no Golden Fleece—

And yet in the wilderness there is only wilderness, no golden fleece, nothing discovered except their own continuing enslavement to worldliness. The purpose of the original sojourn into the wilderness, according to Scripture, was for the Children of Israel to discover their own corruption: "The Lord thy God lead thee these forty years in the wilderness to humble thee and to prove thee and to know what was in thine heart" (Deut. 8:2). In the wilderness, they find absence, not presence.

Jason—sham—too.

In the end even Jason, the captain of the voyage, the self at the heart of the sojourn—call it consciousness or presence—is revealed as a sham. In the heart of the wilderness, only more wilderness, no Christic vision, no Kingdom of Liberty this time, either. Freedom, as Janis Joplin sang, turned out to be just another word for nothing left to lose.

And so the wheel turns and the pattern repeats itself.

A hundred years later, in the Sixties, another generation of Americans, stirred to life by the positive visions of inspired leaders, awoke from the complacency of a paralyzing arminian structure and set out on a journey to remake the world. As these efforts at reform failed, they came to realize that a more radical solution than mere reform was needed. They came to realize that they were an Israel enslaved in an unreformable Egypt, and so they set out with great enthusiasm and excitement into the psychic wilderness in search of a Promised Land. But the wilderness turned out to be but wilderness, no discovery, no crew; and finally even the questing self was revealed to be a sham. The Sixties thus became the latest instance of the American cycle of the sojourn from Egypt into the wilderness in search of the Promised Land. It followed the same pattern of the awakenings of the Transcendentalists of the 1840s and the Great Awakening of the 1740s.

The first act was finding the essential spirit that liberates the victims of a paralyzing rationality from their psychic encagement. The second act was the loss of that innocent essential spirit. Third was the expedition beyond the inherited structures of culture to find a new essential spirit in which a new possibility could be born. Fourth was the failure of that expedition to find its goal. Fifth was the realization that one's comrades were no longer on the journey. The final blow, the popping of the last bubble, was the discovery that even the self, the very "I" at the heart of the journey, the captain of the ship, is also a sham.

Thus liberation itself, when it came, had a pattern that was already well established within the traditions of the culture. Structure had already provided the means for rebellion against itself. Perhaps this is why it was embraced so readily and so widely. But we rebels ourselves couldn't see it. As Levi-Strauss said, "Myths operate in men's minds without their being aware of the fact." Or as Norman Mailer put it, you never know what vision humps you through the night. So one mythos was overthrown within the context of a larger mythos. But there is always a larger mythos, a larger context. We cannot step outside of time and space, nor can we step outside of the conditional nature of consciousness. We can climb out of smaller boxes into larger ones; that is all. We rebels only thought that we were truly free. And perhaps we were, for a moment. If so, that was the moment of terror between Egypt and Canaan, the moment in the wilderness, on the cross, down the void. Freedom was the moment when we stared into the void outside of structure and saw in the deep black holes of Charlie Manson's eyes the projection of our own internal terror: Jason sham too.

So the revolution ended, but that too was part of the pattern.

1

Finding Is the First Act—

I.

"Now the trumpet summons us again"

"AND WHEN THE FOG WAS FINALLY SWEPT FROM MY HEAD," SAID BIG Chief Bromden, "it seemed like I'd just come up after a long, deep dive, breaking the surface after being under water a hundred years."

With these words, and with his ultimate escape from Nurse Ratched and the ward, his long legs carrying him in great strides back to the village and his friends fishing as they had in the old days but now along the white man's dam, Chief Bromden, the narrator of Ken Kesey's *One Flew Over the Cuckoo's Nest,* gave voice to the innocence with which the decade opened. The awakening, a stirring to new life, an exciting rediscovery, was the first act of the Sixties. And this spirit could be found everywhere in those first few years, in traditional politics, in radical politics, in the civil rights movement, in music, and in literature.

Chronologically, the election of John F. Kennedy was the biggest symbolic breaking of the placid surface of the Fifties. By no means, however, was this merely political event the moment of awakening. Kennedy's election was one of many related events that together made up the first act. The civil rights movement, though it had a long beginning, exploded into prominence in the early Sixties. It, more than anything else, set the stage for the drama to follow. But the Port Huron Statement of 1962, with which the Students for a Democratic Society was inaugurated, and the Free Speech movement at Berkeley, were also parts of this pattern. The folk music revival, and with it the coming of marijuana into white middle-class colleges and suburbs, helped spread the awakening beyond politics.

No book introduces the Sixties as well as Kesey's 1962 *Cuckoo's Nest.* Even Joseph Heller's *Catch-22* and Kurt Vonnegut's *Cat's Cradle,* important as they were and published about the same time, failed to escape the paralyzing cynicism of the Fifties and give voice to the romantic optimism of the rebellion. In Kesey's book can be found all of the themes of the decade neatly packaged and wonderfully personified, even to the bittersweet end. More importantly, Kesey ties these themes not just to the immediate era but to the larger sweep of American culture and its enduring images.

The mental hospital stands for the dominant institutions of society, what Kesey called "the combine," a huge machine that shapes everyone to its liking. The hospital ward is not the combine but a factory for the combine in which the broken products of the machine are fixed. Society successfully shapes most of its members to its predetermined patterns, but those who for one reason or another fail to get shaped correctly in the first place go to the ward to be remade into functioning members of society.

Chief Bromden, the befogged Indian, institutionalized in a mental hospital, resigned to his fate, personified the silent generation of the Fifties, but in his awakening and his ultimate liberation from the ward and from the control of Big Nurse Ratched, he became the perfect voice for the awakening generation. Raised by his Indian father and his white mother, Bromden had lost everything when the white men came and took his Indian village to build a hydroelectric dam. When he had lost his home, he also lost his identity, but he refused to adopt the new identity that the white culture offered. Unable to function without some identity, he withdrew into the fog, stopped talking and stopped listening, and ended up on Nurse Ratched's ward, one of the "chronics" thought to be beyond repair.

If the Chief symbolized the repressed victims of the Fifties, the sexist, macho, totally uninhibited Randle P. McMurphy was the perfect avatar of the coming rebellion. Where Bromden meekly submitted to Nurse Ratched's control and allowed a meaningless mop to push him around as if to assist in her anality, McMurphy challenged Ratched from the very start. Where she was intense, he was relaxed; where she was spit-and-polish clean, he was armpit-scratching dirty; where she kept her sexuality hidden behind a starched white uniform, he swaggered around in his Moby Dick underwear. McMurphy didn't argue the politics of institutionalization with her; he confronted her. He didn't tell the other patients how to live; by his example he provided them with an alternative way of life.

The official Leninist analysis of the book, once taught sternly to students of American literature in eastern Europe, was that romantic anarchism is doomed to fail, that the leadership of the party combined with a carefully organized mass movement are the only ways to overthrow tyranny. For them, McMurphy's death in the end is a total defeat. But for American readers, his death is one more example of the power of the individual by his willing self-sacrifice to redeem the world.

For many in the early Sixties, John F. Kennedy, and not Kesey's fictional Irishman, was the symbol of the new era. Young and brash and—we have since learned—also sexually uninhibited, Kennedy stood in the dawn of the decade blowing reveille. Kennedy saw his candidacy as offering not simply a more liberal administration but a whole new approach that would replace grandfatherly paternalism with youthful activism. He imagined himself waking a sleeping nation to the exciting challenges of a new era. Perhaps the troops were already awakening and would have risen without his call. But there it was. Throughout the 1960 presidential campaign, Kennedy over and over again proclaimed that it was time for a new generation to awake to the challenges of a new era: *"Now the trumpet summons us again—not as a call to bear arms, though arms we need; not as a call to battle, though embattled we are; but the call to bear the burden of a long twilight struggle, year in, and year out, 'rejoicing in hope, patient in tribulation'—a struggle against the common enemies of man: tyranny, poverty, disease, and war itself."*

Kennedy was calling to his own generation, those born in the Twenties and Thirties, but it was the generation of the baby boomers born in the Forties and Fifties who were most receptive to his words. As often before in American history, the younger generation heard the call to break out of structure, to brave the new frontier and enter the wilderness once again.

This book is about those visions that hump us through the night. Finding them is the first act. But to find them, we must first open our eyes to their existence. The rational mind must become conscious enough, distanced enough from its own conditioning, to be able to see the shape of those visions emerging slowly out of the fog. At night in sleep, before we awake, hallucinations rule uninterrupted, and subconscious images rise like ghosts from the grave to dance in the moonlight. Then the light of day is unthought of; it does not exist. Only when we awaken can we begin even to know that there is a difference between dreaming and waking. Only after we have opened our eyes and shaken our minds into daytime can we begin to look around and realize how asleep we'd been and then ask what is going on, where we are, and why. Chief Bromden was on the ward for many years, scared to look outside, before McMurphy stirred him awake enough to look out of the window and see "for the first time how the hospital was out in the country."

When he did finally come out of his deep nighttime fog long enough to look out the window, what the chief saw was a natural reality beyond the antiseptic human factory in which he had been institutionalized. He saw the grass, and the trees, the moon riding overhead, a chevron of geese sweeping across the sky; and he saw a young dog just happy to be alive rolling with sheer joy in the grass under the moonlit sky. From the depths of a socially constructed prison, the Chief saw again and remembered the existence of that which we call nature, that life beyond the artificial social constructs that is real, and really there, out of which we came, and within which we live and move and have our being. "If dogs run free," Bob Dylan sang, "then why can't we?" No matter that the dog got up and headed for the same spot of pavement as the headlights of an oncoming car; the moment of freedom seemed worth the risk. Indeed, the risk is barely mentioned. It stays deep in the background. In the foreground, instead, is the Chief's realization that he does not have to remain hidden in the fog but can once again be himself, his true self, his natural self. He can return to his essential nature.

So McMurphy's happy freedom seemed worth the risk, too. Here was a man not ashamed to be himself, spontaneous, uninhibited, unafraid, rolling like a dog in the moonlit grass and loving it. Here was a man who appeared to be completely at ease in his own life. McMurphy's freedom was not simply freedom from the iron control of Nurse Ratched. That freedom existed, but such merely political definitions of freedom are far too mechanical. Nor is it, as the Chief thought, that somehow McMurphy had escaped the brainwashing of the combine, just as he had escaped the brainwashing of the Chinese Communists in Korea; he was still conditioned by a combine, by some combine; we all are. There can be no escaping from the influences of our cultural encagements. Anyone so completely original and outside of any established construct would by clinical definition be insane. As the effeminate acute Dale Harding pointed out, McMurphy was a throwback to an earlier era, a brawling Paul Bunyan / Mike Fink out of the romantic nineteenth-century past. Since McMurphy was as much enslaved to conditioning as anyone, his freedom was his ability to be himself despite it all.

From the perspective of today, McMurphy is horribly sexist and altogether politically incorrect, as was (until his recent death) his creator and alter ego, Ken Kesey. His women are either bitches or whores; he calls the black attendants "coons," and he does not regret a syllable of it. He struts his moment upon the stage, playing the part handed to him, and he hams it up to the hilt. Where the other inmates of the ward are there because they have forgotten—if they ever knew—how to play their roles, McMurphy is not afraid to laugh, to boast, to sing out loud, to take a risk. He has no pretensions that need to be defended. His philosophy, if it can be called that, is a simple, unreflexive confidence in his own abilities and feelings. He is in enviable control. Knowing himself and accepting the given, McMurphy is able unselfconsciously and proudly to be himself.

Him "self"? What do we mean by that? Haven't modern social science, psychology, and literary theory proven that the self is a social construct? A product of environmental and social conditioning? Isn't personality completely contingent?

Yes.

But if that is so, then there is no essential "self." There is no true heart, no core, no soul, no spirit. We are instead each a virtual-reality program, and there is no actual reality we can touch. How then can McMurphy be so happy, so content, playing a constructed role in a contingent universe? Shouldn't he be trying to deconstruct his sexism and his racism? Shouldn't he be letting Nurse Ratched try to show him how to reconstruct himself in order to fit in better with the therapeutic community?

No.

Because whether he realizes it or not, McMurphy's freedom is the freedom to be whatever his self happens to be, however it happens to have been constructed, whatever crimes against humanity it may be perpetuating. It is a life free from doubt, free from neuroticism, free from fear. McMurphy is a happy sinner sent by whatever powers may be to teach the neurotic, whimpering, pussy-whipped acutes of the ward how to be "men." One can read this book as if it were published today as a direct answer from an unreconstructed nineteenth-century American male to the women's movement. When he ripped off Nurse Ratched's starched white blouse and exposed those beautiful swelling breasts, McMurphy deconstructed the construction she had tried to create and reduced her to her original essential nature. As she had tried to prove him to be "just a man," he proved her to be "just a woman."

Nature, then, is the secret that allows McMurphy the freedom to be himself. Nature, what the Chief saw when he looked outside the barred windows of the ward, was what lured the Sixties generation out of the combine. Belief in nature had also been the heart of romantic nineteenth-century American culture; so it is easy to see McMurphy's Emersonian self-reliance as a function of that belief. The two poles of *Cuckoo's Nest,* Ratched and McMurphy, thus signify the two poles of repressed arminian constructionism and amoral antinomian essentialism. Not only McMurphy but the dog in the moonlight and finally even the Chief are symbols of this essentialism, symbols of the alternative to the social constructions of the sterile, antiseptic Fifties ward. After all, what was Beaver Cleaver's father's name?

Is there then an actual reality out there beyond the cages of our contingency? Many modern theorists, such as the deconstructionists, insist that there is "nothing outside the text." According to them, the constructions of culture are all we have, and everything we know and feel can be reduced to some socially constructed source. Hence, to them there is no "truth," nothing outside of the self-referential, self-justifying rationalizations of human discourse. But are they right? Or might some "truth" actually exist? Orthodox Calvinists (quite the opposite of today's evangelicals) had said yes, there is a reality beyond our constructs, but we cannot know it or approach it and must operate in a fallen world separate and alienated from it. The deconstructionists say no, there is no such thing as external "truth." To them, even what we call "nature" is nothing but another human construct.

But the romantic answer to this question is a definitive "Yes! Yes, there is some basic, knowable truth." This reality, insist the romantics, exists in what we call nature, and that nature is both, as the Beatles sang, "within us and without us." What defines a person as a romantic is the belief that this essential presence can be found in the fields and woods and deserts, and not just there but also in the human heart. As the English poet Wordsworth had said back at the beginning of the Romantic movement,

> And I have felt
> A presence that disturbs me with the joy
> Of elevated thoughts; a sense sublime
> Of something far more deeply interfused,
> Whose dwelling is the light of setting suns,
> And the round ocean and the living air,
> And the blue sky, and in the mind of man.

Belief that one's self is an essential self and thus a safe and reliable agent liberates the anxious, fear-ridden neurotic. If one's deepest impulse is the energy of the universe, then the self is founded on the bedrock of existence and can be trusted. Romanticism, as Emerson so famously said, proclaims the freedom to trust oneself.

Such freedom carries with it the dangers that the self may well be made up of socially undesirable and philosophically contradictory if not downright false elements. The orthodox Calvinists and the postmodern deconstructionists may well be right that our personalities are no more than the sum total of the contingencies of our self-interest. In that case, trusting the self might be dangerous. When asked whether his impulses might not be from below, Emerson replied, that if so he would be the Devil's child and "live then from the Devil." Human beings are the products of the times and places and cultural assumptions in which they live, and these assumptions are rarely what anyone in another time and place would call the right ones.

We are thus caught here between two familiar poles. At McMurphy's extreme is the carefree living out of one's constructed self despite its possible failings; at Nurse Ratched's extreme is the artificial attempt to force that original nature behind a starched white uniform and to try to be—and to force everyone else to be—something we naturally are not. McMurphy is antinomian; Ratched is arminian. Good arguments can be made in favor of each position; good arguments can be made that each is wrong.

If in fact the attitudes and assumptions passed on to us through our historical cultures are harmful to ourselves and others, if we have for instance been brought up with racist views, then it becomes necessary for us to stop playing the roles we are most comfortable with and to change them. Such a process is very difficult. How can the self take control of the self? Can you stand apart from yourself and look yourself in the eye? Such change requires first becoming aware that one is playing a role, then finding out that it is a harmful role, then deciding among the many possible alternatives, and finally choosing a different role that will at first not be at all comfortable, because it does not fit. This is how neurotics are made. This is why so many intellectuals are nervous Woody Allens, full of insecurities and uncertainties.

Because they are aware of themselves as actors playing historically conditioned roles, intellectuals are forever watching themselves playing themselves and watching themselves, watching themselves playing themselves. Ashamed of their original conditioned roles, they are forever striving to become that which they are not. Trying to justify themselves or, failing that, trying to find a role that can be justified, like Thoreau they chase the elusive loon of self-consciousness in circles until they drive themselves nuts.

To escape from false consciousness is hard enough; but to find authentic consciousness is even harder. False consciousness, an original sin, is the universal human inheritance. The very fact of being conscious means that each of us lives in a world of meaning, a matrix of ideas about what is real and false, what good and what bad. Animals, which merely react instinctively and do not analyze and choose, do not share this human dilemma. They, like McMurphy, live immediately upon their nature; those dogs run free. But most of us do not. Instead, we are trapped in our belief systems that become our virtual-reality cages, our Egypt, our Matrix.

Traditional religious language has its own discourse for talking about these problems. The fall from grace in the Garden of Eden was the fall from a natural animal unself-consciousness. Once we walked with God in the garden, but after eating of the fruit of the tree of knowledge, our original ancestors became conscious. They realized they were naked, and covered their genitals. Why? Animals after all are also naked. But dogs run free; they do it in the road. Why can't we? Because in falling from grace we set in our minds a false construct of the way we ought to be, and our genitals do not fit that construct. They do not look right. We have acquired an idea of what should be that is not what is. The human mind, as John Calvin said, is a factory of idols, and we believe in those idols, not in the reality of nature. Human self-consciousness is original sin.

Christians claim to be freed from cosmic stage fright by their acceptance of Christ's justification. The mythic figure of Christ signifies to them the possibility of fulfilling the law and being justified, a goal that humans cannot hope to attain by themselves. In the Reformation's formulation of this doctrine, sinners, failing to attain their own justification, finally give up their own efforts and indeed their own personal salvation. They become, as good Calvinists said in the eighteenth century, "willing to be damned for the glory of God" and accept Christ's attainment of salvation "in place of" their own.

This Reformation doctrine of justification by faith freed the neurotic sinner from terror and made life in the world possible. But it also led, in its extreme manifestation, to an antinomian enthusiasm in which the previously neurotic imagined themselves free to be themselves, even if the socially constructed selves were "sinners." This was the liberty, St. Paul said, "in which Christ hath made us free." And the "yoke of bondage" that they had cast off was bondage to some external arminian code of right behavior, what they called "the law." In theory, according to these antinomians, such freedom did not really grant license to follow one's heart wherever it led. To his own question, "Should we therefore sin that grace may abound?" the apostle Paul answered "No, by no means." But his compulsion to ask and answer the question shows the direction in which such theology leads. What many thus called "Christian Liberty" remained an attitude of fear and trembling in the wilderness between the old Egyptian structures and the coming entrance into Zion. But others imagined that they had crossed that wilderness, that they had passed beyond the law, that they had entered into Canaan, and that the impulses of their hearts were from God.

Antinomianism thus freed sinners like McMurphy to be their cheerful sinful selves. It does not matter that McMurphy was ignorant of all this theology. He represents the antinomian spirit that runs through American history from Anne Hutchinson to John Brown to Timothy Leary. He represents all of those inspired souls who were led to believe that their own natural selves, the roles they felt most comfortable with, were grounded in an essential presence.

Antinomian romantics like Emerson or McMurphy did not care whether their behavior was correct according to some external standard. They felt in their hearts that the roles they played were in fact from the very heart and thus fully authentic and in no need of being justified.

They felt free to be themselves and thus able to strut their moment upon the stage with an enviable self-confidence. Free from self-doubt, they were free to be themselves. They may in fact have been leading their more neurotic followers into the valley of death, but since they confidently believed that they knew what they were doing and why, they did not doubt. As Stubb said, "Aye, Ahab, thou actest right. Live in the game and die it!" They may have been racists, sexists, militarists, communists, or religious zealots, but because they sounded no uncertain trumpet, they became leaders of men.

Though no Randle P. McMurphy, John F. Kennedy had much the same effect. Listening to him, watching him confidently enjoy life, young baby boomers began to realize that a different way of life was possible. As the largest single generation in American history entered its adolescence, the time when a crisis of identity often occurs, we had before us the example of a confident attitude that stood in marked contrast to the neurotic worries of conformist, timid parents. Here was a man who enjoyed his life, who played being who he was to the hilt and who wore his personality easily and unself-consciously. Perhaps it was all a public relations gimmick, a trick for the cameras. Nevertheless, it worked. I can remember as a kid watching and admiring as he responded confidently and humorously to the questions at his press conferences, like Babe Ruth or Joe DiMaggio hitting the ball easily out of the field. There was as much of a hunger, a need, in America in 1960, as there had been on the ward when McMurphy arrived. And for the same reasons.

II

"pessimistic, fatalistic, and depressive"

The Fifties had been a deep, long sleep filled with fantasies and fears running all through each other. For the older generation, the decade had been a long-awaited and long-deserved rest. The generation of the Fifties, the parents of the baby boomers, had grown up during the Great Depression and come of age during World War II. They had been forced to sharpen their intellects to stay alive, stay alert, awake, fully conscious, warily watching their environment like a coyote in the desert. In the Fifties, according to conservationist David Morine, nature was seen "as a mean old bitch . . . right out of the Old Testament." And human nature was seen to be just as mean a bitch as its external counterpart and just as much in need of containment. Their struggle to survive in a hostile world had enhanced their need for control, personal self-control as well as collective social control. The New Deal had been an attempt to control the chaos created by the laissez-faire excesses of a free-for-all competitive economy. World War II had been an attempt to control international chaos. When the first atom bomb went off at Alamagordo, a generation's faith in science and intellect, in man's ability to control the very heart of nature, seemed vindicated. The cool, thinking scientists of Los Alamos, my parents among them, had beaten the maddened, hate-filled Nazis and the treacherous, animalistic Japanese. Centralized organization and careful planning, under the gentle care of a paternal government, had seemed the answer to both economic chaos and military fanaticism. In the many horror movies that became popular in the Fifties, the pattern is repeated. Huge freaks of nature mutate in the desert and threaten the peace and prosperity of Smalltown, USA. A kindly old government scientist with a beautiful daughter is called in as an expert. Working hand in hand with brave young army officers, these experts figure out a way to destroy the freaks and restore order. The daughter then marries some nice young hero and the people of Smalltown live happily ever after—secure, peaceful, and prosperous, knowing they are safely looked after.

When the Depression was over and the war was won, the parents of the baby boomers wanted to enjoy the security they had earned. They got secure jobs in the large corporations that had been built up to win the war. They moved into suburbs like Levittown and they made LA what it is today. They stayed to work at Boeing and Lockheed and Grumman, building bombers to protect America from the Russian threat. They settled down and bought TVs, and in the evening after work they gathered around the flickering screen to watch Wally and the Beaver, or Lucy, or Amos 'n' Andy, shows that strengthened their sense of security by reinforcing their view of the world.

Marion Morrison became the fitting hero of the age. According to Joan Didion's portrait, director John Ford was one of the first "to sense that into this perfect mold might be poured the inarticulate longings of a nation wondering at just what pass the trail had been lost. 'Dammit,' said Roald Walsh later, 'the son of a bitch looked like a man.'" So Marion Morrison, an actor, became John Wayne, the symbol of a white male civilization imposing its own sense of order on the wild natural west. When chaos threatened, John Wayne could be counted on to contain and control whatever irrational forces threatened civilization. He represented security, decency, democracy, the American way. Didion remembers her own thoroughly unliberated response when Wayne promised the girl in *War of the Wildcats* that he would "build her a house in the bend of the river where the cottonwoods grow." She confesses, years later, knowing full well how reactionary it is: "Deep in that part of my heart where the artificial rain forever falls, that is still the line

I wait to hear." Whenever Americans feel the need for security, for a strong father figure to love and protect them, John Wayne's movies will be popular.

Americans in the Fifties wanted law and order and security, and they got it. Nurse Ratched, the villain of *Cuckoo's Nest,* represents all of the worst aspects of this need for order. She hides her large natural breasts under a stiffly starched white lab coat. She is always in control, not just of the ward, but of whatever natural self she had. She is cold, distant, manipulating, unspontaneous, and unnatural. She fits her ward to her personality; its machinelike efficiency becomes the model for the hospital, the ideal to which others aspire; and the hospital itself becomes the model for society at large, what Kesey called the "combine."

Of all the institutions of the combine designed to package human personalities into functional units in the Fifties, the university was one of the most important. Only after World War II, with the revolutionary impact of the GI Bill sending millions of young men to college for the first time, did the university system, public and private combined, assume such an enormously influential role in American life. After the GI Bill had educated them, the veterans expected that their children would become college grads, too. A lot of money was spent in the Fifties on the nation's universities and colleges. Not only did the veterans and their children want to go to college and "better themselves," but the expanding economy needed educated employees. The new generation needed to be educated in order to fit into the new technological, mechanized super-corporations that American businesses all seemed destined to become. The system—the entire system—economic, political, religious, planned and unplanned, trapped in its own history—needed organization men to keep itself alive and secure; and for that it needed big factorylike universities. It also needed conformity.

The college students of the Fifties have been labeled the "Silent Generation." At their wildest, they did jam into phone booths and VW Bugs in record numbers; they did swallow live goldfish for laughs. But other than that, they were quiet. This silence, however, should not be mistaken for stupidity. Their complacency was rooted not in apathy or selfishness or fear but in a profound sense of resignation. Growing up in the Thirties and the Forties, this generation had known both the fragility of human institutions and the terror of the wilderness beyond their borders. The Depression had shown how fragile were the economic structures and the theories that had enshrined them. The rise of fascism in Europe and in Japan had brought the world face to face with the beast within. Most educated Americans' belief in the existence of a benevolent God had been shattered after World War I. Whatever romantic illusions managed to survive that holocaust, died at Auschwitz and Buchenwald. Looking back at the Fifties, John Updike wrote, "My generation, coming into its own, was called Silent, as if, after all the vain and murderous noise of recent history, this was a bad thing." To the Fifties generation, silence in the face of existence was not a mark of shame but of knowing.

It is therefore too easy to say that the passivity of the silent generation was rooted in the social constructs of a combine that needed that passivity in order to create compliant employees for the military-industrial complex. No doubt the resignation of many was, if not created, then at least reinforced by the economic realities that can always be found at the material base of any ideological construct. Yet the silence of the students of the Fifties was not as mindless and robotic as this caricature assumes. For one thing, the students of the Fifties, the silent generation, could explain their silence without its being a confession that they were simply weak and ruled by fear. No, they could explain themselves.

Do ideological constructs, our philosophies of life, create our behavior? Are they really the sources of our actions? Or are they rationalizations that merely justify behavior that has deeper, hidden roots? Is our behavior a product of our principles, or are our principles mere rationalizations of our behavior? When Benjamin Franklin, that great American rationalist, was tempted by the delicious aroma of frying codfish to violate his vegetarian principles, he came up with a justification that served the purpose. Seeing a large fish on the deck with smaller fish in its belly, he reasoned that if a fish could eat other animals, then he should be able to eat that fish. After breaking his vegetarian vow and enjoying what he called the best codfish dinner he ever ate, he observed, "So wonderful a thing it is to be a rational creature, because a reasonable creature can find a reason for anything he has a mind to do."

Franklin knew as he happily chewed and swallowed his principles that he was rationalizing, but that did not stop him. Nevertheless, had he not been able to come up with a rationalization, he would not have broken his principles, not even for freshly caught codfish cooked in butter. We human beings may only rationalize our hidden concerns with our philosophical constructs, but still we need them. We will not act without them. And we cling to them, no matter how illogical or irrelevant or fabricated they may be. These are the webs of meaning that give our lives some sense of order, that at least make us feel as if our behavior were rooted in some essential understanding of the world. Determinists of every stripe, whether religious, psychological, or Marxist, often talk as if such rationalizations, because they are only rationalizations, are unimportant. On the contrary, they are crucial. What we profess to believe may not have much to do with what we really believe, but we do not know that; so we think our beliefs to be entirely our own. Otherwise we would not claim to believe. Psychologists and analysts love to explore the real motivations behind human rationalizations, searching through the murky depths for the hidden causes. But of course, even their theories of what lies beyond are part of their own rationalizations and serve their own ends just as ours do us. We all play games. We all live in the fallen world of rationalizations, and illusions, and lies. Trying to uncover the "layers of deceit and sin that lay in my heart," Jonathan Edwards despaired of every getting to the bottom of them, and so he went about the roads of Northampton muttering "infinite upon infinite, infinite upon infinite." Nurse Ratched's greatest sin was that she ignored her own fallen human nature "just like she chose to ignore how nature had tagged her with those outsized badges of femininity, just like she was above him, and sex, and everything else that's weak and of the flesh."

And because we live in the fallen realm, and because we need those rationalizations to justify our own behavior, whatever its true causes, they are important. Some people are convinced more easily than others. Academics and philosophers construct the most complex and elaborate rationalizations for their behavior. This book can be read as one such effort, my own effort to rationalize, to put it into context, to try to understand. Less wordy people construct or borrow or inherit less complex ones. Sometimes the inability to develop convincing rationalizations forces people to examine their appetites and even to change. Sometimes a convincing rationalization is so powerful that it continues to maintain its power to shape behavior long after, generations after, the causes that gave rise to it have ceased to exist. For these reasons, we need to take the rationalizations of the so-called silent generation seriously.

Joan Didion is perhaps as good a spokesperson for that generation as any. In Berkeley in the Fifties, she and her friends did not believe that mankind could be improved by going to the barricades, but instead were convinced that "the heart of darkness lay not in some error of social organization but in man's own blood." She and her classmates were called silent, but "we were silent neither, as some thought, because we shared the period's official optimism nor, as others thought, because we feared its official repression. We were silent because the exhilaration of social action seemed to us just one more way of escaping the personal, of masking for a while that dread of the meaningless which was man's fate." In an act as much confessional as anything, Didion includes in *The White Album* her psychiatrist's brief report of her mental condition. The good doctor describes

a personality in process of deterioration with abundant signs of failing defenses and increasing inability of the ego to mediate the world of reality.

. . . In a technical sense basic affective controls appear to be intact but it is equally clear that they are insecurely and tenuously maintained for the present by a variety of defense mechanisms including intellectualization, obsessive-compulsive devices, projection, and more, all of which seem inadequate to their task and are thus in the process of failure. . . . Patient's thematic productions on the Thematic Apperception Test emphasize her fundamentally pessimistic, fatalistic, and depressive view of the world around her. It is as though she feels deeply that all human effort is foredoomed to failure, a conviction which seems to push her further into a dependent, passive withdrawal. In her view, she lives in a world of people moved by strange, conflicted, poorly comprehended, and, above all, devious motivations which commit them inevitably to conflict and failure.

Didion allows us to read this analysis because she believes it not only an accurate description of her state of mind but also an accurate description of the world. "If I could believe that going to a barricade could affect man's fate in the slightest," she wrote, "I would go to that barricade, and quite often I wish that I could, but it would be less than honest to say that I expect to happen upon such a happy ending."

This outlook on life was an ideological construct, a philosophy; and that philosophy even had a name. Because it shared many of the attitudes of the old Protestant orthodoxy, a sense of the inevitability of fate, of the profound corruption of even well-intentioned human nature, of the insignificance of human effort in an overwhelmingly complex world, of free will as an illusion and behavioral conditioning as the true ruler of the mind, of reason itself as mere rationalization, and of the ever-present threat of madness in the radical undermining of the defense mechanisms of the ego—because of these it was called "neo-orthodoxy."

In Europe, after the bloodbath of World War I had drowned the nineteenth century's romantic illusion of the indwelling presence of God, theologians like Karl Barth had brought back the older orthodox emphasis on man's alienation and separation from God. For the intellectuals, at least, the romantic belief in presence, which had been articulated on one hand by Emerson—who believed his soul at one with the blowing clover—and on the other hand by the romantic Christians—who found Jesus in their hearts—was shattered in the trenches of France. All of the latent evils of human consciousness, repressed under the pressure-cooker lid of Victorian morality, exploded in World War I, spewing entrails and philosophical constructs throughout western culture. After the war, the so-called "lost generation" echoed Hemingway's belief that all the gods were dead. But the God who had died was the indwelling, immanent God, the romantic Jesus of Victorian culture, not the older God of Wrath. The secure and empowering sense of presence was gone, but the profound absence that took its place contained its own theological implications. Many people today think that religion must necessarily be a strong affirmation of essential presence and absolute certainty of belief, but in fact much of Christian theology has been just the opposite. In many ways, what theory is, theology was.

Karl Barth's theological writings, most notably *The Epistle to the Romans* and *The Word of Man and the Word of God,* had a significant impact upon disillusioned American theologians in the Twenties. Barth claimed that all of human culture is illusory, a tissue of lies; that even theology had to be always "a theological warning against theology." The ancient Hebrews' use of the abbreviation JHWH and their refusal to write out God's full name was a confession that our human speech about the greater reality beyond us is necessarily caught up in the corruptions of our human constructions. These theologians did not need Jacques Derrida to tell them that all is vanity, that human words are false constructions, that there is no transcendental presence, and that at the heart of human culture a terrifying absence reigns. All of that they had already read in Calvin. In the United States, Reinhold Niebuhr became the leading theologian and spokesman of this neo-orthodox movement. His brother, H. Richard Niebuhr, became its leading historian.

In reaction against the naive essentialism of much of the romantic theology of the preceding century, neo-orthodoxy revived a Christian discourse in which God is known not by His presence but by His absence. Karl Barth called this the "NO" of the Word of God, a radical undoing of human structures of belief in the face of the absolute, what had once been called the fear of God. To the rare individuals confronted by this terrifying reality, it was a deep experience. But it was not an experience that all humans encountered or could encounter. Those who did experience this profound undoing were the elect, the chosen few, chosen not to some happy immortality in some literal heaven but chosen to taste the fear at the heart of the void where human intentions, human works, human institutions all came apart and were exposed for their inevitable corruption, where the vanity of works and the liberal assumption of inevitable progress were thoroughly debunked.

This spirit marked much of the best literature of the early twentieth century. The black blood of determinism that stains so much of William Faulkner's writing has clear neo-orthodox sensibilities. Faulkner always acknowledged the Old Testament as the book that came closest to what he was trying to achieve. Much of his best writing sets human constructs against the typological wilderness, exposing the profound webs of historical delusion in which we are embedded.

For Faulkner, as for many American writers, this wilderness is a symbol of the gulf between man and God, between Egypt and Canaan. But the wilderness is also the locus where the mystic goes in order to try to confront the other, to step outside of that human cage, or at least to be reminded that we are in a cage. In "The Old People," his preface to "The Bear," Faulkner has McCaslin say about Sam Fathers, the Chickasaw chief, "Like an old lion or a bear in a cage, he was born in the cage and has been in it all his life. He knows nothing else. Then he smells something . . . there for a second was the hot sand or the cane-break that he never even saw himself, might not even know it if he did see it. . . . But that's not what he smelled then. It was the cage he smelled. He hadn't smelled the cage until that minute."

The wilderness exists to remind us of our cages. To say that we ought not speak of an other, a nature, a wilderness, because of our cages is to take away one of the most important symbols of the memory within our culture of our encagement. Perhaps we cannot get out of these culturally conditioned contingent cages, but we can remember that we are in a cage and occasionally rattle the bars. This is just what the premodern orthodox language of the reformed theology was trying to do, to shake us out of our sinful worldliness, our faith in our social constructs and rationalizations, and to force us to confront the terror of the void.

So neo-orthodox attitudes permeated much of the intellectual life of the United States in the years after World War I in both secular and religious forms, at least among the intellectuals. At the level of pop religion, in the pews, American Protestantism in the Fifties continued to preach the romantic Christian revivalism of the nineteenth century. Norman Vincent Peale and Billy Graham never surrendered to doubt. Neo-orthodoxy remained an intellectual and therefore elite movement. But it also had left-wing political allegiances.

Niebuhr was explicitly religious, articulating his message within the context of the language of the Reformation, but his ideas did reach into elite secular culture, even to those who professed no belief in religion. Because Christianity continued to be the dominant discourse in the United States, despite the obtuse secularism of many academics, neo-orthodoxy remained primarily a religious viewpoint. But many who had never even been inside a church found in Niebuhr a voice that articulated the cause of their silence. As Didion indicates, his was the voice of the so-called silent generation. In college towns, at least in the Northeast, bumper stickers appeared that read "Atheists for Niebuhr." In the universities, literary critics of the era applied neo-orthodox readings to Faulkner, Melville, and Hawthorne while praising the Christian imagery of poets like T. S. Eliot and Robert Lowell. Perry Miller's discovery of depths of unsuspected meaning in the writings of orthodox Calvinists like Jonathan Edwards who had once imagined mankind as "Sinners in the Hands of an Angry God" was part of this neo-orthodox movement.

In the Thirties, Reinhold Niebuhr was the minister of an urban church in Detroit, where he tried to combine a left-leaning labor union politics with his orthodox sense of God's sovereignty and man's sinful nature. In his most widely read work, *Moral Man and Immoral Society,* he argued that men as individuals may be capable of moral acts but that man in the mass is too often an unthinking mob, a beast. In *The Nature and Destiny of Man,* his most important work, he traced the conflict between Athens and Jerusalem, the split between the rational and the subliminal, the Enlightenment and the Reformation, the head and the heart. Man strives for a mystic oneness, both to know and to feel, but his sinful nature inevitably causes him to fall back into the separatism of sin. He tries to embrace the whole and, failing to unite them, holds himself at a distance to try to understand with his head; and failing that, tries again to embrace it. History swings back and forth between the two poles of consciousness, between a logical rationality that would know and control and a mystical ecstasy that would love and submit. Progress, if it happens at all, happens despite us.

Niebuhr himself was a tireless social reformer who had outlined what he considered a realistic way of pressuring the inert mass of society into reforms. In 1932, in *Moral Man and Immoral Society,* he had written, "It is hopeless for the Negro to expect complete emancipation from the menial economic and social position into which the white man has forced him, merely by trusting in the moral sense of the white race. It is equally hopeless to expect emancipation through violent rebellion." Instead, he suggested a "technique of nonviolence" similar to that used by "Mr. Gandhi." He noted the "peculiar spiritual gifts of the Negro" for such a campaign: "He would need only to fuse the aggressiveness of the new and young Negro with the patience and forbearance of the old Negro, to rob the former of its vindictiveness and the latter of its lethargy." Studying theology in the Fifties, surely Martin Luther King came across these words and somehow found the way to cross over from words into action.

In its attempt to face a brutal reality as honestly as possible, the old Puritans' orthodox Protestantism had preached a means of acceptance, a way to bear the arbitrariness of fate and the horrors of existence. It had provided a way to survive in the hands of an angry God, making a kind of cosmic sense of human suffering by turning it into a means of reconciliation. Such orthodoxy did more than accept suffering; it sanctified it. This acknowledgment of sin made it possible to endure periods of economic and political turmoil, to face chaos without losing faith, to survive despite the existence of real evil. But in times of peace and prosperity, when such acceptance becomes complacency, it allows social problems to fester, and it brings contempt down upon itself. The original American orthodoxy, that of Calvin, Hooker, and Edwards, had peopled the wilderness by giving profound meaning to and thus glorifying all that the settlers suffered.

But at the same time, learning to confess evil slides easily into learning to accept evil, perhaps even wallowing in it. Of all the images left us by the Puritan era, even including the Salem witch trials, none is more hideous than Stephen Vincent Benet's portrait of the Bible-thumping Christian slaver who "traded in niggers and loved his saviour." Here was a man who had learned how to reconcile Christianity with the reality of human sin, who had rationalized the brutality of the slave trade within the context of orthodox acceptance of evil. Can this breed anything but contempt?

The Sixties, when they came, were a revolt against this neo-orthodox acceptance, this complacency that had not been caused by the theology of neo-orthodoxy but explained by it. Sometimes, however, the merely descriptive explanation appears unwittingly as a prescriptive cause. Neo-orthodoxy did not cause the feelings of alienation and disengagement; it was an attempt to articulate those feelings. But in articulating those feelings, it inevitably reinforced them and kept them alive.

If the Fifties were neo-orthodox, then the Sixties have rightly been called a neo-romantic rebellion against the paralyzing rationality of the orthodox head. Where neo-orthodoxy saw through the rationalizations of the world to the larger motivations in which we are all entangled, the Sixties turned from theoretical constructs to the flesh and blood realities of the world. They cut the Gordian knot of neo-orthodox complexity by crying, as Melville did, "I'm for the heart—To hell with the head." Where the Fifties saw the dangers and the complexities all too clearly, the Sixties damned the torpedoes and steamed full speed ahead.

III

"The power to transform"

Like the neo-orthodox students of the Fifties and the old lights of the Great Awakening, the acutes of Miss Ratched's ward accepted their inability to function in the wider world, and they passively let themselves be pushed around by the combine, that invisible social machine that shapes each of its members to its pattern. To the efforts of McMurphy to stir some rebellion in their souls came Billy Bibbit's stuttering response, "But I just don't think a vote wu-wu-would do any good. Not in the l-long run. It's just no use, M-Mack." And the chief, seeing McMurphy hesitate in his battle with Nurse Ratched, slips back into the safety of the fog, explaining, "Eventually we all got to lose. Nobody can help that."

The acutes still clung to their security: "Why can't McMurphy leave us be? Why can't he leave us in the fog where it's safe?" To which Mc-Murphy cannot respond with logic; logic is the enemy of action. He can only put himself on the line. Frustrated by his inability to stir the guys into taking a stand, McMurphy attempts the impossible. He bets that he can lift a four-hundred-pound control panel, aptly-named. Knowing he can't do it, knowing that it can't be done, they willingly put their money down. McMurphy puts his arms around the cooler and strains mightily. For a moment, as his veins bulge and the cement grinds, it looks almost as if the thing might move. But McMurphy fails; he is forced to let go. Throwing his money down in disgust behind him, he says, "But I tried though. Goddammit, I sure as hell did that much, now, didn't I?"

Like McMurphy, Kennedy also tried. He tried to pull the nation out of the fog, to get people to laugh again, to trust themselves. His own self-confidence and energy constantly on display were an example of the kind of vigor he wanted to impart. He wanted America to believe that the challenges of the new decade could be met and won, from the efforts to put a man on the moon to the long, twilight fight against Communism. The Peace Corps is rightly cited as the prime example of this spirit. It was an effort to do everything that Kennedy believed necessary, to rouse sleepy young Americans from their suburban couches and send them into the jungles of Asia and Africa to resist the spread of evil and to rebuild the world. Like the frontier of the old West, the Third World became a symbol of the need to escape from the suffocating embrace of structure and to confront the wilderness. To have spent a year in Africa became a badge of courage and commitment, a willingness to try to lift the world.

It was also part of the fight against the Communist threat. Kennedy was as much a Cold Warrior as any. Shaped by the experiences of World War II, he saw Communism as a dangerous external threat, and he wanted America to overcome its paralyzing worry about the struggle. The Green Berets were his personal answer to the threat of insurrection by Communist guerrillas in the Third World. His commitment to stopping Communism in Latin America, in Africa, and in Southeast Asia was as much a part of his vision as the Peace Corps. America, he said, had the means and the ability; all it needed was the will. Kennedy did what he could rhetorically to pull Americans out of the fog of their fears and hesitations, out of that fog into which they had withdrawn after World War II.

In *Cuckoo's Nest*, Dale Harding, in the mental hospital to be cured of being gay, speaks for the other inmates, explaining why they remain so passive and so silent. After a particularly humiliating therapy session, he rejects McMurphy's characterization of the event as a pecking party. His words reveal that he believes what society says about him, about his being sick: "You completely disregard, overlook and disregard the fact that what the fellows were doing today was for my own benefit? That any question or discussion raised by Miss Ratched or the rest of the staff was done solely for therapeutic reasons? You must not have heard a word of Dr. Spivey's theory of the Therapeutic Community." McMurphy's task is to make him see that whatever he is, as is, he's still as good—or as bad—as any other man. McMurphy has to raise his consciousness and free him from the paralyzing fears. In a classic statement of egalitarianism, he tells Harding, "As near as I can tell you're not any crazier than the average asshole on the street."

But the patients need the security; they need to feel safe. The Chief complains, "That's what McMurphy can't understand, us wanting to be safe. He keeps trying to drag us out of the fog, out in the open where we'd be easy to get at. . . . Why don't he leave me be?" But it is McMurphy's fate to be an avatar, a Moses, and ultimately a Christ, to bring his people out of Egypt.

But how? How do you liberate souls trapped in the paralyzing cages of God's sovereignty and man's sinfulness? McMurphy's attempt to liberate by example failed. So did Kennedy's. Merely showing the inmates the way proved not to be enough. Another element was needed.

More than Kennedy or the fictional McMurphy, Martin Luther King Jr. was the true Moses of the new age, leading the oppressed out of the fog of bondage and self-hate. If the Sixties can be seen as an essentialist reaction against the orthodox Fifties, King stands as the dominant figure of this romantic awakening. Since the Montgomery bus boycott of 1956, long before Kennedy took a stand, King's voice had been challenging America to live up to its promise and to end the legal segregation that still kept millions of black Americans in servitude one hundred years after the Civil War. His was not simply a political but explicitly a moral appeal.

Just as Martin Luther had attacked the hierarchical rationalizations of his day and had proclaimed that God speaks not to the elite but to the hearts of all believers, so Martin Luther King, an ordained Baptist minister, preached that black Americans are children of God, too, and equally deserving of a seat anywhere on the American bus. He backed up this claim not with logic or law, those tools of paralysis, but with the mystic language of love. God, he said, is with the oppressed: "Unearned suffering is redemptive." And the means of that redemption is Agape, "an overflowing love which is purely spontaneous, unmotivated, groundless, and creative. It is not set in motion by any quality or function of its object. It is the love of God operating in the human heart."

King faced the same dilemma that McMurphy had faced, that nineteenth-century romantic reformers had faced, that adherents of the first Great Awakening had faced, that theologians of the Reformation had faced: how to raise the consciousness of people who had been taught to accept their lot as fate and the will of God, who had resigned themselves to being victims. Negroes, said King, "as a result of long years of oppression, are so drained of self-respect and a sense of 'somebodiness' that they have adjusted to segregation." Worse, they had not simply adjusted themselves to fate, but they had been "skillfully brainwashed," King said, to the point that they actually believed the white man's theory that they were inferior. Like Harding and the other submissive acutes, black Americans had been programmed into believing that they belonged on the bottom. Their virtual-reality programming had been constructed, as James Baldwin said to his nephew, "to make you believe what white people say about you," that you really are a "nigger."

What King had to overcome was what he called "the psychology of servitude." Whether thought of as servitude to white segregationists or to the Nurse Ratcheds of any combine or to the pharaohs of the spirit, whoever and whatever they are, this was servitude to a structure that controlled and commanded from the top down. The rational logic of the neo-orthodox position could not be refuted: irony has intellect on its side. We are all trapped within contingent cages that we cannot break out of. Any logical person can see that resistance is futile. Thus, before the oppressed could hope to stand up to their oppressors, the heart had to revolt against these logical propositions of the head; the spirit had to free itself from the paralyzing effects of its adherence to the given order. The oppressed had to be freed from the belief that they had to out-think their oppressors. Neo-orthodox alienation could not be overcome by logic or what John Winthrop had called "force of argument." Instead, King had to somehow find and communicate an emotional or spiritual essence, powerful enough to overcome fear. And he did: "Somehow God gave me the power to transform the resentments, the fears and the misunderstanding I found that week into faith and enthusiasm. I spoke from my heart, and . . . with the new unity that developed and now poured fresh blood into our protest, the foundations of the old order were doomed. A new order was destined to be born."

I cannot emphasize too strongly the source of the empowerment that made the civil rights movement possible. King's strength, and the strength he was able to impart to his followers, came from a belief in an essential presence he called "God." Even Malcolm X, as intellectually brilliant as he was, found the strength to change his own life and to stand up against the combine, not from ideology or book learning of any sort, but from his faith in Islam. "My sincerity," he said, "are my credentials." That is, his credentials were not a PhD, or membership in a party, or the speculative truth of some doctrine, but his own heart's feelings and his willingness to speak his heart's most honest truth and mean it.

As the philosopher Richard Rorty has said, the ironic position, basically neo-orthodox cynicism, cannot empower. Deconstruction can show the internal contradictions of the old order, but it cannot establish a firm foundation for a new order. The theology of absence can bring one out of idolatry and knock one off a rock of misguided self-confidence, but it cannot establish in that void a new rock on which to stand. Without that sense of divine presence, there can be no empowering. All of the great revolutionary movements of the world have depended upon such a sense of presence, of being at one with some force greater than any individual, call it God or Allah or, as the Marxists did, history. As King so eloquently said, "Human progress never rolls in on wheels of inevitability; it comes through the tireless efforts of men willing to be co-workers with God."

But what did it mean to believe in God?

If we are in fact caught up in constructs, encaged in our contingent cultural conditioning, then even our ideas of God are part of that conditioning. We cannot escape that. Calvin himself said that everything we think we know, even about God, is idolatrous stupidity. We are trapped in our cages, and religion is part of the cultural cage. The silent students of the Fifties accepted their cages as inevitable. They knew they were in cages. They were resigned to Egypt, for they did not believe that the wilderness promised anything but death and destruction. Those blacks "brainwashed" into believing in the psychology of servitude were equally aware of their enslavement to Pharaoh. But they could only pray for a Moses to someday come and set them free, not just from segregation, but from the constructions of the self. The acutes of Ms. Ratched's ward knew where they were and saw no alternative but terror or death. "Why can't McMurphy leave us in here, in the fog, where it's safe?"

But what is outside of the cage? Outside of the fog? In the wilderness beyond Egypt? Is our choice only to bend to the whip and submit to "reality?" Or is there a possibility, no matter how remote, of a state of being beyond these cages? Is it possible to escape the solipsistic maze of contingent human consciousness? No one knows the answer to that. Very few even know that the cages exist; certainly no one knows what is out there beyond them. And those few who have been allowed a peek have returned, as Moses did, shaken with terror. But in that very fear is a sense of something, even if it is a sense of an other, outside and beyond. God can be thought of not as a thing, for that would put Him within the constructs of our mental worlds, but as that Absolute Reality that exists outside of the constructs of our mental cages. As such, He is outside of what science might call rationality, and He is outside of what deconstructionists call the "text." He is that which ultimately exists outside of the contingent brainwashing of our virtual-reality programming.

The belief in God that propelled the leaders of the Puritan community to dare to create a new society was the belief that there is a reality outside of the cages of our cultural constructs, even if we cannot see or speak it. Further, it was for them the faith, and all it can be is a faith, that the power that gave rise to us has its own ends and its own righteousness, which though it may not be ours is more than ours if we could only put aside our own vain desires and let God be God. On Good Friday morning, during the campaign in Birmingham, the leaders of the movement felt they had finally reached a dead end, that they had done all that they could. They had filled the jails, but that was not enough, and now they had no money for bail. They were overwhelmed with a feeling of hopelessness. When his friends turned to him for leadership, not knowing what to do, King went into the bedroom and returned in a moment dressed in his overalls ready to march and be jailed. "I don't know what will happen; he wrote, "I don't know where the money will come from. But I have to make a faith act." His faith act was an irrational act. He stopped trying to be in control and surrendered his campaign to the will of God. King was fond of quoting the prophet Amos, "Let Judgments run down as waters, but righteousness a mighty stream" (Amos 5:24). To trust righteousness over the law is to believe in God.

What broke through the apathy that had frozen the Fifties generation into silence was the hot sword of belief in ultimately righteous forces beyond ourselves over which we have no control but with which we can work to transform the world. One can hear it in King's claim that change never comes in on the wheels of inevitability but only to those who are willing to be co-workers with God. One can hear it in Bob Dylan's cry, "A hard rain's a gonna fall." One can see it in McMurphy's sacrifice of his own life that his friends might taste, however briefly, the freedom he had enjoyed. McMurphy as a Christ symbol signified a pointing outward beyond the combines, all of them, to the belief in a promised land somewhere beyond the wilderness. Even the dog rolling in the grass lived a moment of freedom as he reveled in that brief space between his kennel and the car on the highway. He looked up to the sky and saw the chevron of wild geese and followed them to his death. Should he have stayed in his kennel? Is the possibility of a moment of freedom worth the risk? As President Ronald Reagan was to ask years later, "Should the Children of Israel have refused the wilderness? Should Christ have refused the cross?"

Martin Luther King thus took his stand outside the constructs of his combine secure in the faith that righteousness does reign outside of the laws and traditions of society. He determined to follow it as well as he could, even if it meant his death. Sick of his enslavement in Egypt, he followed his vision of a promised land despite the risks. In his "Letter From a Birmingham Jail," he explained to the white ministers who criticized his acts of civil disobedience that there are two laws, man's laws and God's, and that he was following God's laws.

How does one know God's laws? If the logical speculations of the mind are only rationalizations and therefore not to be trusted, how can one determine what God wants? Where does he or she find the basis upon which to appeal? Where can anyone turn to find answers? In the seventeenth century, the Puritans' attempt to build a Bible Commonwealth based entirely upon scriptural command had proven an unholy mistake. Following the letter of scripture had failed as a guide for building social and political institutions. But if not to Scripture, where else can a person turn to determine God's intent? When King refused a court order to halt his demonstrations, he was putting himself outside the Constitution. If not to the state and its legal institutions, or to the literal word of Scripture, where else can a human being go to find the higher law?

One answer is: to the self, to the heart, to consciousness. Call it conscience if you want. Like the Transcendentalists of the nineteenth century, like the followers of the Great Awakening, like Anne Hutchinson in 1636 and the radicals at Munster before her, King called on the sense of the heart as a guide to righteousness. If one can break through all the rules and regulations, the dos and don'ts and rationalizations of the mind and the legalisms of society, and stand naked for a moment, then, say these essentialists, one should be able to hear the voice of the universe within oneself, Wordsworth's "presence," Emerson's "Reason," Edwards', "sense of the heart," King's "God," and—yes—even George Lucas's "the force."

The believer in nonviolence, wrote King, has to believe that he has "cosmic companionship" in his struggle. Otherwise, there is no power greater than the nation-state, no place to stand outside of the legal structures of the combine. Even those in the movement who "find it difficult to believe in a personal God," he wrote, still have some faith in some essential righteousness that underlies the structures of life: "Whether we call it an unconscious process, an impersonal Brahman, or a Personal Being of matchless power and infinite love, there is a creative force in this universe that works to bring the disconnected aspects of reality into a harmonious whole."

And this creative force was to be found in the depths of the natural self. The still, small voice of conscience was here held out to be not just another socially determined prejudice but actually the voice of God. William Blake called the voice of God the voice of "Righteous Indignation." Whatever word one calls it, one hears it within, in the depths of the mind, in what we metaphorically call the heart. Is this, as the social constructionists say, merely another part of our conditioning and not some essential spirit from the universe? Perhaps it is. But in order for this voice to empower, in order for there to be a place from which to stand up against the Pharaohs of the world, would-be revolutionaries need to believe that it is essential and unquestionably real. The fear that such feelings are part of our constructed sinfulness is what trapped neo-orthodox cynics like Joan Didion in their own cages. "I know it is right because I feel it in my heart" is the romantic sword that cuts through the Gordian knot of neo-orthodox cynicism. This romantic spirit is what gave Moses the strength to lead the Children of Israel out of Egypt; Paul to rebel against the Pharisees; Luther to declare for the priesthood of all believers against the power of Rome; the Puritans to reject the Church of England and brave the literal wilderness; Anne Hutchinson to confront the Puritan patriarchy of Boston; Edwards to lead the Great Awakening; Thoreau to go to jail rather than pay taxes to extend the realm of slavery; John Brown to take up arms against the United States; and Martin Luther King to pull a dispirited people out of the fog to march off to jail for their freedom.

King knew that the problem was primarily spiritual. Because of this, his methods were the same as those used by the church to bring sinners to Christ. The parallel was not merely tactical. Spiritual liberation from the bondage of corrupt worldliness was profoundly similar to political liberation from the bondage of an ideology of oppression. King held mass meetings in the black churches and raised the people's spirits with hymns and freedom songs and powerful sermons. The freedom songs especially were an important tool for raising the emotions and instilling in people a strong sense of presence. When a whole crowded church rocked with the sound and feeling and rhythm of the old spirituals, those who were there felt each other's presence, felt the presence of the music, and felt themselves at one with the spirit who had been there in jail with Paul and Silas.

Hence, the emotional appeal of the civil rights campaign fused with the appeal of music. The music, said Martin Luther King, inspired the people in the churches of Birmingham and Selma. Old religious hymns that for years had filled the hearts of the faithful were rewritten, or reinterpreted, to serve the needs of the movement. Just as King used the structure and the rituals of the black church to infuse the civil rights movement with a sense of God's presence, so he used the songs of the church to fill the souls of the marchers with courage and spirit. Before each important march, between the sermons and the political exhortations, the black churches of the South rang for hours with impassioned music until the stones jumped: "Just like the tree that's standing by the Waters / We shall not be moved," "Oh oh Freedom, Oh oh Freedom, Oh oh Freedom over me / And before I'll be a Slave / I'll be buried in my grave/ And go home to my Lord / and be Free." Sometimes the words had to be altered, but more often than not, the scriptural images fit the times perfectly: "Paul and Silas were bound in jail / Had no Money for to go their bail / Keep your eyes on the prize / Hold on."

In the churches, between the songs, King called for individuals to come forward and commit themselves to nonviolence and to the movement, just as in Sunday sermons he had called for sinners to come forward and commit themselves to Christ. His followers handed out cards that contained the Ten Commandments of the movement, beginning with "1) Meditate daily on the life and teachings of Jesus." The effort to bring black Americans out of the fog of psychological servitude involved the same tactics used by the Baptist churches to free sinners from the fog of Egyptian bondage. "Through these meetings," King wrote, "we were able to generate the power and depth which finally galvanized the entire Negro community." In his book on the Birmingham campaign, King cites examples again and again of how "God gave me the power to transform the resentments, the suspicions, the fears and the misunderstanding I found that week into faith and enthusiasm." King quotes one white businessman: "Am I just imagining it, or are the Negroes I see walking around walking a little straighter these days?"

In retrospect, it is surprising to read King's account of how reluctant the civil rights leaders were about calling on the young to assist their movement, but when they did, the overwhelming response proved that call "one of the wisest moves" they made, King said. Having seen the jails fill up with adults, King and the other leaders turned uncertainly to the young people of Birmingham, not sure they were doing the right thing. The response was immediate. Rather than being afraid to face the police dogs, the young people of Birmingham were only waiting to be asked. And when they were asked, nothing, no orders from their principals, no locking of the school gates, no pleas from their worried parents, could stop them from pouring forth. An awakening was taking place. As King put it, "Something was happening to the Negro in this city, just as something revolutionary was taking place in the mind, heart, and soul of Negroes all over America."

But King's contribution to the spirit of the awakening of the Sixties did not end there. Awakening the black community was only the beginning. From the perspective of American culture and history as a whole, his other eventful role was to awaken not just the black community enslaved in the Egypt of segregation but the white baby-boom generation enslaved in neo-orthodox passivity as well. His call to the young people of Birmingham in 1963 to join in the crusade was heard in neighborhoods, black and white, all over America.

The songs of the civil rights movement played an important part in stirring up emotions and touching the heart. The feelings they brought out were an important part of overcoming the fear that had kept black Americans so long resigned to the fog. These same songs did not remain in the stone walls of the churches of Birmingham, but were sung in the streets as the demonstrators marched bravely into the teeth of the police dogs and the force of the fire hoses. And beyond the South, they were carried onto northern campuses across the nation by the likes of Pete Seeger; Peter, Paul and Mary; Joan Baez; Judy Collins—whites singing to white audiences, spreading not just the political ideas but the emotional spirit of the movement. In the churches, "We Shall Overcome" had been sung about the need of the sinner to overcome sin and the estrangement of the world; in the civil rights movement, it came to mean overcoming not just sin but the particular forms of estrangement signified by legal segregation and racism; in the North it took on additional significance as well. The white students who sang these songs also needed to be freed.

Nor did King do any of this alone. The more militant Student Nonviolent Coordinating Committee, better known as SNCC (and pronounced "snick") was at its inception an equally eloquent voice for liberation from the fogs of apathy and cynicism and despair. I well remember as a white teenager in the early Sixties being drawn to SNCC, and to its affiliate, "The Friends of SNCC," in liberal Massachusetts. To my friends and me, SNCC embodied the true spirit of the civil rights movement, Martin Luther King's moral tactics without his Christic language, a confrontational style that threw the challenge at the face of evil. With SNCC, we found an identity that glowed with a righteous sense of purpose, an organization that wanted and needed our youthful assistance. While King's SCLC went north to raise money among our parents, SNCC came north to the campuses looking for us.

At the beginning, SNCC was thus an integrated organization dedicated to many of the same idealistic goals as King's Southern Christian Leadership Conference. White students stood on SNCC picket lines not just in the South, where most of the confrontations were taking place, but on northern campuses as well. Through this association of white students with SNCC and SCLC organizers, both the spirit and the tactics of the civil rights movement made their way from the black churches of the South to the white campuses of the North.

The founding statement of SNCC is almost as pious as the rhetoric of the SCLC, appealing to religious ideals growing "from the Judeo-Christian tradition" seeking "a social order of justice permeated by love": "Through nonviolence, courage displaces fear. Love transcends hate. Acceptance dissipates prejudice; hope ends despair. Faith reconciles doubt. Peace dominates war. Mutual regards cancel enmity. Justice for all overthrows injustice. The redemptive community supersedes immoral social systems." This is not a faith in ideology or the logic of any systematic analysis. The spiritual hope that ends despair is the essential element that defines this romantic moment of awakening.

When those four black students sat down at that Woolworth's lunch counter in Greensboro, North Carolina, in February of 1960, anyone who had any critical knowledge of politics or history could have told them that they were only going to get their asses kicked from there to the Mason-Dixon line. Those four pioneers had no way of knowing that their action would inspire others to do the same and that these actions building in a wave would sweep away the social institutions of segregation throughout the South. Just as Martin Luther King, when his back was to the wall in Birmingham, put on his blue jeans and marched into jail not as a clever tactic but as a faith statement, so these students too were taking an irrational stand. As McMurphy said after failing to lift the panel, "At least I tried."

What was it Henry David Thoreau had said during the awakening of the 1840s? "If one honest man, ceasing to hold slaves were actually to withdraw from this copartnership, . . it would be the abolition of slavery in America." The Transcendentalists had faith that the righteous individual is in touch with the spirit of the universe and therefore, acting from the righteousness of the heart, could transform the world. A belief in an essential presence replaced the old neo-orthodox emphasis on God's profound absence. So the neo-transcendentalists of the Sixties, like the founders of SNCC, believed that they too could stand up against the combine and, like Samson, tear that building down.

IV

"Put your bodies upon the gears"

Even the principal New Left organization, SDS—Students for a Democratic Society—began in the early Sixties with a burst of hope and moral piety that can only be called evangelical. Its founding document, the "Port Huron Statement" drawn up at a conference of the Student League for Industrial Democracy in Port Huron, Michigan, in 1962, remains an amazing expression of youthful optimism.

Originally drafted by Tom Hayden, who later became famous for marrying and divorcing Jane Fonda, the "Port Huron Statement" begins appropriately enough with a denunciation of neo-orthodox complacency, bemoaning the fact that "the vast majority of our people regard the temporary equilibriums of our society and world as eternally-functional parts." One reason for this, they find, is that the "horrors of the twentieth century, symbolized by the gas-ovens and concentration camps and atom bombs, have blasted hopefulness." Thus, "men act out of a defeatism that is labeled realistic." Unable to imagine actually being able to change the large impersonal world outside of themselves, the complacent students of the silent generation instead inhabit "a privately-constructed universe, a place of systematic study schedules, two nights each week for beer, a girl or two, and early marriage; a framework infused with personality, warmth, and under control, no matter how unsatisfying otherwise."

Joan Didion's "silent generation" is the target here. But the statement aims not at the individuals as somehow weak or evil but at the attitudes and their underlying historic causes. The aim of the Port Huron Statement is to overcome what it calls "the inner alienation that remain the defining characteristics of American college life." The statement recognizes, even if it does not name, the neo-orthodox acceptance of the inevitability of sinful man caught up in the overwhelming complexities of a sinful world. Martin Luther King identified that very term, "alienation," as one of the principal attributes of what he also called "sin," our encagement in artificial constructions and hence our estrangement from whatever ground of being might exist outside our private selves. This alienation, together with a deterministic mindset, had led to a defensiveness, a withdrawal from public life to a private one. This led inevitably to a rejection of any effort to reform the world as hopelessly naive.

According to the Port Huron Statement, the supreme example of this overwhelming, uncontrollable world "contributing to the sense of outer complexity and inner powerlessness" was the large state university with its bureaucratic machinery and mindless conformity. The university came to be seen as both an example of the larger problem and as a means for combating it. If Nurse Ratched's ward served as a model for the way in which the combine tries to shape its victims to its own needs, then the university served the same function and for the same ends. Just as McMurphy could use his presence on the ward to liberate the acutes from their own sense of hopelessness and powerlessness, so the students gathering at Port Huron imagined that the university could serve as the site for liberating an entire generation.

But the example of the Southern civil rights movement, not Kesey's book, provided the students at Port Huron with the model for how to free minds conditioned to believe in their own powerlessness. It is the example of the civil rights movement, declares the Statement, that "indicates that there can be a passage out of apathy." Martin Luther King's call thus was heard well beyond the black churches of the South, and his message was applied well beyond the African-American community. In this, as in so much that occurred in the Sixties, the civil rights movement served as a forerunner and an exemplar, showing not just blacks but other minorities and finally whites that there is a way out of Egypt.

Just as the black churches of the South served as the institutional base for the civil rights movement, the universities could serve as a basis for organizing and enlightening, so believed the young whites who founded SDS. There they could challenge their fellow students and bring the life of the mind alive. "The ideal university," they wrote, "is a community of controversy, within itself and in its effects on communities beyond." And the effect they wanted was what they called a "participatory democracy" in which power rooted in possession and privilege would be replaced by "power and uniqueness rooted in love, reflectiveness, reason, and creativity." Given what SDS ultimately became, the idealism of this statement is amazing.

Yet one cannot read the Port Huron Statement today without a sense of how naïve its optimism was. The document was, first of all, written by white men for white men, and the sexism is so blatant as to be embarrassing. The constant reference to "men" is bad enough, but the offhand reference to the Fifties university world as comprising "two nights each week for beer, a girl or two, and early marriage" has no redeeming sense of outrage or irony. Moreover, it is a remarkably rational document, clearly written with the unspoken assumption that reason and civility could still somehow be relied upon as tools. In its clarity and rationality, the document is wonderfully innocent, like the pure strains and uncomplicated melody of a Joan Baez song. Liberation was only just beginning, and the radicals of 1962 had no idea how much further they would travel before the Sixties ended.

The beginnings of the student movement on campuses across the U.S. cannot even be imagined except as outgrowths of the civil rights movement of the South. The Port Huron Statement wisely credited the civil rights leadership with pointing the way out of apathy, for the apolitical campuses of the Fifties felt their first stirrings of political activism around that issue. From Harvard to Berkeley to community colleges in the midwest, black and white students organized in the early Sixties to raise support for the struggle in the South. The Freedom Rides of 1961 were supported throughout the country by students demonstrating their demands that the federal government honor its insistence that interstate travel be integrated, that the right of the Freedom Riders to travel in safety on integrated buses across Dixie be protected. Around such clear examples of moral and political right and wrong, more and more students began to pull themselves out of the fog of apathy and get involved. By presenting again and again the obviously evil white racists bullying the obviously innocent, nonviolent blacks, the movement created living morality plays that confronted neo-orthodox cynicism and proved that real moral choices could and must be made. Once aroused, the spirit of righteous indignation spread.

The first major campus rebellion of the Sixties, the Free Speech movement at Berkeley, began in 1963 when just this sort of small group of civil rights activists from the campus joined with community activists to demand that the local hotels stop discriminating and hire more black personnel. Tired of ineffective efforts to persuade the local power elite to do the right thing through argument, these students took up Martin Luther King's tactic of nonviolent confrontation. The idea was to create a situation that would force the hotel owners to respond one way or another. To the great surprise of the activists themselves, the picketings and sit-ins, and the arrests that followed, had the desired effect. The hotels ultimately agreed to hire many more minority employees. The response of one of the student leaders was the amazed realization, "My God, we really could have an effect on history." And they could do it "simply by taking seriously the words of the Constitution and the preamble and the Declaration of Independence and all that stuff we believed in with vim and vigor."

Here was the active response of Berkeley students to Didion's generation, those neo-orthodox cynics who were unable to believe that individuals could possibly have any power or control over the larger issues that shaped their lives. These Berkeley radicals, many of them veterans of the Southern civil rights movement, had become infected with the spirit of the Greensboro sit-ins. Black people, more religious perhaps, more willing to believe in some essential righteousness, had demonstrated to the jaded and overly intellectual whites that there was an essential rock within the soul, and on that rock it was possible to take a stand that could change the world.

In the following year, many of these same Berkeley activists responded emotionally when the campus authorities, reacting to the fears of local businessmen, banned the use of tables for political recruiting at the corner of Bancroft and Telegraph, where such recruiting had long taken place. Forbidden their traditional location, the activists moved their tables inside campus, where the authorities felt they had no choice but to take names to try to stop the political activity. What had begun as simple efforts to recruit volunteers for the civil rights struggle suddenly became a different issue, not of the rights of black people in the South or even in the Bay area, but of the free speech rights of the white students themselves. In attempting to prevent the use of the campus as a base from which radicals could attack local businesses, President Kerr of Berkeley and his administration raised the stakes and in the process helped to awaken a generation.

The resulting demonstration on campus against the banning of the political tables brought out thousands of students who felt for the first time not only that their own rights were being abused but that they might actually be able to do something about it. The arrest of one of the leaders, Jack Weinberg, by the local police was prevented when several thousand students surrounded the police car he was in and kept it from leaving for thirty-two hours. During this period, dozens of speakers climbed onto the car and addressed the growing crowd over an open microphone as the local news media, ever in love with picturesque stories, transmitted the images into living rooms and campuses throughout the nation. Members of the crowd, still in the spirit of the civil rights movement, held hands and sang "We shall not be moved."

The stalemate around the police car was broken when the administration finally agreed to establish a committee to review its policy against political activity. This committee worked out a compromise after several weeks that allowed any organizations that did not advocate illegal activities to return to their traditional use of campus property for recruiting. But this compromise left out organizations such as SNCC and even Martin Luther King's SCLC, since both of these organizations supported civil disobedience. The more radical students, still a small minority, felt temporarily isolated. But that isolation ended when the administration, stupidly unable to leave well enough alone, decided to discipline the eight students who had started the original protest. Once again, the middle-class white students of Berkeley felt that their rights and privileges were being attacked, and once again they responded.

Behind much of this anger and willingness to take a stand was a growing frustration, not only with the politics of 1964, but with larger and still ill-defined issues. Mario Savio, the best-known and most articulate of the Free Speech leaders, spoke to this frustration when he angrily reacted to the administration's use of a business metaphor to describe the operations of the university. If this is a corporation, he said, and the regents are the board of directors of a company, then we the students are nothing more than the "raw material" of this production process. We need, he argued, to make the university a place of learning and not a factory for the combine. Echoing Thoreau, he told the crowd, "There comes a time when the operation of the machine becomes so odious—makes you so sick at heart—that you can't take part, you can't even passively take part, and you've got to put your bodies upon the gears and upon the wheels, upon the levers, . . . and you've got to make it stop."

What followed was the first major campus occupation of an administration building, as students filled Sproul Hall with their bodies and forced the university to grind to a halt. Just as they used the civil rights tactics of civil disobedience in their protests, so they also followed the civil rights tactics of going limp and refusing to offer resistance or cooperation when the police came in force to arrest them.

After the police had cleared the students out of Sproul Hall, the administration held a large public meeting at the Greek Theater to try to explain why it had chosen to act as it did. The classical Greek context was all too symbolically appropriate. The meeting was a wonderful example of the rational, analytical approach, and of the profound limits and failures of that approach. The chairmen of the academic departments drafted a letter that deplored the demonstration at Sproul Hall as an act that "obstructs rational and fair consideration of grievances." President Kerr, who liked to call the university a "knowledge industry," still faithful to the assumptions of neo-orthodox realism, criticized the radicals for their apparent belief in some attainable "utopia." The university, he said, supports "opposition to passion and hate, the reasoned argument as against the simplistic slogan." For a person steeped in the ideology of the Fifties, nothing could have been more scathing. But to the students at Berkeley who had tasted some of the fruits of their breakthrough to action, the old assumptions were no longer valid. To them, "utopia" and "passion" didn't seem like such bad words after all. For one of the things these neo-romantics were protesting was an education that "severed the intellect from the heart."

Rather than let the administration simply call its meeting and have its say, Mario Savio, at the end of the proceedings, approached the platform and tried to speak. He was stopped and dragged away from the microphone by armed guards. After the dust settled, President Kerr argued in his own defense that this was "a structured meeting not an open forum." And with that, the differences were clearly set. On one side, arminian order demanded structured order, Nurse Ratched running a smooth ward. On the other side, long-haired, unkempt students, dreaming utopian dreams, wanted openness and passion, regardless of the risks. The administration had proven that all of its high rhetoric about the use of reason was only rationalization intended to disguise the raw police power on which their authority really rested. In the act of dragging Savio away from the microphone, the authorities' belief in rationality itself was discredited.

In the wake of this disaster, the faculty senate passed a resolution upholding the right of free speech on the Berkeley campus. With that simple act, the faculty repudiated the administration, and most of the students felt that their side had won. Power seemed to have shifted from a structured administrative elite ruling from the top down to the body of the whole, not ruling at all but cooperating in a splendid anarchy. It was as if the British redcoats had been defeated once again and the colonists were free to be themselves.

Like Martin Luther King and like SNCC in its early days, the rebels at Berkeley imagined themselves in the mainstream of America fighting for traditional American principles. Jackie Goldberg remembers angrily rejecting the charge that the student rebels were alienated and cynical: "We were so committed and so involved, we risked our careers, our jobs, our education. We did it because we were so tied in to this system, to this country, to this culture. We believed in it so much that we were willing to take risks." John Gage remembers how surprised he was to discover that the university officials had actually lied. Later, they would all be amazed at how innocent they had been.

V

"Stirring the essential heart"

Like all movements, the Free Speech movement also had its own music. Satirical ditties were penned, in the sarcastic style of Tom Lehrer, that ridiculed the administration and the apathetic students who had still not gotten involved. But for those already involved, the music played an important role, as it had in the South, stirring up the passion needed to sustain the rebellion. Joan Baez, fresh from the struggle in the South, was in Berkeley for these protests, singing "We shall overcome" and "We shall not be moved" in a way that instantly united the crowds that sang along with her and united the Berkeley movement emotionally as well as politically with the struggle in the South.

In retrospect, many people have seen rock 'n' roll in the Fifties as the beginning of the Sixties awakening, as a subtle undercutting of the rational complacency of the establishment. Jerry Rubin said that rock 'n' roll was the first big assault on the establishment: "Elvis Presley ripped off Ike Eisenhower by turning our uptight young awakening bodies around. Hard animal rock energy beat/surged hot through us, the driving rhythm arousing repressed passions." But if this was happening under the surface, it was not apparent at the time. On the contrary, in the early

Sixties, rock 'n' roll was condemned by political activists and the socially concerned as commercial and mindless. With redneck Elvis Presley living the life of conspicuous consumption, then sitting in the barber chair and getting his hair cut for his induction into the army, rock 'n' roll in the early Sixties was still identified with the old establishment. Conservative parents, ever suspicious and watchful, sensed the danger, fearing that if Presley's swinging hips showed up on television, their children would eventually end up in a field somewhere screwing in the mud, stoned on dope, chanting animal noises like savages in the moonlight. However much its rhythms ultimately undermined the old authoritarianism, rock 'n' roll's explicit images and lyrics served at first to reinforce the combine, not confront it. The concern of its teenage fans was puppy love, not politics. If Jerry Rubin was right that Elvis Presley laid the foundation for the youth rebellion of the Sixties, it was not evident then.

Folk music, on the other hand, was politically committed and socially involved. It explicitly reacted against the commercialism of Top 40 rock 'n' roll with a natural simplicity and directness and sentiment. Bob Dylan's early music was hard on the ear and hard on the soul, but in its harshness, it forced itself upon the mind and spoke of the possibility of a new beginning, of a return to simple basics from which to start again. It was ugly but honest. "The times they are a-changing" was a bolder, more radical statement of Kennedy's "New Frontier," but the poetic imagery reinforced the political. "Your sons and your daughters are beyond your command," Dylan warned the older generation. "Get out of the way if you can't lend a hand / For the times they are a-changing." In "A Hard Rain's A-Gonna Fall," the apocalyptic sense of imminent change is at once both ultimately destructive of the old world and full of the sense of righteousness about to be vindicated. As in most apocalyptic writings, a sense of despair over the destruction of the old world is more than matched by a sense that a power in the universe that does not sanction apathy and excuses but angrily works toward justice will in the end prevail.

Despite the harshness of such rhetoric, what stands out most in listening to that music today is its innocence, not just in its lyrics but in its sound. A single acoustic guitar, clear and distinct, accompanies Joan Baez's clear and sentimental appeals. Folk music deliberately shunned the commercial accompaniments of large bands and background voices, of studio mix and complex arrangements. By its very simplicity of style, it declared itself to be from the heart, from reality. Its claim to be "folk music," that is, from the people, was itself an attempt to locate its own source not in the commercial constructs of the system but in the soul of the nation. It was part of the essential rediscovery of eternal truths and of the return to nature.

While Bob Dylan sang his apocalyptic, political chants, Pete Seeger and Joan Baez sang old tunes that harkened back to a simpler time even as they carried the songs of the civil rights movement north. But they also sang protest songs having nothing to do with civil rights, songs that touched on issues of importance to northerners: the deadening conformity of suburban life, the injustice of poverty, the stupidity of war. If the complexity of neo-orthodox philosophy had created cynicism in the face of social inequities, the songs of the civil rights movement and of the folk music crowd cut through to the simple feelings of the heart. It was a repetition of an old theme in American culture articulated in an old Shaker song:

> 'Tis the gift to be simple
> 'Tis the gift to be free
> 'Tis the gift to come down
> Where you ought to be.
> And when you find yourself
> In the place just right,
> It shall be in the valley
> Of love and delight.

This stirring up of the essential feelings of the heart was what made the rebellion of the Sixties possible.

The Fifties, of course, had not been without some white dissenters, Beats who had poured forth passionate protests against the sterility of American society. Norman Mailer's 1958 essay "The White Negro" was an important statement, years ahead of its time even as it reflected the era in which it was written. But to say that the Sixties "hippies" were the children of the Fifties "hip" is to ignore some crucial differences. The Beats of the Fifties—Allen Ginsberg, Jack Kerouac, Lawrence Ferlinghetti—prepared the way for the coming, but during the reign of Beat in the Fifties, their message was more neo-orthodox than neo-romantic. The Beats were in rebellion against the sterility and conformity of the combine. They knew they wanted better. But they shared the neo-orthodox assessment of the possibilities of human nature. The Beats, said Mailer, are "white Negroes" because, like the Negroes, they live outside the system, outside society, existing not for some delayed material gratification or hope for some future political utopia but for the immediacy of what he called "kicks." The Negro was not there by choice, but he was there. And the Beat willingly joined him.

If society was a construction of sterility, then the only realistic alternative, according to Mailer, was whatever primal energy could be found in the heart of darkness, in primitivism and in sex, in orgasm and in jazz, which, according to Mailer, is orgasm's expression. One gets a strong sense of need and desperation, of longing and despair, in Ginsberg's "Howl" and Kerouac's *On the Road.* These are prayers for some mystic refreshening to come into the deserts of these lives, but there is no faith that it will come. Instead, as Todd Gitlin shows, the Beats "recognized one another as brothers, all taking cover in the crevices of a society they could not begin to imagine changing." Mailer acknowledges that in the wastes that Hip inhabits, the human passions unleashed would be violent and murderous. He wrote, "The nihilism of Hip proposes as its final tendency that every social restraint and category be removed, and the affirmation implicit in the proposal is that man would then prove to be more creative than murderous and so would not destroy himself." This then is the best he can hope for, that the acts of creativity would outnumber the acts of murder, in this Hip anarchy. Hip, he explains, "which would return us to ourselves, at no matter what price in individual violence, is the affirmation of the barbarian."

Beat culture, extending from the Fifties into the Sixties, was thus one of the movements that contributed to the growing momentum. And almost unnoticed at first, another element added to the growing sense of the dawning of something new and better. At the edges of the growing crowds that attended folk concerts, in the parks of large cities or in the darkened recesses of coffeehouses in Greenwich Village and Harvard Square and North Beach, the distinct smell of burning weeds more sweet than tobacco drifted across the scene.

Marijuana had been well known in the urban ghettos of the North for years. Until 1937, when marijuana was made illegal by the federal government, a brisk market in the weed had flourished openly. A friend once told me that his father, an immigrant from Puerto Rico, had made his living selling grass. In 1938, when he was arrested and called before a judge, he still did not quite understand what was happening. "But your honor," he pleaded, "I have always sold marijuana. That is how I make my living." The judge was not sympathetic.

What was being stirred to life with the politics and the folk music scene was an awakening from a sense of apathy and despair to a willingness to believe in one's emotions and to act on them. Coffeehouses in the beatnik hangouts became places where the different awakenings intersected. There, former civil rights workers discussed their experiences in the South with college students and anyone else who might be interested. They listened to protest songs about politics; and late in the evening, when the straight patrons had all gone home, they lit up their joints. Politics, music, marijuana belonged together. The feelings of political righteousness stirred up by the music were already an intensification of feeling—of commitment, of righteous indignation, of belonging to a cause. Marijuana intensifies feeling. For those escaping from the

grip of a deathly rationality that saw all the problems, all the alternatives, all the inconsistencies, marijuana added to the sense that when
the head and the heart collide, the head needs to stand back and let the
heart hold sway.

Jerry Rubin, who would make a name for himself later in the decade
as a "Yippie," wrote a wonderful essay called "Keep Pot Illegal" in
which he argues that as long as pot is illegal, it will continue to spread
as an underground agent freeing the minds of the young: "Education is
conditioning. Pot deconditions. School makes us cynics. Pot makes us
dreamers. Education polarizes our brains into subjects, categories, divi-
sions, concepts. Pot scrambles up our brain and presents everything as
one perfect mess." And so it did, and does.

Thus, in the early Sixties, adding to the sense of renewal and change,
marijuana served a significant purpose. It was a natural high that did not
leave its users puking in the grass or crashing into roadside trees. It was
outlawed by the authorities. It was natural. It promoted introspection.
It helped to distance the users from the old beliefs as it wedded them
to the new, breaking down old taboos and inhibitions by stimulating the
senses. The most dangerous side effects of grass, so the wisdom went,
were obesity and pregnancy. It thus bound its adherents together in a
brother- and sisterhood of black markets, rediscovered feelings, and forbidden games. According to Norman Mailer, it was the wedding band
that in the late Fifties united the hipster and the spade and produced
the child—the new age—about to be born.

But Beats like Norman Mailer and Allen Ginsberg were over thirty.
In the Fifties, they had remained in Egypt, content to throw stones at
Pharaoh and howl about their enslavement in Moloch. Kerouac remained a slave in Egypt and drank himself to death there; only Ginsberg, the true child of Israel, took LSD and moved ahead with the
younger crowd. What made the Sixties different was that the baby
boomers rejected alienation and despair to embrace the possibility of a
new and better life. Awakened from a long, deep neo-orthodox sleep, a
new generation found romantic hope in the liberating possibility that
one could, after all, as Emerson had said, trust one's essential feelings.
So they set off eagerly and innocently to return to themselves and by so
doing change Egypt into the Promised Land. In the final line of *Cuckoo's Nest,* the Chief determines to head home, saying with obvious joy,
"I been away a long time."

2

The Second, Loss

I

"What is the matter with you guys?"

NOBODY PROMISED IT WAS GOING TO BE EASY. MAYBE SOME ENTHUSIAS-tic Democrats did believe all the hype about a liberal Camelot under Kennedy. Maybe some folkies did dream that they could strum and sing their way marching to utopia. Maybe some young integrationists on the picket lines did imagine that day had dawned when black and white would walk hand in hand together. But the dreams with which the Sixties opened flourished only long enough to release the old romantic vision of essentialism before they were violently blown away.

Having found that they were slaves in an Egyptian bondage, the children of the baby boom enjoyed a momentary hope that, with nature on their side, they could reform the world. They really believed that right was so obvious that they could go to Pharaoh and convince him with reasoned arguments and a few powerful songs to set all of Egypt free. They really believed, in those innocent days, that they could reform Egypt and turn it into Canaan. They never imagined that they might someday have to leave.

For some, the shattering of that hopeful illusion occurred suddenly on November 22, 1963; for others not till 1968; for a few, the myth of Camelot lived on and continues even to this day. But for those who experienced the shattering of the liberal illusion of an easy way to Canaan, a chill uncertainty blew in. The loss of political idealism was only the beginning. In time, as the circles of doubt widened, a growing terror crept into their souls.

At that point, as if the scales had fallen from their innocent eyes, they looked around and began to realize that the world was not the hopeful place they had assumed, that the evil they fought was not simply out there but in themselves as well. From that first realization, when they stepped back and saw for the first time that they really did not know, the edges of their virtual-reality helmets rattled loose. The supreme

78

confidence with which they had recently faced the future began to fray. The entire fabric of their beliefs began to unravel, strand by strand. As King said, "The assassination of President Kennedy killed not only a man but a complex of illusions."

At first, McMurphy thought that he could "put a Betsy bug" up old ball-buster Ratched's butt within a week: "Bug her till she comes apart at those neat little seams, and shows, just one time, she ain't so unbeatable as you think." He took bets from the other inmates that he could get her goat, and then he tried to make the ward a place where he could enjoy some of the freedoms he had been used to on the outside. But his attempt to organize a vote to let the inmates watch the World Series was defeated by Ratched's parliamentary maneuvering. His few successes were fleeting at best. Everywhere he turned, he found that she controlled the strings. He had come onto the ward with a burst of cheerful optimism, convinced that he could reform the place and make it over in his own image in a week. The other inmates, slowly dragged out of their fogs, cheered him on and risked their own tender growth. In his energy and enthusiasm, they sensed somehow a way out of their apathy.

These patients, the acutes of the ward, are like the silent students of Didion's generation. The inmates of the Fifties, intimidated by memories of the Depression and the world war, had become convinced that humans are too evil, society too complex, and conditioning too profound for anyone ever to break out. Human consciousness is so tied up in the web of conditioning, they believed, that escape is impossible. If there is nothing but the constructed web of social conditioning, no place exists to escape to, nothing outside the text. For them, every apparent goal is only another aspect of society's own constructions, another part of the web devilishly disguised to look like freedom only, a matrix inside a matrix ad infinitum. Thus, safety and security were their primary goals. And nothing McMurphy says or does has any real influence upon the acutes' profound sense of being helpless victims of a cruel and angry God. It was, according to one inmate, as in the old orthodox Calvinist world, "A hell of a life. Damned if you do and damned if you don't. Puts a man in one confounded bind, I'd say."

At first McMurphy treats the inmates just as if they were regular guys, as if, said the Chief, he was a politician running for office and everyone had an equal vote. They are amazed by his natural egalitarianism, by the way he shakes the hands of every acute and every chronic, even old Ellis nailed against the wall and standing in a puddle of his own piss. As far as McMurphy is concerned, these guys are no different than the "average asshole out there on the street." And in his own innocence he expects them to react in what he considers normal ways.

But the inmates can see that McMurphy is different. They debate

how it is that the combine didn't get to him. It shaped everyone else to
its pattern of conformity. It made corporation men in grey flannel suits
out of many, except of course for the broken products that ended up on
Nurse Ratched's ward. But McMurphy was clearly neither a product of
the combine nor one of the broken spirits in the combine's dumpster.
He was different. Perhaps, reasons the Chief, it was because he moved
around, because he never stayed in one place long enough for the combine to get its wires around him.

Perhaps. But to say that would be to say that he was not conditioned
by any particular environmental forces, that he was somehow unique
and not the product of any social construction. But McMurphy is a familiar and common type in American culture and not unique at all. He
is a combination of Mike Fink and Paul Bunyan, the ultimate nineteenth-century rugged individual brawling and loving his way across the
continent, standing defiantly alone against the tyrants of the world. He
is the very model of nineteenth-century Romanticism, Emerson's self-
reliant man. He is not uniquely free from social conditioning. He had
escaped the twentieth-century American combine, but he was clearly a
throwback to the ideal of an earlier era. Harding recognizes this when
he defends McMurphy for his lying, cheating ways: "I'm all for him, just
as I'm for the dear old capitalistic system of free individual enterprise,
comrades, for him and his downright bullheaded gall and the American
flag, bless it, and the Lincoln Memorial and the whole bit. Remember
the Maine, P. T. Barnum, and the Fourth of July. I feel compelled to
defend my friend's honor as a good old red, white, and blue hundred-
per-cent American con man."

So McMurphy is a con man, a con-structed man but one who plays to
the hilt a role that was shaped by an earlier version of what it meant to
be American. And that rugged, individualistic, laissez-faire, robber
baron American was as out of place in the safe, secure corporate Fifties
as was the American Indian. That is why both McMurphy and the Chief
ended up on Nurse Ratched's ward with the other misfits and broken
spirits. McMurphy is as much an echo of nineteenth-century romantic
America as he is a foreshadowing of the Sixties counterculture to come.
Both of these romantic eras have much in common, for both stand out
in similar contrast to the orthodox and neo-orthodox eras that preceded
them.

McMurphy is thus the American Adam in the garden, a latter-day
Walt Whitman worshipping the smell of his own armpits and sounding
his barbaric yawp over the roof of the world. He does not, as some neurotic intellectual might, look to nature to justify himself; he is instead
an act of nature. And just as nationalistic American expansionists like
Whitman thought they could reform the world into their own happy

image, so McMurphy sees the ward as a New Frontier—as Kennedy would put it—of challenge. He is himself happily unaware why other people might not be as comfortable in their natural skins as he is. Simply by his own example, he determines to show them that they can acquire his natural self-confidence. That is why he is so horrified when he discovers that the other inmates are not—as he is—committed, but are all voluntary and could walk out the door any time they want. "You're bullshitting me," he screams in disbelief. "What is the matter with you guys?"

His immediate reaction to this confusing news is to withdraw to give himself some time to figure out the meaning of this strange revelation. It shakes him to the core. For the first time, he actually feels their terror and comprehends emotionally where they are coming from, and it both terrifies and confuses him. So, for a while, he plays Nurse Ratched's game. Like the other acutes, he hides in the private world of his own introspections, his confidence all but lost. He cleans the latrines and does what he is told. He goes along to get along. McMurphy seems to have finally learned, says the Chief, to be "cagey," to accept his cage and hide in the fog from the terrors of a mysterious universe outside of his control and beyond his comprehension. The Chief understands what is happening, but Cheswick, one of the most devoted of McMurphy's disciples, cannot believe that his hero would abandon him, and when he realizes that McMurphy will no longer fight, that he is all alone and that there is no hope—none whatsoever—Cheswick drowns himself in the bottom of the swimming pool.

But McMurphy is too much McMurphy. That old frontier conditioning, however it got into him, is much too strong to be denied for long. He cannot conform despite his efforts, and he comes to realize how profoundly his new friends need him. He comes back into the fight. But this time, the stakes are higher; something heavier needs to be done, something more radical. The early days of liberal reform are over, lost; well-intentioned efforts to control events have collapsed. Simple example is not enough. The New Frontier has turned out to be but a borderline, the beginning of passage into the wilderness. The Sixties have begun their deconstructive spin.

II

"To Peep Over the Parapet"

In *The Best and the Brightest,* his study of the origins of the Vietnam War, David Halberstam tells of an early confrontation in the Kennedy administration over the wisdom of getting the US involved in Vietnam.

David Riesman, a sociologist from Harvard, was disturbed by the hubristic talk of counterinsurgency and limited war. He distrusted the New Frontiersmen's naive optimism that somehow it would be easy to reform the place. He asked a group of Kennedy's aides if they had ever been to Utah. Utah? they said, no, why Utah? Have you ever been there? Halberstam recalls: "No, Riesman answered, but he had read a great deal about the Church of the Latter Day Saints, and it occurred to him that his friends did not know much about America, about how deep the evangelical streak was." According to Halberstam, Riesman, a student of the American Civil War, "had always been disturbed by the passions which it had unleashed in the country, the tensions and angers just below the surface, the thin fabric of the society which held it all together, so easy to rend." Sometimes the old primal constructions cannot be overridden or controlled. When awakened, the hidden demons of the self may be more dangerous than imagined. Sometimes it may be better to let sleeping visions slumber.

The constructs in our heads are not just those of our immediate culture. We have of course the known beliefs and values that we articulate and defend, but these are mere rationalizations. Such speculations of the head are controlled by the inclinations of the heart. Of course we are free to think and to do what we want, but the real question is: why do we want what we want? What controls our desires? To say that we freely choose is naive. Every act of choice is based upon some contingency. It cannot be otherwise. We can do what we want, but we cannot control our wanting. As Jonathan Edwards said, "Liberty is the power anyone has to do as he pleases without considering how his pleasure comes to be as it is."

To stand in front of the counter at the ice cream store and decide which flavor to buy, or which candidate to vote for, is an act of will. But the will's decision is based upon factors already in place, buried in the recesses of memory and experience. We do not really control our own decisions; the factors determining our decision-making are all part of our programming. Because we sense these decisions being made in our minds, we imagine we are making them. But in fact, as Jonathan Edwards said, we no more control the ideas that come into our minds than we control the sounds that come into our ears or the sights that come into our eyes. Instead, our decisions are based upon well-developed, complex constructs in what psychologists call the unconscious. Whether we realize it or not, we have each given our heart to some god or gods, and those gods control us.

Liberals, being arminian, tend to reject such analysis. One of the classic definitions of liberalism includes a belief in the freedom of the mind to make rational and intelligent choices, to be in control. To the extent that they acknowledge an unconscious, liberals see it as a demon best kept under control. They assume a model of human consciousness in which free will's rational arguments, not the inclinations of the heart, determine behavior. They believe that people, being both rational and basically good, can be persuaded by argument and education to do the right thing. In Freudian terms, they believe that the ego can control the id. Liberals, as James Baldwin said, are innocent.

Those people we call "radical" rather than "liberal" tend to emphasize the deeper roots of social problems. The word itself is from the Latin "radix," which means "root." Recognizing that individual behavior is all too often based upon unconscious constructs over which the rational intellect has no or little control, radicals reject the liberal faith in reason. They reject such arguments as mere rationalizations, like the excuses of Franklin that let him enjoy his fish. They see through the superficial constructs to the underlying motivations out of mind, such as the money, power, and status that they say are the ultimate roots of our behavior, the gods that really control us.

Despite these insights, however, most radicals share the liberals' assumption that we can change the old ways and construct a better world. They, too, believe that humans can seize control and change the greater circumstances of their lives. But they believe this has to be accomplished by means other than moral suasion and reason. They reject the liberals' faith in rational argument and logic. Because we humans are programmed to respond to the unconscious desires produced by the processes of social conditioning, rational arguments, they say, tend to be a waste of time. As John Winthrop said back in 1629, "Force of argument . . . may enforce a rational mind to some present act of mercy," but it cannot change the heart. Instead, they argue, changing the environment in which people are raised can reform human behavior.

Radical attempts at social engineering are based not on Winthrop's orthodox idea of original sin and the need for mystic conversion but on a model of human consciousness coming from Enlightenment philosophers John Locke and Jean-Jacques Rousseau, a model that says humans are born a "tabula rasa," neither good nor bad, and are shaped by their social environment. Today's radicals hold the latest extension of the belief that in order to change the heart, since liberal reason cannot hope to work and Christian mysticism proved a failure, what you have to do is to change the environment. For if you can change the circumstances that shape human consciousness, then you can create new cultural contingencies that will eventually produce better people. Even if such cultural engineering fails to affect the current generation, surely it will create better people out of the younger ones.

But radical attempts to engineer utopia have repeatedly proven themselves to be dismal failures. The Plymouth Pilgrims soon learned the folly of trying to live in a utopian communism. Explaining the reason for his change to a more practical individualism with private ownership of land, Governor William Bradford in the 1640s sneered at "the vanity of that conceit of Plato and other ancients applauded by some of later times; that the taking away of property and bringing in community into a commonwealth would make them happy and flourishing, as if they were wiser than God." To a Puritan like Bradford, the communitarian illusion is the product of people who believe, like Nurse Ratched, that they are somehow above all that is weak and of the flesh, that they can somehow step outside of conditioning and know what is best for us all "as if they were wiser than God." The communitarian experiment at Plymouth failed not because the colonists were lazy or counterrevolutionary, explained Bradford, but because all humans are trapped in the constructs of the world and subject to original sin. When he saw that the hope for human perfectability was folly, he pragmatically adjusted his theory to fit the facts rather than hang the wretched sinners. But most radicals through history have gone at it the other way around, trying to force sinful human beings into the square holes of their utopian theories. The French Revolution's Robespierre wasn't the last radical to end up hunting for conspirators who must have somehow foiled his theoretically perfect plans to re-create the world. In our own century, the failure of "scientific socialism" to create "The New Soviet Man" stands as a bloody lesson in the futility of trying to change human nature from the top down.

Does the failure of utopian efforts at social change like Soviet socialism prove that we are not socially constructed? No, it does not; but what it does show is that the cultural constructions are much deeper and have a greater hold on the human mind than even the radicals are willing to admit. Cultural constructions such as gender roles may not be "essential" in some hard-wired or biogenetic sense—they may not come from God and nature, part of the universe and therefore unchangeable—but like the instincts of animals, they may be so deeply rooted in the evolution of human consciousness as to frustrate superficial attempts at eradication. One does not have to be an essentialist to believe that both cultural and biological constructs are embedded in us as deeply as the beaver's desire to build dams. To make people aware of this conditioning, and then to change it, may be harder than imagined.

We humans are so deeply encaged in all these constructions that only the innermost walls of the cage are visible to us. We have our individual political and social beliefs, our opinions and preferences and prejudices. But these are only the bricks on the dungeon's interior walls. We also have unacknowledged assumptions that we so take for granted we do not even know they are there. In Edwards's language, we do not know the gods we really worship. In Norman Mailer's language, we do not know the visions that hump us through the night. Most of life we take for granted. We get out of bed in the morning and put our feet on the floor without wondering if the floor will be there. We put on the required clothes for our daily tasks without asking why. We see the world outside ourselves as other and assume an identity in a body basically unchanged from that which we had the day before. We play our gendered roles. Our social identity is built on a foundation of unconscious assumptions about the meaning and purpose of our existence. Yet all of this is part of our conditioning, the hidden substructures of the physical, biological, and socially constructed cages in which we are caught.

Were we to wake up one morning and put our feet down and the floor not be there, or if we could not remember why we have to put on these strange cloth garments lying by the bed, or we couldn't remember who we were or where or why, the effect would be terrifying. Suddenly the context we had always taken for granted would be gone. Like people in an earthquake who feel the solid earth suddenly turn to shaking jello, we would have our very identity called into question. Terror is the only word for the emotions created by transgressing the margins of identity and staring into the howling wilderness outside the security of one's socially constructed cage. The void outside our familiar paradigms is more terrifying than the mind can bear. Even Emerson, the great American romantic who claimed to believe in the essential presence of God in the soul, once wrote:

> I dare not peep over this parapet
> To gauge with glance the roaring gulf below
> The depths of sin to which I had descended
> Had not these me against myself defended.

To defend the self against the depths of sin in the self is to protect the structures of one's identity and one's sanity.

The theme that ties *Cuckoo's Nest* together is the idea of the combine, that collection of social forces that shapes, or constructs, everyone in society, any society, to a uniform image. Those judged to be outside of the combine, those who do not conform to the beliefs and values of the majority, are said to be not just wrong but in extreme cases "insane." Emily Dickinson said it well:

> 'Tis the Majority
> In this, as All, prevail—
> Assent—and you are sane—

Demur—you're straightway dangerous—
And handled with a Chain

Too great a change can propel one beyond the frontiers, not just of politics and social acceptability, but of sanity itself.

When McMurphy exclaims that his new friends aren't really crazy, at least "no crazier than the average asshole out there on the street," he challenges the common definitions of sanity and insanity. His world is not divided between the sane and insane but crowded with different assholes all believing different things and seeing the world in different ways. His let-it-all-hang-out egalitarian attitude is able to accept diversity. He is able to liberate the acutes from their psychology of servitude by showing them, not how to conform to society's idea of political or moral correctness, not how to fit into the prevailing paradigm, but how to ignore society's great shaking finger of shame and, like him, just be themselves.

He is able to do this not because of his superior intellect or his ability to reason and reach logical conclusions; he is able to do this because he has no use or respect for intellect at all. He knows, instinctively, that the mind merely rationalizes, that all of the intellectual pretensions of Harding—the gay inmate—are nothing more than hot air, and that at bottom everyone, including himself, is basically "an asshole." Nathaniel Hawthorne used the term "brotherhood of sinners" to refer to the same idea. Before him, the phrase was "original sin." We are all created equal not because we are all potential gods but because we are all equally confused, equally selfish, equally prideful, equally the helpless victims of forces beyond our comprehension and control, sinners in the hands of an angry God.

Thus, Harding is never "cured" of being gay. Instead, he stops believing in the combine's putdown of him as somehow inferior or sicker than the "average asshole on the street." He learns to reject the hierarchical definitions of sane and insane that had convinced him to go into the hospital in the first place. He accepts that what once he had viewed as insanity is simply another screwed-up way to be. In this, he foreshadows changes in society itself. In 1962, when *Cuckoo's Nest* was published, the American Psychiatric Association still included homosexuality in its list of mental diseases. Each year, at its annual convention, a larger and larger group of members voted to remove it, until finally, in 1973, a condition once seen by these doctors as a mark of insanity became simply an alternative lifestyle. Insanity, it would seem, is not necessarily a mental condition but a political and social category that can be changed by a majority vote.

Depending upon how deeply entrenched we are within our particular identities, we tend to call people with radically different identities "crazy." Catholics think Baptists are crazy, and Baptists return the compliment. Virginians wonder what must be in the water in Massachusetts, and Yankees shake their heads in disbelief at denizens of the Bible Belt. Americans wonder what the French see in Jerry Lewis, and many Europeans are convinced that Americans as a whole are quite nuts. Muslims denounce America as the Great Satan, while Americans cannot fathom how Muslim women can possibly tolerate walking around in those abayas. East and West can barely communicate.

Someone from ancient Persia suddenly transported to our world would think he had gone insane, or that we were all insane. He would be right. Someone from our world transported back to his would be equally out of place and literally "out of his mind." Was Galileo insane? You bet, but only within the context of his day, because he believed things totally outside the accepted view of his time. In our time, he would seem insane for some of his other views. But whether he was or would be really insane is the wrong question. Insanity is relative, not absolute. It is not a disease like smallpox that can be clinically diagnosed. It is an assessment of a state of mind relative to the majority that in this prevail. A thousand years from now, our behavior and beliefs will surely seem as insane to some time traveler as the ancient Persians' superstitions do to us. So the terrorists think that we are insane, and we return the compliment.

We are each and all sane within our own separate identities and "crazy" to people who have other beliefs, but if enough of us share similar crazy beliefs, then within the context of that belief system we are "sane." If one person believes that some dead Jew, executed for crimes against the state, actually rolled away a rock and rose from the dead and will be resurrected and give eternal life to those who believe in him, that guy is likely to get locked up. If millions of Christians affirm the same, that is OK, because we recognize those beliefs as part of an accepted religious system. Even the official handbook of the medical profession, the *Diagnostic and Statistical Manual*, or *DSM*, states quite clearly that beliefs or "experiences of members of religious or other subcultural groups may be difficult to distinguish from delusions or hallucinations. When such experiences are shaped and accepted by a subcultural group they should not be considered evidence of psychosis." There is, it seems, safety in numbers.

What had begun in the early Sixties as an innocent challenge to established authority eventually opened into a much wider questioning of the combine. What began as a questioning of political assumptions broadened into a questioning of more fundamental beliefs. This questioning of basic assumptions widened in ever-enlarging ripples until, by the end of the decade, the country itself seemed to be sailing over the edge. Liberalism had failed to reform Egypt through the means of good liberal reason, thus leaving the door open to other possibilities. Even middle-class white America, never terribly secure in the Fifties, stumbled at the threshold of the new decade and never quite regained its footing.

III

"The end of innocence"

So the Kennedy administration with its naive optimism also stumbled at the threshold. Like McMurphy with his early attempts to control the ward, the Kennedy liberals found themselves unable to take control and establish their new order. In 1961, the invasion of Cuba by Cuban exiles, overseen by the CIA, bogged down in the mud of the Bay of Pigs. It was a humiliating moment for the young president, as he was forced to confess both his failure and his dishonesty in denying anything was afoot the night before the disaster. At Geneva, Kennedy was again humiliated when Nikita Khrushchev lectured him in public. In 1962, in what may have been Kennedy's finest hour, the Cuban missile crisis almost brought the world its first nuclear war. And by 1963, it was becoming apparent that Congress did not share the president's desire for social or political change. Conservative Southern Democrats controlled the key committees of Congress and buried every serious reform Kennedy attempted. His Camelot was an illusion that existed mostly in the glitter of the media and the dreams of his constituents. Domestic politics and problems with this conservative Congress even had him urging Martin Luther King and the civil rights campaign to go slow, to wait, to back off from the clearest moral confrontation of the day. On top of that, the administration's bold adventure in counterinsurgency in Vietnam was going so badly that by early November of 1963, as Buddhist monks burned themselves to death in front of American news cameras in Saigon, the US administration was letting it be known that a change of government would not be unwelcome. The coup d'état of November 2 and the death of Vietnamese president No Dinh Diem, put into office and embraced by Eisenhower, began the disastrous political disintegration of the never very stable South Vietnamese state. On November 22, John F. Kennedy himself was blown away.

To the extent that the young baby boomers had come to identify with the young president, his death was also the death of their youthful innocence, the death of the liberal faith that a political Camelot was possible. With his assassination, the sense of identity that had begun to crystallize around the public image of the president also began to crumble. His death was the death of the father, not just to the young but to millions across the nation. Psychiatrist Frederick Goodwin has written, "The unraveling of our shared sense of national well-being began with his assassination." Goodwin argues that when Kennedy was killed, "we had no one to turn to, for the entire nation was immersed in shock and grief." He sees in the subsequent events of the Sixties and the behavior of the baby boomers a classic example of the anger and denial associated with unresolved grief. As such, Kennedy's assassination had an importance that transcended mere politics. On the thirtieth anniversary of the assassination, amidst widespread public recollections of the pain, one woman clearly recalled, "It was the first time in my life I remember feeling that hollow inside." The hollowness she referred to had a public as well as a private dimension. Kennedy's death was one of the first great shocks that started the disintegration of the combine. In *Before Our Time,* Henry Idema recalls, "Bitter disillusionment began to pervade my generation like a plague. Deep in our psyches, that feeling has never truly disappeared; it has never been exorcised. . . . The destruction of our innocence shouldn't have been so quick, so violent, so final." As Martin Luther King wrote, "The assassination of President Kennedy killed not only a man but a complex of illusions." Ken Kesey never stopped talking about "that hollow place inside, that hole we all have."

If, in fact, many of the events of the remainder of the decade can be understood in psychoanalytic terms as mass examples of the kind of denial and grief that often follows the death of a father, this certainly underscores the psychic importance of the event. But to isolate Kennedy's death as the only cause, or even the main cause, of the destabilization of the social constructs inherited from the Fifties would be to ignore too many other factors. It was an important factor, but its importance comes not from its own weight but from the accumulated weight of a whole series of similar events, all of which lead to the same disintegration. In many ways, the history of the Sixties is the history of the slow unraveling of the entire structure of beliefs that had characterized the Fifties. In the Sixties, John Wayne was slowly deconstructed.

Even after the assassination itself, the events surrounding it continued to push innocent liberals to a deeper doubt than they had ever expected. The Warren Commission's conclusion that the assassination was only what it appeared to be on the surface, the work of one gunman acting alone, appeared as a typical example of the kind of superficial analysis that refuses to look under the surface for fear of what might be found. Questions kept coming up about the ability of one bullet to do so much damage to two people and still be found intact, about Lee Harvey Oswald's ability to shoot that well, about the mysterious deaths of the people involved in the day's events, about the murder of Oswald in full view of the cameras while in police custody only two days later. It was just too much to believe. And the result was a growing paranoia, a growing sense of doubt eating away at the edges, a foreboding about what was really going on and why.

But it was in the civil rights movement, the greatest source of the essential optimism that had fueled the romantic revolt against neo-orthodox cynicism in the first place, that the sense of loss struck home the hardest. Martin Luther King's Southern Christian Leadership Conference and the younger, more militant Student Nonviolent Coordinating Committee had done even more to generate a sense of hope than had President Kennedy, and the blow SNCC struck was in some ways even more painful for young baby boomers than the president's death.

In *Why We Can't Wait*, a book built around his magnificent "Letter from a Birmingham Jail," King pleads with white Americans to open their hearts to their fellow citizens of color. We Negroes are Americans too, he says. We are just like you and we want to be a part, an equal part, of this magnificent country. King cites all the heroes of the mainstream Protestant American pantheon, Luther, Jefferson, Washington, Lincoln. He waves the flag as boldly as any other Patriot. He cites the Constitution and the Declaration of Independence with pride. He begs white Americans to open their suburban doors and let black Americans join the combine.

Yet almost as a deliberate refutation of his own triumphant nationalism, King concludes by undercutting his optimism with a razor blade of doubt, suggesting despite all his hopeful words that it would take more than freedom songs to get inside the soul of white America and transform its deeply rooted racism. In his chapter "The Summer of Our Discontent," King attacks American racism in language that stands in vivid contrast to the soothing words of the rest of the book. "The Revolution," he wrote, "is now ripping into roots. For too long, the depth of racism in American life has been underestimated." The nation, he said, was "born in genocide," and from hatred of the red man to enslavement of the black man, American racism has stood in violent contrast to the democratic ideals Americans profess. "It is," he wrote, "this tangled web of prejudice from which many Americans now seek to liberate themselves, without realizing how deeply it has been woven into their consciousness." Thus King was more than willing to appeal to the core beliefs of American nationalism in pursuit of his political aims, but even as he seemed to reinforce America's noble image of itself, he raised questions that cut to the heart.

As he had earlier called segregation "an existential expression of man's tragic separation, his awful estrangement, his terrible sinfulness," so here again he suggests that racism is nothing less than an expression of sinful human nature. As such it is a symbol of our deepest alienation, not just from each other, but from ourselves and from God, not something that can be cured by education or by economic or political reforms. Congress can do nothing but prevent its worst effects; it cannot touch the disease itself. To eliminate racism, he suggests, white Americans would have to first liberate themselves from themselves, cut themselves off from their own consciousness—a seemingly impossible concept. Thus even as he sought to convince white Americans that their Negro neighbors were Americans too and ought to be included within the circle of American community, doubts that played around the fringes of his words crackled like lightning on the horizon.

Even more important ultimately in the growing revolt against the old constructions was the effect of King's policy of nonviolent civil disobedience. Defended as a necessary tool to create a crisis and to foster a creative tension in the community, civil disobedience was a deliberate breaking of the law and suffering for it in full view of the cameras, so that individuals watching would be forced to take sides and to confront their own unacknowledged assumptions and "rise from the bondage of myths and half-truths to the unfettered realm of creative analysis and objective appraisal," King said. As such, civil disobedience required a belief that white Americans had a conscience that could be touched. Civil disobedience as a tactic thus depended on that early Sixties belief in the possibility of redemption. King may have harbored neo-orthodox doubts about the nature of man, but he was a Baptist and willing ultimately to place his cautious faith in the existence of some essential goodness in the heart of human consciousness, after all.

In doing so, he also raised the question of authority. If King's conscience could stand up against the laws of the United States of America, against the Constitution and the rule of law in the name of this higher principle, then this empowering act contained radical possibilities. Just as Martin Luther at the time of the Reformation, by positing the priesthood of all believers, had called into question the temporal and ecclesiastical authority that held society together in his day, so Martin Luther King woke a whole generation of Americans from the deep sleep of neo-orthodox pessimism and passivity. In both cases, the Martin Luthers had appealed to the same principle, to the conscience of the individual as a source of authority ultimately greater than that of church, state, or tradition. There are, wrote Martin Luther King, "two kinds of laws: just and unjust." Just laws are laws that uplift the human soul; unjust laws are laws that "degrade human personality." They are distinguished, not by any objective yardstick, not by law, not by Scripture, not by tradition or communal experience, but by the human heart itself.

King repeatedly protested that he was not an "anarchist" but a person responding to a higher law. He well knew that by setting himself outside of the formal boundaries of the law, he risked being called an antinomian, an anarchist, or even a "Commie." But he also knew that to remain enslaved to an unjust law would make him an accomplice to sin. Instead, breaking from Niebuhr and daring a romantic essentialism, he called upon the long antinomian tradition in Western culture "from the refusal of Shadrach, Meshach, and Abednego to obey the laws of Nebuchadnezzar," to the revolutionaries of 1776, to Henry David Thoreau. His was a stance within the constructs of Protestantism but outside the constructs of the America of the Fifties. He set himself, as a preacher should, outside of the mores of his community in order to call that community to a higher vision. King raised the possibility of a cosmic standard from which judgments could be made, and from that mountaintop, many people began to see themselves and their country differently.

James Baldwin's 1963 *The Fire Next Time* offers a dramatic example of the radical shift that was taking place. In the introductory "My Dungeon Shook," his letter to his nephew, Baldwin makes it clear that he is forcing a different angle of perception. Where Martin Luther King had called on middle-class America to make room in its suburbs for the Negro, Baldwin tells his nephew, James, "The really terrible thing, old buddy, is that you must accept them." In this book, the center has shifted. No longer is the white American combine, that John Wayne culture of the Fifties, the standard that marginalized blacks must come up to. No longer is it a question of a superior white America opening its doors charitably to poor, underprivileged minorities. Instead, white America is suddenly on the margins and James is where it's at. Even more frightening for James, it is, says his uncle, up to him, not to make himself acceptable, but to "accept them and to accept them with love. For these innocent people have no other hope. They are in effect still trapped in a history which they do not understand."

Trapped in a history which they do not understand, white Americans are therefore, and Baldwin uses the word like a whip, "innocent." He is talking here, of course, not about the KKK or the white citizens council. Those groups know what they are doing, at any rate. He is talking about the well-meaning white liberals, those who support civil rights and send checks to Martin Luther King. Originally published in *The New Yorker,* this essay was addressed to the liberal establishment, both the centrists like Kennedy and the more progressive white friends, such as SNCC and the folk music crowd. These people, he says, are innocent of their own conditioning, innocent even of the fact that they are conditioned. It is they who need to be freed to face the reality outside of their liberal constructs. But, says Baldwin, they cannot face this reality because they cannot face the dangers inherent in acknowledging their own constructions: "The danger in the minds of most white Americans is the loss of their own identity." So profound is this fear that they do not even know it controls them. Imagine, Baldwin tells his nephew, that "you woke up one morning and found the sun shining and all the stars aflame. You would be frightened because it is out of the order of nature. Any upheaval in the universe is terrifying because it so profoundly attacks one's sense of one's own reality."

White people, says Baldwin, have constructed a reality in which they feel safe. They have so constructed "the details and symbols" of life that even well-meaning liberals act so as to make black people believe in their own inferiority and whites in their superiority. But this manipulation of mere symbols is so far from the objective truth that white people "are losing their grasp of reality." They need to understand their own history if they are ever to be freed from their delusions. But even this may not be enough.

In an essay on Norman Mailer, Baldwin draws a wonderful picture of himself, "a black boy from the Harlem streets," and Mailer, "a middle class Jew," circling each other like fighters "trapped in our roles and our attitudes." But, says, Baldwin, knowing you are trapped in a role does not mean you are free from it. Roles exist because we need them. The identities we construct are not arbitrary but are constructed because they help us to survive. In time we all become our roles. "One does not, therefore, cease playing a role simply because one has begun to understand it." The liberals assumed, as Freud had, that bringing unconscious material to consciousness somehow gives us the power to control and to change who we most profoundly are. But Baldwin denies this possibility. Even knowing our roles, and even hating them, we still find ourselves trapped in them.

So innocent white Americans, even if they could become aware of the roles they have constructed, and the ways those roles are destroying other people, have a hard awakening to undergo. On them, it is indeed a hard rain that's gonna fall. Baldwin tries to assure his nephew that such an awakening is possible, but to do so he has to resort to biblical metaphor. He quotes a line prominent in the freedom songs of the civil rights movement: "The very time I thought I was lost / My dungeon shook and my chains fell off." As Paul was rescued from prison, so the Children of Israel had been rescued from Egypt. But the possibility of whites being rescued from their own white America is on that level of sacred history, not on the level of education, not on the level of liberal reform of the laws, not even on the level of political revolution, but on a level more profound and more personal. And yet, hard as it might be, it is crucial for this awakening to occur, because as Baldwin tells his nephew, "We cannot be free until they are free."

In "Down at the Cross," the second essay in the book, Baldwin details
his own awakening. He describes how his upbringing on Harlem's
streets and in its churches had conspired to make him a "nigger" and
how he had resisted that conditioning even in the face of his father's
fear that by daring to step outside the role white people had constructed
for him, he was putting himself in the path of destruction. But Baldwin,
determined to escape the crude conditioning forced upon him, instead
exposes the reasons why white Americans had constructed such a thoroughly insane "labyrinth of attitudes."

White Americans, he says, belong to an antisexual culture. They are
so out of touch with their own sensuality that they are in fact out of
touch with themselves. Their singing has no soul: "One dare not specu-
late on the temperature of the deep freeze from which issue their brave
and sexless little voices." Even the bread they eat, the "blasphemous
and tasteless foam rubber" fluffy white batter-whipped Sunbeam bread
so prevalent in the Fifties and Sixties, was a symbol of how afraid white
people were of any sensual experience.

Symbolism is in fact at the heart of the racial problem described here.
We are all to each other symbols; as Emerson said, we are symbols and
we inhabit symbols. Unknowingly, we see hidden meanings in even the
simplest facts. Part of the invisible world that shapes our thoughts are
the symbolic meanings we unknowingly attach to everything. The pieces
of printed green paper in our wallets are seen by us as dollars. We accept their symbolic significance unthinkingly, treating them as if their
symbolic value were real and not merely a socially constructed fiction.
In a similar unconscious reading of symbolic meaning, suggests Baldwin, to whites black people appear as walking emblems of the very sensuality they are afraid of in themselves. Hence the stereotype of the
oversexed black is a projection of whites' fears of their own repressed
sensuality. Says Baldwin, echoing a theme originally articulated by
Ralph Ellison in 1953, "The white man's unadmitted—and apparently,
to him, unspeakable—private fears and longings are projected onto the
Negro." Nor is fear of the sexual and sensual all that is projected.
Whites also fear death and project that fear onto blacks as well. Hence,
black people come into the vision of white people not simply, or "innocently," as people with dark skin, but as walking totems of death and the
darkest fears about sex. The need to repress these fears of sex and death
within themselves leads whites to repress the black people who are the
symbols of these fears and whose social repression thus becomes an outward expression of their own psychological repression.

The only way a white man can be freed from this insanity, says Baldwin, "is to consent in effect to become black himself, to become a part

of that suffering and dancing country," to leave the clean, controlled, repressed white suburbs and to join nephew James in his world.

McMurphy's declaration to his fellow loonies in the looney bin, "You guys are no crazier than the average asshole out on the streets," carries the same message. Apart from the artificial roles that have been constructed for us, we are all the same, not divine heroes as Emerson would have it, but all assholes, all "niggers," all ultimately insane. The Nurse Ratcheds of the world may imagine themselves above all that is weak and of the flesh and hide their oversized badges of femininity behind starched theoretical uniforms, but they too are ultimately controlled by essential feelings over which they have no control. This is the egalitarian basis of his democratic spirit, and it's American as "The Oprah Winfrey Show."

In 1963, the country also began to become aware of Malcolm X. Here was another black voice, angrier than Baldwin's, that seemed all the more threatening because of its undeniable logic. A large part of the rhetorical power of Malcolm X came from the tension in his language between the fiery emotion at the core and the icy control on the surface. Just as an extremely hot boiler requires an extremely well-constructed furnace to contain its energy and put it to use, so Malcolm X's speeches were a tight structure containing a fiery anger. Here was a man who could not be dismissed as just an angry hothead. He was too logical, too well educated, too articulate. He spoke to black audiences, but whites got the message: "If George Washington didn't get independence for this country non-violently, and if Patrick Henry didn't come up with a non-violent statement, and you taught me to look upon them as patriots and heroes, then I have studied your books well."

Malcolm X reinforced that decentering so evident in Baldwin, that shifting of the center away from white American culture. Rejecting his family name, Little, as a remnant of slavery and a symbol of identification with white American culture, he called himself simply "X," the unknown. Unlike other converts to Islam, who readily accepted new Islamic names, Malcolm X was not willing to embrace a new identity that quickly. Having just escaped from the long nightmare of oppression within one cultural construct, he was determined to stand alone in the wilderness between constructs as free and independent as a man could be before succumbing to anyone else's cage.

His ultimate conversion to Islam, when it came, was a conscious rejection of the white man's Christianity, a signaling of the acceptance of a world view then totally alien to the United States. But even then, he made the fateful decision to identity with the world Muslim community rather than Elijah Muhammad's Nation of Islam, the Black Muslims. Their vision was too narrow and, ironically, too American.

Malcolm X was against civil rights, he said, because civil rights were the rights that adhere to the citizens of a particular country. The word "civil" is from the Latin "civis" and refers to the city; civil rights are thus the rights of the city. To ask for civil rights is to ask to be part of the American city and nothing more. What we demand instead, he wrote, is human rights. Those involved in the human rights struggle don't look upon themselves as Americans. "They look upon themselves as a part of dark mankind. They see the whole struggle not within the confines of the American stage, but they look upon the struggle on the world stage." There, whites are a minority and people of color are the majority. As long as the "so-called American Negro" thinks of himself as an American asking for civil rights, he will always be part of a minority, but if he should begin to see himself as a black person on the world stage, he will be empowered by this greater identity.

This is why Malcolm X can be thought of as a prophet and not just as another speech-making politician. He tried to expand the consciousness of the people, to force them to see outside of the structures that they still took for granted. Any mouse can be taught how to quickly find its way to the cheese at the end of the maze; the mouse who successfully learns how to do that is an educated mouse. But the mouse who realizes he is a mouse in a maze and stands up on his hind legs and crawls out and over the top of the maze to freedom has had his consciousness liberated. Seeing one's predicament from a higher perspective, having one's mind opened up to new possibilities—this is the role of the consciousness raiser. This is why Malcolm X was such a threat. That . . . and the fact that the tension between the nuclear core of his anger and the tight titanium shell of his self-control made him a potential nuclear explosion, something anyone listening to him could feel.

He may not have used the Christian imagery that characterized Martin Luther King's speech, but Malcolm X nevertheless can be seen as one of those who forced people, white and black, to see that they were as enslaved in a Matrix as the Children of Israel in Egypt. Malcolm X, along with Baldwin and others, was adding to the larger call to break out of structure and to dare stand alone in the wilderness. As with King, it is clear that Malcolm X could not have taken that stand had he not found a faith in some essential force, a reality greater than mere matter, a force that King called "God" and he called "Allah."

For well-meaning white American liberals, secure in their superior righteousness, rhetoric like that of Baldwin or of Malcolm X was a rude fist in the face. What had begun as a self-righteous condemnation of the sins of the segregated South had suddenly and with force backfired and turned into a condemnation not of a few bad apples down South but of the whole damned American barrel and eventually even of themselves as well. With King, liberal whites got so much unctuous political flattery that it was easy for them to skip over the page in which King begins to question; Baldwin, however, forced them to confront those accusations. But if Baldwin's book and Malcolm X's speeches were a fist in the face, SNCC's attack on its own white membership was a kick in the liberal groin.

SNCC, the Student Nonviolent Coordinating Committee, which had begun in 1961 by espousing the same moralistic, integrationist vision as had King, soon lost its early Christian innocence and ultimately did more than any other organization to bring an end to the innocent first phase of the movement. In 1966, the leadership of SNCC changed and a younger, more radical group announced that thenceforth whites were no longer welcome.

In a position paper titled "SNCC Speaks for Itself," Stokely Carmichael let even the many liberal and radical whites who had been allied with SNCC know that they were all racists: "Any white person who comes in the movement has these concepts in mind about black people, if only subconsciously. He cannot escape them because the whole society has geared his subconscious in that direction." Here was true radicalism, a ripping into roots, an overturning of the unspoken assumptions that had ruled unquestioned.

Even the self-declared radicals, in what was called the lib/rad coalition in those early days, still assumed that problems could be solved rationally, that social change really could occur, if only people listened and learned and worked together. The problems the nation faced were serious problems, but they were also somehow fixable. There were segregated schools in Georgia, racist rednecks in Mississippi, police dogs in Birmingham, discriminatory labor unions in Detroit, ethnic thugs in New York. But these were social problems, the results of social causes, and therefore problems that could be dealt with in the political and social realms.

But racism, said SNCC, is not another rash on the skin; it is a cancer throughout the body. The problem of civil rights was not a black problem; it was a white problem, because whites were the problem, all of them. The racism of Birmingham's Bull Connor was different only because it was visible; the liberals' racism was invisible, even to them. Yet they were just as racist. "The conscious white intellectual and radical who is fighting to bring about change is conscious of the fact, but does not have the courage to admit this. When he admits this reality, then he must also admit his involvement because he is part of the collective white America." The solution, said SNCC, was in white northern liberals leaving the South and heading back to the white suburbs they had come from, "where that problem [racism] is most manifest." They had to stop looking outward toward others' sins and look inward to themselves instead.

The reaction from the whites who had worked closely with blacks in voter registration drives in Mississippi, who had been beaten on the Freedom Rides and arrested in the sit-ins, who had given money to SNCC, the SCLC, and the NAACP was a predictable roar of outrage and pain. Even those who had not actively participated in the Southern freedom movement reacted as if they too had been rejected. Hurt and angry letters, together with refusals to make further financial contributions, flooded into SNCC headquarters. At one meeting, attended by both blacks and whites who had long worked hand in hand with SNCC's new leaders, Stokely Carmichael declared that he had never known a white person he could trust. According to the *New York Times,* "A young white man who had considered himself Mr. Carmichael's friend rose from the audience. 'Not one, Stokely?' he asked. Mr. Carmichael looked directly into his eyes and replied, 'No—not one.'"

On its editorial page, the *Times,* ever the voice of rational white liberalism, called SNCC's turn to Black Power "a hopeless, futile, destructive course expressive merely of a sense of black impotence." Reflecting the neo-orthodox attitudes of the older generation, the *Times* went on to say that SNCC's statement was really "a young man's statement. The authors express a yearning for identity and status that seems as much personal as racial. There is almost no recognition of the ambiguities and indefiniteness of real life." One can hear clear echoes in this of Joan Didion's belief that at bottom all barricades are personal.

But to the militants then in control at SNCC, such philosophical musings were mere rationalizations. They had their hands on a solid truth, albeit a painful one, and they were determined not to let go. White people, even liberal well-meaning white people, even radical whites, were racist, "if only subconsciously." The white liberal could not evade this ugly reality, "because the whole society has geared his subconscious in that direction."

Here was a challenge thrown down, a mirror held up defiantly. Here, when the white liberals and intellectuals were forced by the likes of Baldwin and Carmichael and Malcolm X to consider the possibility of their own sin, innocence was lost. With this, the liberals' moral condemnation of the sins of the South washed back onto the condemners. Once innocent liberal whites began to learn just how profoundly the whole society had geared their subconscious minds in ways they did not even realize, the cracks in the combine began to spread northward. Liberal whites had to endure taunts like comedian Dick Gregory's: "In the south they don't care how close you get as long as you don't get too high, and in the North they don't care how high you get as long as you don't get too close." What had begun as an attack on the sins of racist Southern whites had become an attack on the larger sins of the nation and the very same liberal whites who had risen with such righteous anger against those sins in the first place.

The civil rights movement thus became the major catalyst to a larger and wider questioning of the assumptions and values of American culture. What had begun as an attack on particular sins of a particular region of the nation widened into a greater questioning, once it had captured the nation's attention and drawn in the young members of the baby boom. Once we realized that the problem was not just outside of ourselves but in our own minds as well, the whole structure of belief came into question. Points of view that traditional American society once viewed as so far outside its consensus as to be "crazy" now came to be taken seriously. Once that tab was taken, the trip was on and there was no going back.

Nor did this process end with the revelation of subconscious racism. At the end of its statement, SNCC added a new international dimension: "Again we feel that SNCC and the civil rights movement in general is in many aspects similar to the anticolonial situations in the African and Asian countries." Here was a widening of the ripples of doubt, a spreading of the cracks in the combine, to include America's role, not just at home but abroad. Here too was a rejection of the liberal and even the radical assumption that somehow America was still the scene of the battle and the pearl to be won. Just as Baldwin had told his nephew that he and not white America was the true center, SNCC declared, "Whites are the ones who must raise themselves to our humanistic level. We are not, after all, the ones who are responsible for a genocidal war in Vietnam; we are not the ones responsible for neocolonialism in Africa and Latin America; we are not the ones who held a people in animalistic bondage over 400 years. We reject the American dream as defined by white people and must work to define an American reality defined by Afro-Americans."

Thus, just as Malcolm X had argued that blacks needed to stop defining themselves within the limits of their old American identity, the new leaders of SNCC, too, began to raise their heads above the maze and to look around at the world stage. When they did, they began to realize that there might be options other than remaining in Egypt and trying to persuade Pharaoh to reform.

IV

"Lies in the heart"

In his 1964 "Talking Vietnam Blues," folk singer Phil Ochs, one of the leading voices of protest throughout the Sixties, begins,

Sailing over to Vietnam,
Southeast Asian Birmingham.

The symbolism was catching. The need for order is personal and national, but also international. As white Americans had repressed their own emotions, projected those controlled emotions onto black Americans, and then tried to repress those black Americans, these same white Americans saw the Vietcong insurgency in South Vietnam as another eruption of disorder threatening their sense of control. The same psychology that led them to bring out the dogs in Birmingham led them to send the marines to the Mekong Delta. White Americans feared the disruption of their carefully constructed combine, whether at home or abroad. On the surface, of course, Vietnam and Birmingham had nothing to do with each other. But on the symbolic level, where the heavy hitting occurs, both sides sensed what was going on. Logical liberal whites could sense a tremor as the cracks in the American combine deepened and spread. And the militants of SNCC reflected their fears back at them: "The murder of Samuel Young in Tuskeegee, Alabama, is no different than the murder of peasants in Vietnam."

Even before Vietnam became the supreme example of American power stripped of its innocent pretensions, other hotspots across the globe foretold the story. In the Congo, in what seemed almost a scene out of some Tarzan movie, white troops landed in 1962 to save missionaries from savage natives who seemed to have gone berserk. On the surface, the need to maintain law and order and to exercise civilized control seemed plain enough, but the symbolism was disturbing, at least to a few. White European civilization, liberal and rational, once more had to assert firm control over dark and savage emotions.

In a more publicized and lengthy colonial war, the French attempt to crush the Algerian rebels may have had a more lasting impact. Here, for the first time, the story of the rebels was presented, not in the linear newspapers that the older generation read but in the movie theaters, where the baby boomers were learning about life. The 1966 film *The Battle of Algiers* was a sympathetic telling from the rebels' point of view, not of the logic of their politics or ideology, but of the depths of their emotions. Together with Franz Fanon's influential book *The Wretched of the Earth*, this movie made it possible for Westerners to imagine what the West looked like from a vantage point outside of the combine.

In the early years of the Kennedy administration, the adventure in counterinsurgency had been seen in a distinctly heroic light. We were going to rescue South Vietnam from Communist oppression, just as we had helped to defeat the Communists in Korea and the Philippines and saved the French from the Nazis in World War II. The Green Berets were going to be our answer to the Communist guerrillas. They too were going to learn the language and live among the people they were there to protect. The villages would be organized into "strategic hamlets" where the local people could feel protected and safe while their army hunted down the Vietcong and their politicians built the foundations for an American-style democracy. The same American intellect, organization, and control that had won World War II and defeated the Depression would defeat the irrational tide threatening Vietnam.

Kennedy's secretary of defense, Robert McNamara, had been one of Ford Motor Company's "Whiz Kids," the management experts who had through sheer intellectual brilliance refashioned American business into a marvel of economic engineering and success. He, more than anyone else, with his rimless glasses and engineer's efficiency, embodied the idealistic liberal belief that intelligent, logical humans could solve problems and control events. According to Stanley Karnow's history of the Vietnam War, "McNamara had been a brilliant corporation executive who could scan a balance sheet with unerring speed and skill. When he made the first of his many trips to Vietnam in May, 1962, he looked at the figures and concluded optimistically after only forty-eight hours in the country that 'every quantitative measurement . . . shows that we are winning the war.'"

But by late 1963, even that brave adventure had lost its early glamour. The advisors had failed to turn the South Vietnamese army into an effective fighting force, and the South Vietnamese president, Ngo Dinh Diem, had failed to live up to his billing as the George Washington of his country. The strategic hamlets ended up looking more like concentration camps into which unwilling villagers were herded in front of American television cameras.

All of this was a shock to the nation. And again the pattern was one of an initial enthusiasm for a righteous crusade being undermined and exposed, and innocence lost. White-robed Vietnamese Buddhists, the very people we imagined we were there to protect from godless Communism, solemnly sat down in the streets of Saigon in front of American news cameras, stoically waited while gasoline was poured over them, and then lit their matches, to protest the oppression by the Catholic Diem family. It was not police dogs chasing children, but the pictures out of the streets of Saigon had as powerful an effect as the pictures out of Birmingham that summer.

For some, the bitter shock when the enthusiasm of finding a meaningful crusade gave way to an abrupt loss of innocence led to a long and winding road. McNamara himself, reading the balance sheet with a sharp eye, realized by the end of 1965 that victory was not possible. He saw the approaching breach in his fortress and made one last attempt to prevent the dark, irrational red tide from pouring over the borders. He proposed building an electronic fence, a barrier of sophisticated detection equipment and mines that would be monitored by acoustical and visual systems, a technological Maginot Line. The project was actually begun but abandoned when others realized how futile it was. When he was finally forced out of the Johnson administration in 1968 by tougher die-hards who still believed they could win the fight, McNamara had lost the symbolic struggle against his own emotions.

For that reason, Robert McNamara has become something of a living symbol of the old literal-minded liberalism, the belief in rationality and self-control. He was the computer nerd, the whiz kid, the genius who proved that human beings could control the universe, that ego could control the id. He epitomized everything that the liberalism of the Fifties, the scientific, icy Nurse Ratcheds, stood for. He had been at a budget meeting in the Pentagon when he got the news that Kennedy had been shot in Dallas. After a brief delay, he had gone on with the budget. His iron self-control was notorious. Between 1966 and 1968, he was a walking contradiction, a man who had committed himself, and his nation, to a cause that he knew could not be won. His public persona and his private self were two different people, saying different things to other people, and to himself, on the same day. Against the terror of what he knew to be true, he exercised a self-control that can only be called madness and could not be sustained. Even LBJ worried about his having a nervous breakdown. It was, writes biographer Paul Hendrickson, "the struggle between technology and the soul, and the pathologies of Washington power, and the manner whereby public men stand behind masks, and what happens when the head does not listen to the heart."

When he finally left the Pentagon, a symbolic three days of painful transition impressed many of those who witnessed them. On the first, February 26, 1968, while the Tet offensive was raging in Vietnam and Americans were desperately fighting to hold onto even the American Embassy in Saigon itself, McNamara said only a few words at a brief farewell event. But according to witnesses, he could barely contain his emotions and almost cracked as he finished: "Mr. President, I cannot find words to express what . . . lies in my heart today . . . ." At "lies in my heart," he broke and could not choke back the tears. Writes Hendrickson: "Such a perfect unintended double play. You have to think God designed it. Call it song for the life. Call it coda for the close." Call it the universe being in sync. The next day, at his farewell address, this paragon of self-control shocked those listening who thought they knew him: "He reeled out the familiar statistics, how he had dropped more bombs on Vietnam than on all of Europe in World War II. Then his voice broke and there were tears in his eyes as he spoke of the futility, the crushing futility, of the air war." According to one witness's retelling, "And with such fury and passion and tears he's lashing out at the whole war, his voice rising and cracking and the room swelling with all of it." The liberal dream that we can in fact control events and change the world, that we can in fact control the irrational, was lost. McNamara's fate was that of his generation: "You could say he had no sense of man's irrational side, even though he could be highly irrational himself. He was motivated to help create rational utopias, or something close to that idea, and the world disappointed him: Why weren't they more like he was? What he lacked, or lost, was intuition. For all his brains, he couldn't fathom his own heart."

For others, such as the white liberals kicked out of SNCC, the loss of innocence, the loss of the liberal belief in progress and human control, came as a slap in the face. For the young marines sent to Vietnam in the holy crusade to stop Communism, the transition from heroics to tears, for those who had the time to realize it, was brutal. Most of the literature of Vietnam, from *Born on the Fourth of July* to *Dispatches,* documents this seduction and violent awakening of the innocent. Others, of course, never made that transition but continued to believe in the liberal dreams of Camelot and the New Frontier.

V

"structured meetings . . . open forums"

Inevitably, the loss of the first bright glimmerings of liberation from the combine had political repercussions. This was the transition, whenever it occurred, that pushed liberals into radicalism, that turned Kennedy liberals into SDS rads.

The Free Speech movement at Berkeley had been a clear example of a kind of activist civil rights moralism applied to a white campus. As such, it was more in keeping with the idealism of Martin Luther King than the radical anger of Malcolm X. Most of those who participated expressed themselves at the time with a kind of innocent enthusiasm born of the idea that they were making the American political dream of participatory democracy work. They were comfortably at home with the idealism of the Port Huron Statement of SDS and the nationalistic rhetoric of King's Christian preaching. But something happened.

Jentri Anders recounts in the video "Berkeley in the Sixties" how she was walking away from the final rally of the Free Speech movement with a smug feeling of satisfaction for a job well done when she heard Mario Savio's voice at the microphone saying, "Wait a minute, people. Don't go yet. We've still got a war to stop."

It was the war, more than anything, more than the death of Kennedy or the revelation of the depths of white racism, that revealed how profound the gulf was between the beliefs of the older generation and the assumptions of the new. Like the assassination of Kennedy, the war with all its unbelievable stupidity and brutality shocked many young idealists into radicalism. At Berkeley, the students had been protesting against a huge educational bureaucracy that had seemed to be stifling individual initiative and creativity. Suddenly, the university turned out to be not alone but only one institution of a whole society geared like Nurse Ratched's ward to control its inmates. "The war," wrote Mickey Kaus, "was the perfect realization of the New Left's fears. Here was a big impersonal bureaucracy that was not only stifling individuality but actually killing people."

The transition of SDS from the romantic visions of the Port Huron Statement to its later more radical incarnation was a gradual process. No one moment defined when SDS changed, but the constant confrontation with the government and with supporters of the war pushed the students in SDS further and further out onto the margins and then over the borderline. More than any overt act by the Establishment, it was the insistence on reasoned argument, now seen against the madness of carpet-bombing whole villages with napalm, that revealed how empty the liberals' rationalizations were.

We all live within our structures of belief. We could not live without them. But there are different degrees of complexity and commitment. Intellectuals, almost by definition, are those individuals who have built the most elaborate and convincing cathedrals, who can rationalize and justify their behavior to a greater depth and a greater degree than ordinary folk, and who get all too often lost in their own castles. Their words may be sophisticated and even noble, but at bottom they are engaged in as crude a defense of privilege and power as any Southern sheriff defending his way of life. This is why Jefferson told his nephew to take a moral problem not to a professor but to a plowman.

Indeed, the Berkeley administrators and the government administration, in defending their actions, sounded to the young rebels much like sheriffs they had confronted on the picket lines in the South: "If ya'll be reasonable, won't no one get hurt. But if ya'll step out of line, boy . . ." Once this comparison was made, respect for the old order was impossible. There is no point in arguing the benefits of integration with Bull Connor. No matter what you say, he is committed to the old order and is not about to change. His defense of segregation has nothing to do with any speculative ideas of the mind.

Todd Gitlin, author of *The Sixties: Days of Rage, Years of Hope*, a political history of the New Left, remembers having been persuaded to change from liberalism to radicalism by the words of philosopher H. Barrington Moore, who argued, in effect, that "protest, to make sense, . . . has to take the form of destructive criticism of a destructive system." That is, one cannot protest from within the system one is protesting. If it in fact is a destructive system, it will inevitably justify itself. Instead, it must be confronted from the outside.

The good liberals, first of the Kennedy administration and then Johnson's, continued to talk of the need to contain Communism, of the excitement of counterinsurgency, of winning hearts and minds, of defending democracy. They continued to talk this way long after it was clear that the Vietcong were not puppets of some international conspiracy to take over the world, that this was a nationalistic struggle more akin to the Algerian revolt against French colonialism than to anything out of World War II.

Antiwar liberals, and there were many still within the system, argued point by point against each of the administration's attempts to justify the war. But it became apparent that such arguments were a waste of time, and as these liberals began to realize just how deeply the Cold Warriors were committed to their own rationalizations, they began to look on their own government as if from outside the gates of the asylum. Once pushed outside the community that assumed its rationalizations in fact made sense, these protesters became radicalized. And, leaving good liberal reason behind, they became impassioned.

VI

Breaking through to the other side

Thus for many young liberals still flying high on New Frontier idealism, it was the Vietnam War, bombs after bombs after bongs, that brought us down like the squeal and crash of death on the highway; it was Vietnam that shattered whatever was left of Kennedy idealism and radicalized the Sixties generation. All of those mellow dreams of righteousness and reform, conjured up by the civil rights struggle and the New Frontier, lingered only for a moment, like the sweet smoke of marijuana exhaled slowly into the air. But marijuana wasn't the only forbidden drug, and not all those drugs produced pleasant dreams. There were some bombshells of another sort waiting to explode.

Richard Alpert stands as the ideal representative of how hallucinogenic drugs helped to transform the Sixties. At the beginning of the decade, he was an ambitious, eager, upwardly mobile Jewish boy from Boston, worldly, secular, liberal—the very epitome of the eagerness of the era. By 1963, when he and Timothy Leary were finally kicked out of

Harvard, he had become something else entirely. He had, in the phrase that Leary would make famous, tuned in, turned on, and dropped out. How this happened illustrates a process that was repeated a million times among the children of the baby boom.

Alpert's description of this transformation in *Be Here Now* offers a succinct account of the experience. In the early Sixties, Alpert was a scholar in clinical psychology at Harvard who in his own words "came out of a Jewish anxiety-ridden high-achieving tradition." He had passed all the exams, read all the books, and gathered all the degrees necessary for success in academia. In a very short time, he had climbed to the very pinnacle of the academic ladder. Everyone thought he was a genius. His family was very proud. And yet he felt what he called a "slight panic in me" because he knew deep down that he didn't really know a damn thing: "Every time I went to a family gathering, I was the boy who made it. I was a professor at Harvard and everybody stood around in awe and listened to my every word, and all I felt was that horror that I knew inside that I didn't know. Of course it was all such beautiful, gentle horror, because there was so much reward involved."

Alpert's whole life, from his personality to his academic career, was a flimsy fabrication, a barely stable patchwork of sophisticated lies constructed out of the elaborate academic rationalizations with which he handled the world. And yet this was not clearly apparent to him at the time. At worst, he had a dim sense of unease at the edges of what appeared to him, his family, his friends, his jealous colleagues to be the very model of a bright young man who was in complete control. He uses the word "horror" to describe this vague unease, but his use of that word takes place after the fall. At the time, like Kennedy, like the enthusiastic crusaders of the civil rights struggle, like the righteous students who founded SDS, like McMurphy when he first arrived in the ward, Alpert really believed in himself. Becoming a religious zealot was not a part of his plans.

His Judaism, he confesses, was more political and cultural than religious: "The spirit escaped me somehow." So he had no idea what to expect when his colleague Timothy Leary told him about the magic mushrooms of Mexico. But he was intrigued by Leary's descriptions of the inner space where they took him. So he took some psilocybin in pill form at Leary's home in Newton, Massachusetts.

After enjoying the way "the rug crawled and the pictures smiled," he saw a figure in the darkness, a hallucination that he interpreted to be that part of himself, the Harvard professor, that had somehow separated itself from him. Then, one by one, each of the forms in which he identified himself—professor, lover, social sophisticate, even his very "Richardness"—appeared before him and then dissolved. And then he felt his very body begin to dissolve. At this point, he said, "A scream formed in my throat. I felt that I must be dying," and the panic mounted almost uncontrollably. Then a voice in his head seemed to ask him, ". . . but who's minding the store?" With this experience, Alpert had lost his innocent faith in Alpert. He realized, not just academically as he always had in his lectures, but emotionally, that his persona was indeed a fabrication, an illusion, a phony, a sham. With this experience, his old structure of belief was shaken, his old personality impossible to sustain. When everything one once believed is revealed to be an artificial construct, what is left? Where is there to go? If we are nothing but social constructs, and those constructs are removed, what can possibly remain?

The answer that Alpert discovered, greatly to his surprise, was that underneath all the little "i's" of his constructed personality there remained, at the center of the drama, a calm "I" that was watching the whole scene with bemused interest, a larger self outside of himself, an "i" at the eye of the storm: "Instantly, with this recognition, I felt a new kind of calmness—one of a profundity never experienced before. I had just found that 'I', that scanning device—that point—that essence—that place beyond. A place where 'I' existed independent of social and physical identity. That which was I was beyond Life and Death. And something else—that 'I' Knew—it really Knew. . . . It was a voice inside that spoke truth."

What Alpert imagined he had discovered was nothing less than the essential soul that the nineteenth-century romantics had imagined pervaded all of life. He had found that God within, that eternal presence which neo-orthodoxy denied. He had found that divine companion whom Martin Luther King depended on and Malcolm X had prayed to. In a flash, he discovered that the whole academic world was an empty construct based on chasing shadows, that truth wasn't to be discovered by the busy brain reading articles and running around to conferences but by the brain's letting go and letting itself be replaced by the experience of the soul within: "Sola fides," faith alone.

Like Alpert, Timothy Leary began his trip on the straight and narrow path of academic careerism. Also professor of clinical psychology at Harvard, Leary took his first LSD trip in November of 1961, an event he describes in revealing detail in *High Priest*. Although he had experienced psilocybin mushrooms and peyote in Mexico, Leary was apprehensive about taking the more powerful factory-produced drug. There was something comforting about the fact that the magic mushrooms were a natural product that had been used for thousands of years in Indian cultures. With them he felt relatively safe. LSD, he knew, would be a different kind of experience.

Finally persuaded to give it a try, Leary licked a spoon that had been stuck into a mayonnaise jar filled with a paste made of powdered sugar and the potent chemicals. Half an hour later, he had left Timothy Leary, Harvard professor, American, homo sapien, far behind. "Tumbling and spinning down the soft fibrous avenues to some central point which was just light," he could from that distant height look back and see what he called "the entire cosmic drama. Past and future. All forms, all structures, all organisms, all events, were illusory, television productions pulsing out from the central eye." The world then appeared to him not as the reality it had been but as "ever changing stage props." He watched the world as if from the distance of the first cell or the first atom at the beginning of time, evolving slowly through the eons into the forms and structures in which that primal light manifested itself.

Walking into his daughter's room, he confronted for the first time the impossibility of being in the world and cosmically, chemically removed from it at the same time. His daughter sat on her bed listening to rock and roll and doing her homework. She looked up and said, "Hi, Dad." He slumped against the wall, unable to relate to "the father-daughter game." Here they were, acting their predetermined parts in the cosmic play, "the plastic doll father and the plastic doll daughter both mounted on little wheels, rolling by each other around and around on fixed tracks." This he knew as "a complete vulgarization of the real situation—two incredibly complex, trillion-cell clusters, rooted in an eternity of evolution, sharing for a flicker this space time coordinate." From that remarkably cosmic perspective, Leary saw the egocentricity, "the sham," of his whole routine.

Like Alpert, Leary had experienced under the influence of LSD just how constructed his entire personality was, not just his worldly personality with its likes and beliefs, but the entire structure of self from personality to body to species consciousness. It was as if the virtual reality helmet he didn't even know he had on had suddenly been removed. Once he had seen what he called "the illusion, the artifice, the flimsy game-nature of the entire universe," there was no going back. "I have," he wrote, "never recovered from that shattering ontological confrontation."

This chemical confrontation with the constructed nature of the self may have been shattering, but it was also profoundly empowering. It removed Leary and Alpert from the old constructs of self in society, of "America," of "Harvard," and let them realize how shallow even these powerful fabrications were. But it also put them in touch with a sense of an essential presence under those fabrications, a more certain reality than these atheistic academics had ever imagined they might experience.

At first, when Alpert and Leary returned to their academic environment, they interpreted the new drug's liberating experience within the framework of the assumptions of the old, familiar, university world they knew so well. The experience was seen as an extension, albeit a dramatic one, of the kinds of intellectual games they had always been playing. Just how naive Leary and Alpert were about their new discovery can be seen in the enthusiasm with which they introduced their rational, academic colleagues, and their graduate students, to this new experience. In the early Sixties, this new drug seemed but another means by which the human spirit, awakened at last from the fog, was emerging to rediscover a wonderful light. It fit into a pattern already established by the civil rights and other movements for progressive, liberal change.

Alpert at one point tripped with a black member of the faculty. Up to that point, he said, he had always been "a very liberal person about Negroes, which meant that you didn't have feelings. It was a phony kind of liberal thing." On acid, Alpert was able for a brief period to transcend his constructed perception of Madison Presnell as "a Negro," with all of the symbolic and historic freight that designation carried. "It was just that he was wearing that skin and I was wearing this skin. It was no more or less than that." Thus, for Alpert, this new drug seemed so much a part of the spirit of the times.

Leary and Alpert's innocent enthusiasm was shared by many who were also first tasting of the hallucinogenic experience. In a famous experiment at Boston University, Walter Pahnke brought a group of seminary students together in church one Sunday and gave half of them psilocybin and the other half placebos. The results of the "miracle at Marsh Chapel" persuaded him, and many of them, that they had found a new means to produce a direct, personal encounter with the divine. The new experience, although drug-produced, was seen to fit nicely into a romantic reading of traditional American religion. Rather than something radically new and different, the hallucinogenic experience, at least at first, merely reinforced an optimistic, romantic view of life.

After first dropping acid at Leary's house in Newton, the Beat poet Allen Ginsberg and his friend Peter Orlovsky burst naked out of the bedroom, declaring, "I am the Messiah. I've come down to preach love to the world. We're going to walk through the streets and teach people to stop hating." Ginsberg then actually tried to call both President Kennedy and Soviet Premier Krushchev to "settle all this about the bomb once and for all." They were disappointed when the operator was unable to put Ginsberg through. This was innocence carried to the point of being a satire of itself.

But once the two Harvard professors had realized that even Harvard's magnificence was a manufactured illusion, they began to slide outside of the combine. And as they moved closer to the border, they began to spin out of what society considered control. The essential experience provided by LSD was, to say the least, decentering. That is, by providing an essential center not tied to the worldly constructs of society, it removed its users from some other-directed dependence on the opinions of society. The world in which they had achieved success no longer mattered to them. Instead, another reality seemed to summon them.

Like converts to a new religion, they wanted to share their experience with as many people as they could, down to and including their graduate students. Their colleagues were aware of them and their friends as a clique growing into a cult. Their personal use of the chemicals they were supposed to be studying clinically was considered highly unprofessional, their sharing it with students highly unethical. And yet to them, it seemed the only right thing to do. Their beliefs were based on an experience that could not be adequately described. There was no way to communicate it with a seminar paper read at a conference. It was more experiential than intellectual, and thus beyond Harvard's accepted forum.

Alpert recalled vividly the day that he and Leary were kicked out of Harvard. Everyone felt sorry for him; everyone felt it was a horrible tragedy. And yet he felt not that he was being kicked out of the garden but that he was being released from the ward. He stood there and thought to himself, "I must really be crazy, now—because craziness is where everybody agrees about something except you." And yet, he wrote later, "I felt saner than I had ever felt, so I knew this was a new kind of craziness or a new kind of saneness."

With their tripping on LSD, Leary and Alpert gradually lost that sense of connection to the world and personalities with which they had grown up. They lost their reliance on the structures of the world. Once they had discovered with the help of drugs just how superficial their thoughts and perceptions had been, these trippers had lost their faith in the world of reason. Instead, they turned from the liberal faith in the mind's ability to know and to control. The way in which the drug had revealed to Alpert the phoniness of his older rational liberalism about Negroes provides a good example of the process. Like the Vietnam War, LSD provided a more concentrated and intense dose of the experience that many whites had gone through when confronted by SNCC's radical denunciation of their racism. LSD provided another argument in the lesson that the liberal crusade was not under the control of reason, that human beings are not rational creatures motivated by enlightened self-interest, that something entirely different and very strange was going on.

Martin Luther King and John F. Kennedy, Bob Dylan and Joan Baez, marijuana and LSD—all had played parts in awakening the young baby boomers of the early Sixties from the cynical silence that had paralyzed their elders. The beginning of the Sixties was characterized by the finding of an essential something in the human heart, a righteous indignation and a sense of shared purpose, a vision, a belief in hope. Confidence in a self that believed it did know the truth, that it could distinguish right from wrong, honesty from lies, reality from mere illusion, was a powerful stimulant. This innocent phase lasted long enough to awaken millions of the single largest generation in American history just at the point when adolescents begin to question the received wisdom of their parents and to search for identities of their own.

The early phase of the Sixties had all the aspects of any mass enthusiasm. There was, in the liberal optimism of the New Frontier and the sit-ins and the Freedom Rides and the earnest sincerity of guitars strummed in smoky coffeehouses, a boyish enthusiasm that championed the values of American culture, freedom, equality, and justice. Martin Luther King's quoting of the founding fathers seemed then the perfect note, combining the new crusades with the nation's best ideals.

But Kennedy was killed. Later, his brother Robert and Martin Luther King were killed. Vietnam became an apocalypse. Racism turned out to exist not just down in Birmingham but inside our own heads. America came to be seen not as a noble experiment, temporarily gone astray, but as itself the problem. And acid pulled the rug out from under all constructed beliefs and ideals. Not only was the first enthusiastic innocence lost, but confidence itself was lost.

These experiences, of course, did not affect everyone, nor did those affected experience these changes all at the same time. Many people never experienced any of these; some only a few. Some went partway and no higher; others lagged far behind. Yet when we talk about Pickett's charge at Gettysburg, we can discuss it as a movement with a beginning and a middle and a high-water mark even if over half the men never made it to that height. This is a very general pattern, and the transitions within it are located at specific times with specific persons, texts, or events, merely for convenience and for the sake of telling a good story. A great many liberals, who like President Clinton believed in Kennedy and his New Frontier, remain to this day still stuck in that early stage. Clinton's claim that he never inhaled becomes believable when seen within the context of his desire to be identified with the John F. Kennedy of 1962. He never got beyond that first stage. If he had inhaled, he might have left the New Frontier behind and proceeded with the real pioneers of his generation into the wilderness instead of the White House where, like McNamara, the conflict between his passions and his intellect destroyed him.

Despite McMurphy's heroics, his efforts to lift the control panel, to stir life into the brainwashed shuffling prisoners of the combine, to dole out a life for them "to dream themselves into," he ultimately loses. His disciple Billy Bibbit, though momentarily liberated through the natural magic of sex, returns, like a coward, to his stutter; and then, like the Judas he is, squeals on McMurphy and kills himself. McMurphy goes down fighting, but he goes down, as did King, both Kennedys, Malcolm X, Jimi Hendrix, Jim Morrison, Janis Joplin, and a host of others.

At the very end of the novel, the Chief, having smothered McMurphy's lobotomized body, goes to the window through which he had once longingly rediscovered the nature that exists outside. He breaks through that very window to the other side. He escapes from the ward, and his long legs carry him away in confident strides. He imagines heading back to the village of his childhood, to see the guys fishing from the old weirs off of the dam that had destroyed his tribe. He wants to join them in their attempt to rebuild the garden. But Kesey lets us, the readers, know that as he runs across the land, the Chief is heading in the same direction that the dog had headed, toward the highway with its murderous machines.

Is freedom worth the risk? Perhaps it is not even a risk, but an inevitability. McMurphy, says the Chief, is like a prizefighter who keeps on fighting, even when he knows he is doomed. He fights to hold open for a minute the possibility of freedom before the combine closes in again with its rules. It does not matter whether these restricting rules are old moral codes or new political correctness. Either one is a covenant of works, an attempt to control from structure, from the top down, from the outside. In his fight, McMurphy gives up his own life for the sake of the possibility of freedom. He points beyond his own literal existence to the hope of some new possibility, some Promised Land. The crucifixion of the self is the destruction of the old belief structures, a clearing away of the old lies, if only—as Norman Mailer said in *The Deer Park*—to "let it come and clear the rot and the stench and the stink, let it come for all of everywhere, just so it comes and the world stands clear in the white dead dawn." If the death of the ego is the final letting go, then perhaps that apocalypse is the price of freedom. Perhaps Janis Joplin was right: "Freedom is just another word for nothing left to lose."

Kesey's message is classic. It is the message that Moses signified when he led the children of Israel out of Egypt; it is the message of Christ's sacrifice; it is the message lived out by all of those children of the Reformation who left Europe to cross the ocean and enter the American wilderness; it is the message of the pioneers who left Boston and New York and the Shenandoah Valley to travel in covered wagons to Kesey's Oregon: do not be afraid to leave, to let go, to lose your old self. Don't waste time trying to reform Pharaoh. Instead, abandon the rot and stench and stink of structure and let go and dare to break on through to the other side.

3

Third, Expedition for the "Golden Fleece"

I

"If dogs run free, why can't we?"

AFTER THE FIRST ACID PANIC HAD SUBSIDED, AFTER THE FIRST HORRI-
fied reaction to loss had darkened into night and been endured, there
was, instead of despair, a calm. And then a new light slowly dawned: the
old world was dead! School's out forever! The old morality, the old politics, the old authority, the old ways, all gone, all dead—and a new morning awaited. The times were still a-changing, but that change had taken
a dramatically new direction. People's eyes suddenly and for the first
time opened; the mice had discovered they were mice in a cardboard
maze. Rather than figure out new and better ways to get to the exit, they
realized they could simply climb out and escape.

After being locked up in the ward for so many years, when the Chief
finally looks out and sees for the first time that he is in the country, he
is reawakened to the reality of a world outside himself, a different place
only dimly remembered. But slowly he does remember that he was once
a person, that he once had an identity, that he once felt at home. He
remembers being a boy, a child of nature, an Indian playing along the
falls, spearing salmon, living in a village with others, at one with life. He
remembers that before he lost that identity and was forced to try to
pretend another, he had once dwelt in Paradise, before the Fall. All of
this comes back to him as he watches the puppy in the yard outside of
the window rolling happily under the moonlight in the grass.

He had grown up an Indian shaped by Indian culture and Indian values. When his tribe had lost its land to the government, the entire structure of his existence had fallen apart. With nothing left, no identity, no
sense of self, no constructs, the Chief had withdrawn into the fog and
hidden from the emptiness. Nurse Ratched made it her job to fill that
void with new values, new constructs, a whole new identity. As an army
nurse she had seen how this is done, how raw recruits stripped of every
vestige of their old identity, from their clothes to their hair to their self-

114

respect, can be taught to believe in the values of the state, their old individual identities gone and their new identification given wholly over to the collective cause.

If, after all, as the neo-orthodox theologians had argued, and as the Marxists and behaviorists concurred, "we" are nothing more than the sum of our socially conditioned responses, if we have no true selves but are only layers of socially constructed responses, then what Nurse Ratched was trying to do had parallels not just in Parris Island but in Moscow and Beijing. If the individual is a bourgeois illusion, the creation of random forces and not essential, then any alternative identity provided by the state, or the party, or the army, or the ward, is just another identity, no more or less authentic than the first. Indeed, some would argue, such a rationally planned personality, being free of the irrational contingencies of life, should be more socially constructive, more cooperative, and thus happier. Authenticity and truth, goes this argument, are bourgeois illusions designed to avoid the need for humans to take control and create by themselves a social utopia. Nurse Ratched simply wanted to deconstruct the old failed personalities and reconstruct new more socially-constructive ones. What could possibly be wrong with that?

And yet the personalities formed by those first irrational, accidental contingencies of life remain surprisingly strong—stronger than anything that comes after them. They hang on in memory no matter how brutally they might be deconstructed. When people talk about their "real" selves, they are usually referring to their first childhood identities. One's original language and accent are always foremost. When in 1989 and 1990 the Red Army left the street corners of Bosnia and Kazakhstan, the original tribal identities of the people there came back in a rush. When the recruits leave boot camp and finally the army, they go home. When the Chief looked out of the window and saw the dog, he remembered who he had been. His old identity began to return, and at that moment, "he" was free to discover "himself" again. At that moment, he was free from any and all external attempts to deconstruct and then reconstruct him. He was free to look out the window and turn his head once again to his old irrational original home. He was liberated from his enslavement to the human combine and free to return to his own original, irrational nature.

Like Faulkner's caged bear, at that moment when the Chief had smelled a reality outside his barred window, he had become aware of the bars. Like the Jewish slaves of Exodus, he became aware that he was a Child of Israel enslaved in an Egypt, and he set his heart on returning to the Promised Land called home. By doling out his own life for his friends to live, by sacrificing his life for them, McMurphy had awakened them to a life they had forgotten existed, an essential sense of reality within themselves. The Chief watches as the dog chases wild geese that are flying across the moon. He watches as a car coming out of a turn heads toward the same spot of highway to which the dog had headed. But the Chief cannot let himself worry about the significance of this when he is caught up in the joy of rediscovery and return.

If the awakening of the early Sixties from the paralyzing structure of the Fifties had been exhilarating, then this new awakening from structure itself was ecstatic. After 1963 and with increasing momentum throughout the decade, baby boomers by the thousands dropped out of the structures in which they had been raised, and like the dog, and finally the Chief, followed the wild geese to freedom.

But how? How does one avoid structure? How does one escape from the many layers of cages that society has constructed around us? If there is a soul, a profoundly essential human self that is at one with the nature out of which we all originally came, how does one strip away the artificial layers of social conditioning and get back to it? And how does one know when this Promised Land has finally been gained? Emerson said a man can do this "by unlocking at all risks his human doors and suffering the ethereal tides to roll and circulate through him." He never did say how.

Some of the most obvious things to avoid are large institutions of any kind, like the army, or the university, or the Democratic Party, or the Communist Party, or multinational corporations, or the church. These are the institutions of the state, the apparatus, the combine that shapes us. These "granfalloons," to use Vonnegut's term, are to be avoided. They, and closer extensions of them like the family, are the enemy that originally created the lies that now encumber.

But there are also structures of the mind. Once one has freed oneself from the external constraints, like the institutions of the state, the inner struggle is the hardest one of all. The external structures exist, after all, in order to implant internal controls. A police state only works if the police become successfully billeted in every person's head. If every time people feel like acting, some inner voice, some "conscience," warns them not to—for whatever reason—then the rules of the external structure have become internalized and control is complete. Freedom thus means not simply freedom from the external structures but also freedom from all those ideas, beliefs, attitudes, feelings, everything. If these beliefs and attitudes are what constitute the self, even the original self, then freedom means a freedom from that self. The arminian need for rational selfcontrol is a cage. Beyond those bars, only an empty space waits to be explored, worlds where no man has gone before.

Some went ahead of the crowd; others never ventured out at all. In

Newport in 1965, Bob Dylan was scheduled to play for the annual Newport Folk Festival. For the folk music crowd, this festival had become a ritual of great importance, an opportunity for fans and singers alike to be together and define themselves as a collective entity with a clear identity. Here, old labor songs like "Joe Hill" connected the singers and the crowd both to the past with its rich history of American protest and to the righteous poor, the "folk" of their music. Older songs like "Barbara Allen" reached even further back, establishing a lineage with deep historic roots. The blues of black musicians like Muddy Waters put them in touch with the black roots of America, while songs from the civil rights movement connected them to the contemporary struggle in the South. Newer "folk" songs expanded that protest to include the Vietnam War and the narrowness of the bourgeois American life.

For this crowd, natural, relaxed, blue-jeaned, and lipstick-free, "commercial" was as much the enemy as the military, and Top 40 pop songs were seen as the product of a corrupt society against which they measured their purity. To them, rock 'n' roll still meant Elvis Presley's redneck South and misguided, unpolitical rebels without a cause. It meant antisocial, anti-intellectual greasers, car-stealing hoods from the projects with no political or social conscience. It meant adolescent immaturity, puppy love, and sentimental self-indulgence. Musically it meant a noisy, cluttered sound produced by businessmen in studios who cared only for profit. In contrast, the clean, innocent sound of a catgut guitar string was their defining note. It was perceived as uncorrupted, uncommercial; and it was granted entry straight to the heart.

For this crowd, a young folk singer like Bob Dylan was a star. Older folk singers, like Pete Seeger, who had worked with Woody Guthrie and been a Communist and blacklisted by Joe McCarthy, were icons, heroes from out of history. But Dylan was one of their own. His honest unpolished voice was believable. His guitar and his harmonica were equally authentic. He was from the American heartland, and his words pulled together the past, the present, the civil rights struggle, the growing antiwar movement, and the yet un-articulated feelings of a generation. That he avoided the explicitly political messages of a singer like Phil Ochs and instead chose to communicate poetically, through metaphor and symbol, merely heightened his appeal. Pete Seeger's words were nakedly literal, accessible, and concerned with the immediacy of politics. Dylan's were poetry and suggested themes that transcended the here and now. Somehow, without saying so, without anyone even knowing what was happening, he caught the mood of the awakening. If anyone then had been told that the appeal of a song like "A Hard Rain's A-Gonna Fall" was religious and apocalyptic, the speaker would have been dismissed as somehow hopelessly lost in the past. Dylan belonged, so it seemed, not to the Top 40 deejays, not to the old John Wayne America, not to the religious moralists, not to the Republicans or the Democrats. He belonged to them.

Thus, on that July night in Newport, when Bob Dylan came on stage with an electric guitar and a backup band, and proceeded to sing "Like a Rolling Stone" and "Maggie's Farm," the purists in the crowd sat stunned and then rose in anger against this betrayal. Pete Seeger went to his car and put his hands over his ears, trying to block out "that sound." They were, writes biographer Paul Williams, "that portion of Dylan's audience who felt threatened by his continuing growth, many of whom sincerely believed that 'rock and roll' equalled commercialism equalled sellout to the establishment." Forced to choose between folk purity and his continuing growth, Dylan left innocence behind and headed east of Eden. Many of those in the crowd, including many who had booed him, soon followed, leaving very few behind to continue singing "Barbara Allen" and "We Shall Overcome" on their acoustic guitars.

This change from "Barbara Allen" to "Maggie's Farm" had in it a move more significant than the mere technological innovation of electric sound. With this turn to the loudness of electric guitars and the complex rhythms of rock, Dylan took his poetry to a new level and a new world. Folk had about it too much of the rationality of the old ways. For all of its appeal to sentiment, one could still actually hear the individual notes being plucked and understand the words. One could locate it in history. It was, within its own world, safe, comfortable, even conservative, securely located in a familiar social and political context. Folk music came out of the arminian side of the brain. It was a part of a liberal milieu that was, like Kennedy liberalism, trying to establish or even reestablish sane rational order in an insane world.

But rock 'n' roll was chaos from the first chord. It was loud and confusing and designed to drive its listeners out of their rational little minds. It came from the other side of consciousness. With an electric guitar, said Santana, "You're always cursing, you're always praying, you're always making love." Dylan knew this. He knew that the change was taking place, that it would be necessary to leave the comfort and familiarity of rational structures behind, and he went through the door first. His appearance that summer night in Newport was his way of beckoning the others to join him, signifying to them even as he did that the new journey away from Maggie's Farm would not be a comfortable little folk song but a long strange and even frightening trip. "How does it feel," he sang, "to be without a home, to be on your own, without direction known, like a rolling stone?"

In retrospect, we see that this change was taking place in any number of ways. The Beatles arrived for their first tour of the United States only a few months after Kennedy was killed. The extreme enthusiasm with which American teenagers turned to them for solace, or perhaps for diversion, was noted even then, in 1964, as suggesting something beyond the obvious. And at that point, the songs the Beatles sang, like "I Want to Hold Your Hand," were part of the innocence of the early Sixties. Yet, like Bob Dylan and much of the baby boom generation, the Beatles also experienced "continuing growth" and soon left such innocence far behind.

Historians tell us that in the first Great Awakening, in 1741, young Americans greeted an earlier British import, the evangelist George Whitefield, with similar manifestations of extreme enthusiasm. Then, too, the older generation was at first astonished and then alarmed. And then, too, the movement turned out to be not a fad but the beginning of something that would radically shake the foundations of the culture—in Walt Whitman's words, "a barbaric yawp over the roofs of the world."

II

"Going Furthur"

In 1965, New York writer Tom Wolfe grew curious about these changes stirring in the land and headed out to California to discover for himself if there might be a book in all this. There was. *The Electric Kool-Aid Acid Test* has become a milestone for students of the Sixties, a book that captures a moment from inside with as much precision and feeling as could be expected. Despite all its faults and the outsider status of its New York, over-thirty author, this book manages to capture much of the excitement of a generation discovering itself suddenly outside of the cage and free.

It begins deep in the middle of the story, with Ken Kesey getting out of jail, but it reaches back to the beginnings, to Kesey's joy of growing up a "superkid" in the protected Fifties, of his coming to live the quasi-bohemian university life at Stanford, comfortably on the margins of American structure, until he innocently responded to an ad posted on the wall looking for students to take part in an experiment with a new drug, LSD.

By 1965 in California, LSD had already led the avant-garde of the baby boom generation into the next stage. By then, the beatnik thing was dead; the relevant political commitment that had characterized the early innocent Sixties had somehow become corny. As Wolfe put it, "The whole old-style hip life—jazz coffee houses, civil rights, invite a spade for dinner, Vietnam—it was all suddenly dying." No clear alternative had yet arisen to take its place, but the means of transformation was readily available. No one knew what was on the other side of the psychedelic door, but everyone who discovered the door wanted to go through it. The power of this experience reduced everything before it to insignificance.

Wolfe's book catalogues the antics of Ken Kesey and the Merry Pranksters, pioneers of the psychedelic journey. Wherever others would later go, the Merry Pranksters had already been. In 1964, they had covered an old yellow school bus in Day-Glo paint, mounted loudspeakers on the roof, and set out on a journey to the East. The immediate purpose of the journey was to get Kesey to New York to be on hand for the publication of his second novel, *Sometimes a Great Notion.* But there was another purpose, and its symbolic importance soon overwhelmed all other considerations.

They named their bus "Furthur," and they planned to take it further than any bus had ever been taken before. They planned to take it into the very heart of human consciousness, to open themselves up to whatever truths lay hidden within and to sweep as many people as they could along with them. Theirs was an experiment in consciousness-raising. While they explored the depths of their own individual souls, they would careen through America's small towns and cities, waking people up to the possibility of escaping from boring lives and crossing the border with them. The bus, said Wolfe, had great potential for "altering the usual order of things," and thus "there was going to be holy terror in the land."

Kesey called the trekkers together at the beginning to explain the purpose of their trip. They were, he said, going to let it all hang out, right up front, and no one was going to deny what anyone else was doing. If a person was an asskicker, then that person was going to kick ass: "Everybody is going to be what they are, and whatever they are, there's not going to be anything to apologize about. What we are we're going to wail with on this whole trip."

"What we are"? Well, what are we? Do we even know? What is the reality of human nature? What is human consciousness? What is the nature of the mind? As even Scripture asks, "What is man that thou art mindful of him?"

These very questions are what drove Kesey's ancestors, the original English colonizers of New England, to lay bare the ultimate self. "Why came ye into the wilderness?" they asked themselves. Why, for the same reason that God led the Children of Israel into the Sinai wilderness— "To humble thee and to prove thee and to know what was in thine heart." It was to reveal them to themselves that they might know the depths of their own being and in so doing discover that ultimate bottom layer of consciousness. They wanted to discover the truth of the human heart. They wanted, as one Puritan minister had said, not "seemings" but authentic feeling, the bottom-line Truth; they wanted to experience God. Having discovered that the structures in which they were enmeshed were corrupt and artificial, that the world is an illusory Matrix and that what appears is not what is real, they wanted to leave the old world to discover for themselves whatever might be the Truth. They actually believed it possible to experience this God in consciousness.

They failed when their Israel, instead of riding the wave of the spirit, solidified into repressive human structure. But a hundred years after the first arrival, the grandchildren and great-grandchildren of the original settlers arose again in what historians call the First Great Awakening to break out of that fossilized structure in an effort to try again to reach whatever true experience lies waiting in the soul. They succeeded, temporarily, at least in breaking free of the old structure. Some of those enthusiastic converts, like the patriot Sam Adams, went on to lead their new Israel out of the English Egypt in 1775. But eventually the new institutions they created also solidified into rigid structures of state and church and mind.

This is why Henry David Thoreau, a hundred years after the first awakening, spent his famous two years at Walden Pond trying to drop out of structure. "I went to the woods," he said, to find out if life were, as the Calvinists preached, "mean," or—as indeed he hoped—"if it were sublime, to know it by experience." Society covers up the inner truths with its false and artificial layers. We must strip ourselves of such lies. We must "simplify, simplify, simplify," in order finally to throw off all that trash and uncover the core. "Let us," he wrote, "work and wedge our feet downward through the mud and slush of opinion, and prejudice, and tradition, and delusion, and appearance" until we arrive "at a hard bottom and rocks in place which we can call *reality.*" This is the goal of the escape from the structure of Egypt, not to exchange one cultural cage for another but to escape all cultural cages and return to a real original natural self.

Thus Kesey, one hundred twenty years after Thoreau's experiment at Walden Pond, was trying to do the same thing Thoreau and the earlier mystics of earlier awakenings had done. As he led the Merry Pranksters on "Furthur," Kesey was playing McMurphy. But as McMurphy he was also playing the role of evangelist of the awakening of the Sixties. For just as McMurphy had swaggered his original self unself-consciously through Nurse Ratched's ward, Kesey intended to let himself be himself across the whole of the United States of America. Like Emerson, he did not believe that he was at heart the child of the devil. He rejected the doctrine of original sin and believed instead that the original self was bound to be good. But in either case, like Emerson he would let his all hang out there for all to see, whatever the cost. He could do this because he believed that underneath whatever thorny layers might intervene he would find—they would all find—the luscious meaty heart within, the Truth. And by displaying this to America, they would awaken the entire land. To horrified conservatives, they were radical freaks out to destroy the institutions, and values, and structure that had kept America strong and free. But despite their long hair, freaky appearance, and wildly exotic language, the Merry Pranksters were in their quest as American as John Winthrop, Jonathan Edwards, Johnny Appleseed, Henry David Thoreau, or the first Oregon pioneers.

To escape structure was the goal. And one of the means of escape was LSD. But LSD itself was only part of a much larger pattern. When Martin Luther King had stood outside of the law and challenged America in the name of a higher law, he had forced open the door. He may have forced it open only a crack, but the crack soon widened. The radicalism of the black nationalist movement helped to widen it. The realization of the universality of white racism helped to widen it still further. The stupidity of the Vietnam War helped to widen it even more. Poetry helped widen it. Rock 'n' roll helped widen it. Drugs helped widen it.

Those who passed through that door appeared to many of the people left behind to have gone crazy. Indeed, to abandon the structures of belief by which most people define sanity is the equivalent of going crazy, to become—in the language of the day—freaks. Frank Zappa defined the term as well as anyone: *"Freaking out is a process whereby an individual casts off outmoded and restricting standards of thinking, dress, and social etiquette in order to express creatively his relationship to his immediate environment and the social structure as a whole. Less perceptive individuals have referred to those of us who have chosen this way of thinking and feeling as 'freaks'; hence the term, 'freaking out.'"* Counterculture baby boomers, in this sense, were already freaking out even before LSD arrived to provide the final shove.

One of the adjectives invented to describe the effects of LSD is "psychomimetic." This means that the drug imitates a psychosis; it makes one experience what it is like to be crazy. Numerous clinicians have attested to similarities between LSD psychosis and different forms of schizophrenia. Kesey knew this when he worked at a mental hospital in Oregon. He knew it when he wrote *Cuckoo's Nest*. One of the features of people with schizophrenia is an inability to distinguish between the literal and the symbolic, or at least an inability to judge the same things "symbolic" and the same things "real" that the majority of us do. In this, in some ways, they see better than the sane. As the Chief says, "It was real even if it didn't happen."

How so?

Everything is symbolic and radiates with symbolic meanings, although most of the time we are unaware of them. We read these symbolic meanings as part of the actual object rather than part of what we are reading into the object. Colors, shapes, smells, tables, chairs, people, everything—all suggest meanings and have associations beyond themselves. Our experiences teach us what to expect, and we react often to what we expect rather than what we see. Blacks and whites cannot look at each other without seeing everything they have imbibed about racial difference, and on top of that, as Baldwin said, whites see in blacks walking symbols of their fears of their own dark natures. It took tripping on LSD for Richard Alpert to see his Negro colleague not as a "Negro" but as another person wearing a different shade of skin.

Money is a good example of this. The twenty-dollar bill in my pocket, if held before you, appears to be a twenty-dollar bill. Seeing it, you see its value as money. You see what it can buy. You see what it means. The last thing you see is a small rectangle of paper with green ink and lettering. Thus we see the symbolic meaning of the bill and not its literal reality. And indeed the bill only has value because other people see the same symbolic meaning. Our whole economy is dependent upon everyone's seeing this symbolic value and believing in its power. The bill has no value in itself. It cannot even be redeemed for its worth in silver anymore. Its value exists only in the minds of the people who are looking at it and projecting their beliefs upon a little piece of humanly constructed reality. And if it were not for this mass belief in symbolic meaning, if we did not believe in the same stories, our entire economy would collapse. It is ironic that money, the thing materialists say is the only thing of value, is in fact a spiritual entity. It is our shared belief in the same stories, and nothing more concrete, that is really the foundation of the economies of the state.

In *Cuckoo's Nest*, the Chief stops one day and really listens to the insane babblings of old Colonel Matterson: "The flag is . . . Ah-mer-ica. America is . . . the plum. The peach . . . Now . . . the cross . . . is Mexico . . . Mexico is . . . the wal-nut." Then he realizes that the old man isn't so crazy after all. His rambling nonsense begins to make sense. "I want to yell out to him Yes I see. Mexico is like a walnut. It's brown and hard and feel it with your eyes and it feels like a walnut! You're making sense old man, a sense of your own."

The world, as the Puritan poet Edward Taylor had once affirmed, is "slic't up in types." That is, everything in the world is both its literal surface and its symbolic significance. The literal always comes radiating symbolic meanings like arrows that point to other possibilities of meaning. What is more, those other meanings are the more important. The literal is only a surface illusion, a kind of mask. The symbolic meanings are the first step beyond the literal into that higher reality. To read them is to read the poetry of the world. It is also to step back from the literal world and to view it from an entirely new and liberating perspective. Like Ahab, if we are to reach beyond the illusion of the world, this cage in which we are trapped, we must strike through that mask.

One of the things that strikes Wolfe at the beginning of *Electric Kool-Aid Acid Test* is the way that in this emerging psychedelic mindset, "Everything in everybody's life . . . is significant. And everybody is alert watching for the meanings. And the vibrations." When he goes to the Haight-Ashbury, Wolfe runs into a kid repairing an old desk that has a drop-down lid that opens out. The kid pinches his finger in a hinge and then launches into a tirade about the meaning of the design of the table, about how it is part of the "bullshit thrust" that "opens out into your life," a symbol of "fuck you!" Then the kid extends his monologue to the symbolic meanings implicit in the design of other tables. The simple kitchen table there, he says, is "a symbol of a woman with her shanks open, balling it, in dreams—you know?" Old Colonel Matterson would have simply looked at the table and muttered, "Fuck da wife." Both were poets articulating their perception of the symbolic meanings of the world they perceived around them. The symbolic is the first step out from the literal.

Thus, just as Moby-Dick was Ahab's symbolic hole in the veil of the world, all objects seen poetically—that is, seen for their symbolic rather than their literal significance—become "pasteboard masks" that if seen through might reveal the invisible world beyond. To step from the literal perception of the world through this door was to step from the arminian side of the brain to the antinomian, from literal consciousness to symbolic consciousness, from folk to rock. If the Fifties were fearful, repressed, analytical, and literal, this is where the Sixties became thoroughly romantic.

III

"Holy Madness Divinest Sense"

In the Sixties, Norman O. Brown was the philosopher of this symbolic consciousness, the man whose books tied so much so beautifully together. *Love's Body,* in particular, has to have been the single most important theoretical work of that decade, both foreshadowing and overshadowing all the theory that came out of France in the decades that followed. Not everyone who carried the little paperback book around actually read it. Not everyone who read it actually understood it. But its ideas got around. They trickled down from the writings of those who did absorb them, and they provided a philosophical basis for helping to understand and put in context the changes that were going down.

Brown, a professor of philosophy and classical literature, began his odyssey with the 1959 publication of *Life Against Death: The Psychoanalytic Study of History*. In that book, he makes it clear from the beginning that he is looking for an alternative to the neo-orthodox theology that had dominated the intellectual life of the Fifties. In the preface, he begins, "In 1953 I turned to a deep study of Freud, feeling the need to reappraise the nature and destiny of man." He didn't identify the study—it is not in any footnote—but *The Nature and Destiny of Man* was in fact the title of Reinhold Niebuhr's neo-orthodox classic. For those who cared to notice, the direction of Brown's book was thus made explicit. Brown goes on in his opening paragraph to make it even more clear that he is trying to construct an alternative to neo-orthodox attitudes: "Those of us who are temperamentally incapable of embracing the politics of sin, cynicism, and despair have been compelled to re-examine the classic assumptions about the nature of politics and about the political character of human nature." He asks the reader for a "willing suspension of common sense" in order to allow the possibility of "a new point of view." Critical analysis, he wrote, can come later.

The very methodology is a radical departure. To suspend common sense, to suspend rationality itself, to allow any other part of the mind even temporary ascension, is just what the cautious conservative Fifties feared. After all, the history of the twentieth century, only halfway through, had already proved that the human heart was a furnace of depravity, that nature was an irrational beast, and that safety lay only in fortifying the castle of rationality and refusing to yield an inch. Even today, the idea that common sense should be suspended seems ridiculous, until we recall Einstein's saying that common sense is nothing more than childhood prejudice.

Brown acknowledges the danger. But he sees an even greater one in continued repression. Freud had argued in *Civilization and its Discontents* that the id had to be repressed and the ego kept supreme, but Freud also realized that in time, this act of repression would destroy humanity. The pressure cooker would either burst in a collective explosion, as it had in World War I, or individuals would destroy themselves. Defending itself against the irrationality of the unconscious, the rational mind becomes life-destroying. To protect itself, it attacks and kills, and what it kills is its own emotional roots, thus leaving itself to die unnourished. Since repression ultimately leads to death, what Brown proposed, then, is nothing less than the abolition of repression, letting it all hang out.

Because the abolition of repression would free the unconscious emotional side of the psyche and let it out of its deep, dark cave, Brown identifies the abolition of repression with what the Christians call the "resurrection of the body." The arminian tendencies of the brain, with their reinforcing of structure, are under the control of the death instinct and at war with the universe. The antinomian, or Dionysian, side is the side of life reborn and once again at one with the universe. This life instinct demands "union with others and with the world around us based not on anxiety but on narcissism and erotic exuberance," says Brown.

This is the transition from the literal to the symbolic, from the rational head to the mystical body. In Freudian terms, it is the transition from an anal-compulsive personality, with libidinal function restricted to "particular bodily organs," to the opening up of "polymorphous perversity," in which the human person delights in the full life of all the body. We need to escape from the cages not just of tradition and culture and conditioning, argues Brown, but we need to escape from the cage of rationality itself.

This, he argues, is the true original meaning of the gospel. This is even the true meaning of the theology of the Reformation. But the enlightened mysticism of Martin Luther and Jacob Boehme had lost out to the dark, rational side. As the fires of the Reformation had cooled, structure had once again taken over. Moral codes had replaced mystic feeling. Protestantism had lost touch with the reality of the unconscious. The arminian wing of Protestantism had eventually embraced law-and-order moralism while the once-antinomian evangelicals had succumbed to an equally dead literalism. Today, the liberals fund archeological expeditions to find the literal city of Jericho, while the fundamentalists insist that Jonah really was swallowed by a literal whale. In their different ways, both are equally worldly and equally literal. The torch of mysticism and symbolic consciousness long ago passed out of organized religion to the poets and philosophers. But even if it passed out of the churches, the torch at least was passed. The antinomian desire for freedom burns brightly at times, then flickers dimly for a while. But it is always there as part of the duality of consciousness.

In fact, this life force is always in constant combat against the literal and rational restrictions that would contain and channel it. According to Brown, "The struggle of consciousness to circumvent the limitations of formal logic, of language, and of 'common sense' is . . . never ending." As the Chief said of McMurphy, the "thing he was fighting, you couldn't whip it for good. All you could do was keep on whipping it, till you couldn't come out any more and somebody else had to take your place."

Life Against Death was a significant book, and it had a powerful impact. But it had one fatal flaw. It attacked rationality and common sense, but it was itself written as a logical treatise, in the traditional Western linear style. Even as it attacked rationality, it reinforced by its own medium the very thing it claimed to be confronting. The book called for an escape, but it had not yet itself escaped. This, Brown knew, was a problem, and so he continued to develop his message.

In 1960, at the Phi Beta Kappa speech at Columbia University, Brown came out even more boldly. Realizing that others might think him mad, "at the end of his tether," he nonetheless bravely declared, "It scares me but it deters me not." For our real choice, he affirmed, is not between rationality and madness, but between "holy and unholy madness." Such holy madness is the means of getting out of repression. Madness here is nothing more than the repressed world's perception of freedom. It is not to be feared but to be embraced, for "it is not possible to get the blessing without the madness; it is not possible to get the illuminations without the derangement."

Thus he called on the scholars of Columbia to abandon academia, to leave books behind, to forgo the mechanized tools of civilization: "Fools with tools are still fools, and don't let your Phi Beta Kappa keys fool you." To reinforce his message, he reached back to the earlier American romantic age, to Emerson and his Phi Beta Kappa address, "The American Scholar," and to Emerson's distinction between "Man Thinking" fully alive with all his power and the mere bookworm trapped in the web of words. And to put even that historical reference into context, Brown reached back further still, to the mystical Christianity of the seventeenth century, to argue that to read in the spirit is to read with the eye of symbolic consciousness, not literal language. "For the power I seek," he said, "is also Christian," a Dionysian Christianity, an apocalyptic and fiery light sent from God.

The fruit of this beginning was the small paperback published in 1966 titled *Love's Body*. Unlike the earlier book, this one was not linear but organized—if that is properly the term—as a series of epigrams and paragraphs, quotations with explications, ruminations placed under different headings with only their own invisible logic as a guide. Among the many events pushing Brown to embrace his own radical speculations was the Cuban missile crisis of 1962, an event that he read as the death instinct almost succeeding in its effort to bring self-destruction down upon humanity. If this were so, then a dramatic turnaround in human consciousness would be necessary, and soon, if humanity were ever to survive the side effects of repression. Since the risks of maintaining so-called rational control seemed to be nuclear Armageddon, the risks of abandoning rationality and repression for the mystic depths seemed far less dangerous.

In the section titled "Boundary," Brown refers to Freud and a host of others in arguing that the "external world and inner id are both foreign territory—the same foreign territory." Ultimately, consciousness was and is one—one body—but the Fall was into the illusion of separateness. Thus, isolated, lonely individuals remain trapped in their separate beliefs and are kept from knowing. "To give up boundaries," he wrote, "is to give up the reality-principle," which is anyhow a false boundary. It is to cross over into what the rational mind can only perceive as madness. But it is a "holy madness," akin to Thomas Hooker's "shiveredness of soule all to pieces," to Emily Dickinson's notion that "Much madness is divinist sense," and to Melville's that "man's insanity is heaven's sense."

One avenue of this crossing over, according to Brown, is through symbolism: "To make in ourselves a new consciousness, an erotic sense of reality, is to become conscious of symbolism." With symbolism, it should be possible to make connections instead of separations. Even sex, he says, is not at bottom physical or biological but symbolic. If all of the world is "slic't up in types," then even sex is "a symbolic representation, or adumbration, of that mystical body in which we are all members of one body," a return to some preconscious, Edenic state of unity in which mind and matter are no longer a duality but an orgasmic unity.

And then, in the end, even words, even his own words, are dismissed as part of the problem. Words are the mind's way of forming meanings. Meanings are rationality's way of creating structures. Structures are cages. Words are thus the bars of the virtual-reality cages we humans have constructed to protect ourselves from our own true nature. In Eden before language, humanity was at one with God, with the totality, not defined by the damnation of rational consciousness that dissects and separates. Original sin was the coming of self-consciousness.

When Adam ate of the fruit of the tree of knowledge, he became aware. In becoming aware, he and Eve realized they were naked and covered themselves. They had acquired a sense of how it ought to be, a structure of beliefs that did not match the reality of their bodies. But rather than changing their ideas to fit reality, they covered their bodies. In this they demonstrated that they placed their new belief systems as superior to the truth. And then they turned that new belief system into structure. According to Brown, in a simple sentence that says everything, "The fall is into language." The deconstructionists would later waste thousands of pages and fail to say it as well.

The reason, Brown says, is because the "true psychic reality, which is the unconscious, cannot ever be put into words, cannot ever be translated from the silence into words." The silence is the void; the noise of language is the human attempt to construct itself a castle on a foundation of sand. The world we imagine we inhabit is the world of our own creation and perception. Calvin was right: "All we can conceive in our own minds concerning God is an insipid fiction," for the human mind is "a perpetual factory of idols." The world, Brown wrote, "is the veil we spin to hide the void." The last line of the book sums it all: "The antinomy between mind and body, word and deed, speech and silence, overcome. Everything is only a metaphor; there is only poetry."

IV

"Something is happening but you don't know what it is, do you, Mr. Jones?"

From the classics and from Christianity, Brown created a theology for the Sixties that one way or another filtered out and down to the unwashed hippie horde. His words created a context that helped to explain the new consciousness as it evolved. Ironically, it provided a comforting structure despite the fact that the theme of the book was the need to escape from just such structure. But the mind, even as it lets go, is still too afraid of letting go. It needs a hand to hold as it slides back into the deep blue sea. It was possible for college students, college dropouts, older trekkers, to read Brown and drop out of the straight world and then drop some Orange Sunshine and say yes, this is what is happening; this madness that I feel is not the insanity my father feared but a "holy madness." The censor is dissolving, and the rational is letting go and letting the irrational life force take over. True or not, such thinking provided a context of meaning, however vague, so that the terror implicit in removing the virtual-reality helmet was somehow more bearable, and despite its terror, welcome.

One saw Brown's philosophy even in the underground cartoons that helped to communicate outside the traditional avenues of hierarchical structures of learning. Kesey himself referred to these underground "comix" as "righteously disturbing stuff." Willy Murphy, one of the greatest of the underground satirists, had a wonderful one-page comic titled "Big Blow-out in the Donut Shop." In it, a very spaced-out freak is talking to two fools in a greasy spoon. "But like I got this flash, man," he says, "that its just all this ego and striving and desire that is like the film or whatever that keeps us from ever seeing it. So like we can only reach the one cosmic mind if we can find the calm center in the dualities of life. And like free ourselves from all these paired opposites, between love and hate . . . good and evil . . . even faith and doubt . . . like nothing even like really needs to be done, y'know. . . ." And he fades away to a wisp and disappears. In the final panel, one of the two fools, staring at the empty seat, says, "Dude's got a beautiful head."

Here then was that next stage of consciousness that, according to Tom Wolfe, had left the old political world of civil rights and righteous protest behind. Not that politics ended or many people coming along were not still caught up in those older stages. Each new advance is led by a small pioneering contingent, braver, or stupider, than the rest. And every old stage retains its believers, people who build a structure around an initial insight and, having found a new structure to cling to, never get beyond it.

The political radicals of the New Left had split with the old Kennedy liberals back in 1965. Todd Gitlin, the historian of the New Left, identifies a speech President Kennedy gave at American University in June of 1963 as the last hope of what he called the lib/lab coalition of liberals and labor radicals that had been a driving force for change in the early Sixties. After that, and after Kennedy's death and LBJ's ascension, the Mississippi Freedom Party's confrontation with the Democratic Party at the Atlantic City national convention in 1964 ended any chance that liberal machine Democrats and the New Left could ever understand each other. And Vietnam was a growing wedge that forced the two even further apart. Still, New Left radicals and Kennedy liberals, divided though they were against each other, both remained committed to a basically materialistic worldview and to a basically arminian desire to seize control. The New Left as a political force was in many ways only a more radical continuation of the old mentality, politically progressive yet still not up to the kind of radical otherness that Brown and Kesey advocated.

But even at the heart of the New Left, the new consciousness in search of an antinomian surrender of control was developing a critique of radical political activism. There was a space even within SDS that was beyond politics. To engage in the world actively is to accept its literal reality and to take it at its face value. To look at the world poetically, symbolically, on the other hand, removes one from its literal surface and places one on some external height looking back down, in the world perhaps but not of it. It is the last breaking of the shell of conditioning. The movement that had begun with Kennedy and accelerated with Martin Luther King and then the Black Power movement, and Vietnam, and dope, was a breaking down of the old beliefs, the old absolutes, the combines of the mind that control us. The new consciousness was a stepping outside of the old construct altogether into a realm that saw the political radicals as just another group of players of the old determined games.

A wonderful example of this is provided by Wolfe. At the Vietnam Day Committee's huge antiwar rally on the campus of the University of California at Berkeley in 1966, Kesey made his symbolic move. Here, after all, was Berkeley, the place where the student rebellion had begun, the place that symbolized New Left politics and the continuation of the civil rights struggle into white America, the very liberation of the baby boomers from the old politics to the new. Vietnam was, after all, a "Southeast Asian Birmingham." The fight was the same; the rally was gathering at the church and the march to the Oakland Army Terminal was to be their march to Selma Bridge.

But to Kesey, as Wolfe said, "there were so many reasons why this little charade was pathetic." So after a series of speakers had climbed to the microphone and roused the rabble to a frenzy of righteous passion, Kesey came on and exposed not the war makers, not the fascists in Washington, not "AmeriKKKan" imperialism, but the game being played by the antiwar marchers themselves. Instead of adding his bit of energy to the buildup of martial fury, Kesey instead tried to stand back from the scene and look at it from his elevated perspective above even the politics of the movement.

At the microphone, he whipped out his harmonica and started playing "Home on the Range." Then he told the crowd to look at itself. "This is what they do," he said between chords of deer and antelope playing, "They hold rallies and they march. . . . They've been having wars for ten thousand years and you're not going to stop it this way . . . Ten thousand years and this is the game they play to do it . . . holding rallies and having marches. . . . that's the same game you're playing . . . their game . . ." And he went back to "honking" on his harmonica.

According to Wolfe, the martial spirit almost went out of the crowd. The organizers had all they could do to keep the crowd focused on the job at hand, to remind them of the war, to get their indignation roused against the war, to point them in the direction of the army terminal, and to march them into a confrontation with the war machine. Kesey's call to a higher consciousness meant stepping beyond even the politics of antiwar marches and confrontation. It meant not just seeing how foolish the games of the Pentagon and the politicians are, but seeing how foolish all our games are, to step back from the world of action and reaction and watch ourselves playing our games, to stop the world and get off.

There, then, was the question, the door held open: to stay in the world with its familiar liberal battles, with the humanitarian call to brotherhood; to end the suffering of victims everywhere; to engage with the forces of the state and the economy in the hope of somehow, someday, improving the material existence of the people of the globe; or to realize just how much all this political activity and striving and progressing is a sham, a dance of illusion, a mere symbolic playing out of something else, something higher/deeper/mysterious beyond the veil. Kesey held open the door and said, Screw the old world; let's explore the new. Let's light out for the territory with Huck. To fight them with the old familiar weapons is to play their game. And if you play their game, they have won, for you are on their board, in their world, accepting their reality as ultimate.

So, just as many kids at Harvard and MIT and Ohio State dropped acid and dropped out, many SDS members also dropped acid and dropped out. Or perhaps it would be truer to say that they dropped acid and never looked at politics the same way again. They never again took their own rhetoric quite so seriously. Eventually, even the New Left contained an ongoing argument between its literal, political wing and its acid freaks. Some even managed somehow to combine the two, to continue a form of political action in the world, against the war, for civil rights, without surrendering to the world, or at least without seeming to.

Jerry Rubin was one of these political freaks. He was able, at least in his own person, to bring together the hippie drop-outs like the Merry Pranksters and serious political revolutionaries like Eldridge Cleaver of the Black Panthers. Throughout the late Sixties he was there, at Chicago, at the House Un-American Activities Committee (HUAC), identifying himself as a "Yippie," which he said stood for "The Youth International Party"—and the press, ever serious, believed him. So "Yippie" became the name for his brand of exhibitionism. And his book, *Do It!*, captured that spirit beautifully.

Rubin begins the book as he began the Sixties, as a clean, neat, scrub-faced Jewish boy proudly shaking Adlai Stevenson's hand. Originally liberal, rational, patriotic, with short curly hair and a tie, his was the classic Sixties pattern. He got involved in civil rights, then in the Free Speech movement at Berkeley, then in dope. Yet the language he uses to describe this change echoes Jonathan Edwards's Great Awakening more than his rabbi's Judaism: "We're born twice. It's your second birth—your revolutionary birth—which is the important one. I was born in the FSM in Berkeley in 1964."

An important part of this second birth was his rejection of the attitudes that he had absorbed from the experience of his parents and their generation. He rejected that attitude of fear and the need for rational self-control that was so well articulated by the advocates of neo-orthodoxy. His elders told him that history had ended, that nothing else was possible, because "man is selfish, greedy, tainted by original sin." He laughed and proceeded to ignore his parents' fears. Where they saw crowds as irrational beasts reminiscent of Hitler's Germany, Rubin loved the energy of crowds surging out of control. He rejected his parents' fear of the irrational and instead exited from the liberal, rational side through the door.

And in going through that door, he left behind not only his rational parents but much of the New Left radicalism as well. "For years I went to left wing meetings trying to figure out what the hell was going on," he wrote. "Finally I started taking acid, and I realized what was going on: nothing." The ideologues, the Marxists and the Maoists and the Trotskyites, the political theory intellectuals, all of them were just as repressed, just as "Puritan" as any Fifties conservative. They were all trying to do the same thing, to get in control. HUAC and the Communist Party were equally arminian.

Joan Didion's brilliant portrait, "Comrade Laski, C.P.U.S.A. (M.L.)," captures this anality sharply. Laski is an old Red, not a representative of the New Left but the oldest of the Old Left, still engaging in the ideological wars of Stalinists and Trotskyites, still faithful to the Communist dream of a party of educated elitists at the head of a tightly controlled state. A child of the Fifties herself, as neo-orthodox as Niebuhr, motivated by a profound dread of the void outside her text, Didion identifies immediately with Laski as he squares his little red book to line up along the edge of the table. She writes, "To understand who Michael Laski is, you must have a feeling for that kind of compulsion. One does not think of him eating, or in bed. He has nothing in common with the passionate personalities who tend to turn up on the New Left." Instead, Laski is a man in total control, even if to stay in control he has to construct a world of such discipline and paranoid alertness that he himself becomes a machine, like the combine.

As one of those "passionate personalities," Rubin broke from the ideological left and threw himself into the emotional other. His break with communism was in fact also a family break. The other radical outcast of his family, his Aunt Sadie, tried to persuade him to cut his hair and join the old Communist Party. He tried to explain to her that long hair was the symbol of a new revolutionary identity. "Aunt Sadie, long hair is our black skin. Long hair turns middle-class youth into niggers. Amerika is a different country when you have long hair. We're outcasts." But old leftie Aunt Sadie didn't get it. Why would anyone want to be a "nigger"? Why would anyone want to wallow in sensuality and dirt? Why, she asked him, don't you cut your hair and take a bath?

"Aunt Sadie," he replied, "Man was born to let his hair grow long and to smell like a man. We're descended from the apes and we're proud of our ancestry. We're natural men lost in the world of machines and computers." Here the political theater of the streets acknowledged its debt to the theoreticians. Here was the anti-intellectual radical echoing the ideas of a Norman O. Brown. "Long hair," wrote Rubin, "is the beginning of our liberation from the sexual oppression that underlies this whole military society."

And here another debt is, if not acknowledged, at least made clear. For in the romantic revolution of the nineteenth century, another group of Americans had tried to break away from a deadly rationalism and return to nature, to their own internal nature, to let it all hang out, to get back to the essential truth of the self regardless of the social cost, to get on the bus. Emerson and Thoreau were acting out the same pattern of behavior and belief as Rubin and the Yippies were. They were on the same journey for the same reason. "Aunt Sadie," said Rubin, "We love our bodies. We even smell our armpits once in a while." Walt Whitman, the New York poet of Emerson's romantic movement, in his over-analyzed and under-experienced *Leaves of Grass,* had used exactly the same words that Rubin, the Jewish boy from Brooklyn, used a hundred years later: "The smell of these armpits aroma finer than prayer."

It all came together for Rubin after the 1967 march on the Pentagon: "The Marxist acidhead, the psychedelic Bolshevik. He didn't feel at home in SDS and he wasn't a flower-power hippie or a campus intellectual. A stoned politico. A hybrid mixture of new left and hippie coming out something different." And that something different was a born-again revolutionary who had experienced not ideology but what Norman O. Brown had called the resurrection of the body. "Speculative knowledge," as Jonathan Edwards had called it, is a dead letter. "The Sense of the heart" is living experience; it is felt emotion. It alone is real. In crossing over from arminian rationalism to a pure antinomian romanticism, Rubin left all that old liberal rational structure and order behind. "Our generation," he said, "is in rebellion against abstract intellectualism and critical thinking. We admire the Viet Kong guerilla, the Black Panther, the stoned hippie, not the abstract intellectual vegetable."

After creating pandemonium by throwing dollar bills down on the members of the New York Stock Exchange, Rubin turned on the other practitioners of rational control. He agreed to attend a debate hosted by the militant Trotskyite Socialist Workers Party. But he found it as dull as a college lecture on economics and even more tightly controlled, each speaker given exactly thirty minutes to make a point, ten minutes to rebut—and finally, "the masterdebaters give three minute conclusions." When Rubin's turn came he said nothing but played on a phonograph Bob Dylan's "Something is happening but you don't know what it is, do you, Mr. Jones?"—and they didn't.

V

"Breaking through to Now"

The search for the golden fleece, in New Left politics and in the counterculture, took many forms, but underpinning them all was the implicit understanding that Israel was trapped in Egypt, that before the goal could be obtained, whatever symbolic form defined it, there would have to be a break out of the cages of constructed culture, out of rationality itself. Egypt could not be reformed; Pharaoh was not going to listen to reason. Israel had to head into the wilderness before there could be any hope of reaching the Promised Land.

To put it this way, of course, gives a Christian slant to the search. But Christian discourse was only one among many. It happened to have been the language within which most Americans, Afro and Euro and even Asian, have expressed these ideas. One thus finds these ideas in American culture expressed in the forms and imagery of Christianity more often than in any other forms. This Christian discourse thus becomes an important lens through which to see American culture. Kesey's *Cuckoo's Nest* used explicit Christian imagery to make its points. But these points can also be found in the language systems of other religions, including psychoanalysis, art, literature, and even politics.

In his depiction of Kesey and the Merry Pranksters, Tom Wolfe soon realized that "the unspoken thing was religion." The word "religious," he wrote, was the best to describe "the mental atmosphere they shared." The sense of a cosmic mind behind all the illusions, one unseen reality to which all the symbols that make up the world seem to be pointing, was an implicit part of being "in sync." To let go of control of one's own self and to accept that larger force, to submit to it, is to cross over from Egypt into the wilderness. It is the beginning of the journey.

The parallel that Wolfe makes is to Herman Hesse's 1922 *Journey to the East,* an account of a journey much like the Merry Pranksters' on Furthur. For Hesse, the goal of the journey, his Golden Fleece, was the bringing of "the past, the future, and the fictitious into the present moment." We are never in the moment but always looking back at it or forward to it. The very fact of consciousness keeps us watching ourselves watching, and so we are never fully there in the moment as it happens. The original fall from the immediate perception of things in the world as they really are was the fall from God's reality to the secondary texts of our human consciousness. To close that gap would be to return to Paradise, to walk again with God in the garden, no longer separate, no longer fallen. It would be to end the alienation that separates us from our environment and from each other. It would in Christian terms be the entrance into Canaan, the return to the Garden of Eden, where Adam and Eve once walked with God before succumbing to the cage of self-consciousness.

The journey is thus a religious one. Religion, after all, refers to any set of beliefs and practices that claim to concern the relationship between human life and whatever it is that is in fact true. Not all religions are defined by arminian codes of morality and behavior. Some are, but not all. As Niebuhr explained, there is both a "Christ of culture" and a "Christ against culture," a Christianity that upholds the social status quo and a Christianity that stands forever outside of and against it. The former is based in essentialist notions of knowing some cosmic truth; the latter is based in the undoing of all human knowing in the terror called the Fear of God. Even those like Comrade Laski who construct an elaborate belief system in order to make sense of a chaotic world, to create what they believe is an ultimate world view, are religious. Marxism is as much a religion as Catholicism. But those who are trying to break out of artificial codes of behavior and reach some as-yet mysterious truth on the other side are also religious. Where all religions begin is with experience—romantic monists with an experience of presence, orthodox dualists with an experience of absence.

For Kesey and the Merry Pranksters, the experience that defined them was psychedelic. According to Wolfe, all religions "began with an overwhelming new experience, what Joachim Wach called 'the experience of the holy,' . . . the sense of being a vessel of the divine, of the All-one. Those who have this, by the intensity of their shared experience, become a cult with a charismatic leader and a following. In time this cult becomes institutionalized. Then a code of behavior based on the teachings of the charismatic leaders is formed. Soon, there are only histories of those who first had the experience and no one left who remembers the experience itself."

The psychedelic experience, brought on by the taking of LSD or psilocybin or in whatever other way, was such an experience. It seemed to dissolve all of the mental constructs of rationality and push consciousness through the door into the other side. Aldous Huxley had described this as a "door of perception" that opened in the mind and allowed a temporary glimpse of the universe outside the tiny prison of rationality. It provided a means to get to the place where seekers since the Fall from Eden had been trying to return. With it, one had no choice but to abandon all rational control and float with the currents of the universe, for the first time truly letting go and being in-the-now.

Richard Alpert's transformation into Baba Ram Dass was a result of this paradigm. A secular Jew and not a Christian, Alpert turned to the

East to find a form in which to express his new experience, and he found it in India. That he needed a form, that he needed a language, that he needed a tradition with a history, all show that even in the letting go of form and structure, the human mind needs some sense of structure within which to achieve structurelessness. Up until the last letting go, the rational side of consciousness needs a hand to hold onto. Thus he and Leary formed their own religious cult, the League for Spiritual Discovery, and set up a retreat at Leary's estate, Millbrook, in New York.

When Kesey and the Pranksters careened down the Millbrook driveway in Furthur, rock 'n' roll music blaring out of the loudspeakers attached to the top of the loud Day-Glo bus, they created a confrontation between two different approaches to this new experience. The Californians were surfing on the top of the wave; the Easterners were diving into the sea beneath them. Neither understood the other, and by his own account Tom Wolfe didn't understand either one.

Acid, to oversimplify, somehow took the tripper for a few long hours away from all the layers of constructed belief and revealed the persona of the tripper as a constructed act, a player in a cosmic drama, author unknown, and then left even that revelation behind. The tripper saw himself or herself behaving and reacting for unknown reasons in unexplainable ways. The self, the worldly everyday self, was revealed as performing on the surface of an infinite regression of layers of complex motivation. The tripper was revealed to be wildly yet unknowingly pursuing all kinds of bizarre gratifications without being in control at all, dancing madly to an unheard tune.

The response of Kesey and his California friends to this was to dance ever more madly to the tune, to let the music carry them where it would, to ride the wave. They thus intended to go with the flow, freeing their spirits as completely as they could and not letting the devils of the superego or the intellect step in and tell them to stop. They were intent on letting the self dare its true dance, letting it do its thing.

This utter abandonment of rational self-control involved a letting go so thorough that the individual was left completely at the mercy of all the surging, competing, rushing forces that poured forth from within the soul. In the language of an earlier era, they were, like the romantics of the nineteenth century, ignoring the potential danger and pursuing a complete Emersonian self-reliance, regardless of the cost. Asked what would happen if the spirit he gave himself to were not of God but of the devil, Emerson had answered that he did not believe his spirit was evil but if it were, he would "live then from the devil." But he would be true to himself first and not to some other. In the struggle between the head and the heart, the neo-orthodox analysis was here reversed. The head became the evil source of manipulative control, the Nurse Ratched of the mind, while the heart, human nature at its most basic, was personified as the spontaneous, joyful, loving, self-sacrificing Randle P. Mc-Murphy.

Kesey himself of course had a hard time living up to his own vision. Wolfe goes to considerable effort in his book to show that Kesey, the "Chief" of the Merry Pranksters, insisted on retaining control not just of himself but of his friends and followers. He set the agenda for the group. He authorized the use of the group's communal acid. He decided where they would go and what route they would follow. Is this hypocrisy? Perhaps it is. But perhaps it is also an indication of just how hard it is for humans, even when they try, to let go, to get out of the constructs by which we order our perception of the world, how impossible a task to return to the garden.

Wolfe defines this return as the overcoming of "the 1/30th of a second movie-screen barrier of our senses, trying to get into . . . NOW." This 1/30th of a second distance between the moment and the mind's perception of it is the distance that human self-consciousness creates. It is the product of the Fall. The enemy here, the snake in the garden, is rational consciousness itself, the mind's thinking, analyzing, ordering, rationalizing process. The enemy is not consciousness exactly, for even animals have consciousness, but self-consciousness, which is a uniquely human curse. This distancing is what separates us from the animal world and from each other.

Because we are aware of ourselves being aware of ourselves, we naively believe in our own beliefs. Because of this, we stand apart from the NOW, analyzing it, judging it against the standard of our own expectations. In the garden, Adam and Eve walked unself-consciously with God. But when they ate of the fruit of the tree of knowledge, they became self-aware and covered their nakedness with fig leaves. They showed that they had a new standard of right and wrong in which their God-given bodies were suddenly seen as shameful. Having set up their own beliefs as superior to the given, they tried to hide their true selves from God. This arrogant presumption was the pride for which they were expelled from the garden.

The goal of the Merry Pranksters in letting it all hang out was to overcome that 1/30th-of-a-second reflexive self-consciousness that is the wall separating fallen humanity from a true participation in existence. To them, all of the phenomena of consciousness were merely projections of some unseen other, all of life but a dance to the cosmic music. Their goal was to turn off the noisy, chattering brain and to flow with the rhythms. If you are lost in the woods, Emerson had written a hundred and thirty years before, you should throw down your reins and let the dumb beast you are riding carry you home. If you are to destroy the

Death Star, you must unhook yourself from the computer and trust the Force. If you are to be carried away by the flood, you must step entirely outside of any restraining rational structure. You must leave arminian self-control behind and surrender to the waves of antinomian emotion. You must go "mad."

Leary and Alpert on the other hand were, as Wolfe said, into an intensely meditative trip. Their approach to this new experience, taken from the ancient traditions of the Far East, was to sit quietly and watch the infinite layers of consciousness flow from them. Just as Alpert, before he became Baba Ram Dass, had sat in his Newton home and watched his several different selves appear before him and then disappear, so he believed that there were more and deeper levels of consciousness that could be explored. His model was that of the Buddhist monk sitting in contemplation, letting the conscious part of the mind sink slowly down, like a deep-sea diver, into the dark undersea trenches of consciousness, hoping to come at last to some solid bottom. Where the Merry Pranksters stressed the need to abandon oneself to the human dance, the Easterners stressed the need to get away from the surface and to sink back into the source of the music.

Each of these two approaches had its own separate insight into one of the great dilemmas of the religious life. Once one has been awakened to the ideal realm beyond the literal, once one has experienced the revelation that this material existence is but a virtual-reality dream, how does one continue to be a self in the world? The New England Puritans liked to talk of the need to awaken worldly sinners to this profound revelation. During the awakening experience, the convert was often pictured as a "mad man," out of his head, either in mystic terror or mystic joy. In such moments, the mind became, as Edwards said, "swallowed up in God." But the saints, having been awakened and having been converted, were expected to return to the world, to their calling, and continue to live as if they were, as they repeatedly said, "in the world but not of it."

This meant neither surfing ecstatically on the surface nor disappearing beneath the waves, but being in both realms at once. It meant living in the detailed particularity of the world as if the virtual-reality program really mattered, but still having one's mind on the infinite ideal. It meant living in the dream even while knowing it to be nothing but a dream and being aware of the cosmic dreamer, the ultimate programmer, whose dream it is. The Romantics of the nineteenth century also imagined themselves bearing this same dual consciousness. As Emerson's friend Octavius Brooks Frothingham said, *"whenever orthodoxy spread its wings and rose into the region of faith, it lost itself in the sphere where the human soul and the divine were in full concurrence.*

Transcendentalism simply claimed for all men what Protestant Christianity claimed for its own elect." One hears echoes of this also in Walt Whitman's proclamation in "Song of Myself" that he was at once both particular and universal, "I Walt Whitman a kosmos, and of Manhattan the son." Emerson said, "We must skate upon the surface of reality." That is, we must live in the world even though we know we're not of it.

The assumption, largely unspoken, in much of the literature of romanticism—of earlier eras as well as the psychedelic Sixties—is that the perceived world is not real but ideal, that the old platonic belief in philosophic idealism is true. Jonathan Edwards had believed that matter is all in the mind, and the mind itself but an idea in the mind of God. For these mystics, ultimate reality, the foundation of all existence, was not some material substance, not some tiny subparticle of atomic material, but consciousness itself. God exists, not in matter or in space, but in mind, where we and the world we inhabit are perceived. Ralph Waldo Emerson affirmed this ideal view of the universe, that the world exists only in the mind as idea. What we perceive as the real world is in fact a matrix; we exist as in a virtual-reality game, projections of some master program. This is a notion to be found in many religions. The perception of idealism is in many ways one of the experiences upon which religions are founded. It is what separates a spiritual conception of reality from a materialist one. A sense of this, however vague, is what makes some people suspect that we in fact are not in control and that even our sense of being in control is part of the subtle programming. This is why mystics, to the confusion of people who think the world is all there is, disparage "worldliness," urging instead that though we must live in the world, we need not be "of it." Life may be, as Alpert said, "the only dance there is," but it is still but a dream in the mind of God, a Matrix that only seems to be real.

Alpert's search for the source of the cosmic music took its form from the religions of the East. Even journeys out of structure need a structure. His parents' Judaism was too worldly and did not seem to him to offer any understanding of this mystical stuff. Christianity seemed too dogmatic, too moralistic, too committed to its own institutional answers to even think of religion as a question. But the East of Buddhism and Hinduism was different enough, exotic enough, to satisfy that need for a different door that might lead to a place outside of the constructs of his own self-referencing culture.

Alpert's and Leary's ultimate goal was the same as that of Kesey's Pranksters, to merge with the flow of the infinite, but theirs was a more cautious approach. Unlike the Pranksters, they acknowledged the need to have a structure within which to experience structurelessness. A pure antinomian anarchy was too much for them. Like Emerson himself, they wanted to have the experience but also to know it consciously, to have both mind and body, to be able to experience the infinite and to remain in the world as well. Eastern and other techniques of meditation seemed to offer a guide to this experience. Ancient texts like *The Tibetan Book of the Dead* seemed to suggest some already-explored routes into the wilderness. Leary's estate in New York itself was a symbol of the security of structure within which these dangerous explorations could be made, a magnetic force field within which the fusion explosion could be controlled.

One can see in this cautious essentialism of the older professors a refusal to let go of some contact with the real. Kesey and the Pranksters also started off, as so many did in the Sixties, seeking the essential self within, but they soon found themselves careening toward what we now call a post-modern nihilism that abandoned the hope of establishing any essential grounding and instead went with the flow. Leary and Alpert really believed that truth could be found. Kesey and the Pranksters were already surfing the chaos of image, reflection, confusion, in which we are all being rolled. But then, Leary and Alpert were over thirty.

When the Day-Glo-painted school bus with the loudspeakers on the top arrived at Millbrook unannounced with music blaring, Leary was in a deep trip and had left orders not to be disturbed for any reason for several days. Leary's friends did not know what to make of these California crazies. Nor did the California crazies know what to make of what they called the "Crypt Trip." Wolfe wrote this conflict off as East versus West, or Old World aristocratic snootiness versus American populist worldliness. But there was more to this; the Westerners were surfing on the surface of consciousness, while the Easterners were plumbing the sea in the hope of finding some solid bottom. The Westerners were reveling in the creation, while the Easterners were seeking to know the Creator. They were reacting in two different ways to the same experience, taking two different routes to the Promised Land. But whichever way one sought it, discovering the Golden Fleece required a surrender of self-control and a perfect melding of the individual human mind with the divine mind of universal consciousness.

VI

"The sun is but a morning star"

The highest tide of Sixties romanticism did not come all at once. For some, the climax came early in more private epiphanies; for others the high tide came much later, and for some, in lonely pockets here and there, the tide still surges. But between the "Summer of Love" of 1967 and the Woodstock Festival of August 1969, can be found most of the enthusiasm of this awakening.

One of the symbolic moments of psychedelic intrusion into mainstream culture, the example that seemed to suggest that the national mind was indeed becoming liberated, was the publication in 1976, long after the tide really had turned, of the *Golden Guide to Hallucinogenic Plants*. Written in the accessible paperback style of all the other Golden Guides, from Birds to Stars, this well-illustrated little booklet made the use of hallucinogens seem altogether a normal part of human culture as it traced the use of different natural hallucinogens from ancient times to the present. Simple drawings of Native Americans and others taking hallucinogens in their natural forms embellished the relatively straightforward text and suggested that taking hallucinogenic drugs had always been perfectly normal. Once the publishers found out what they had created, the book did not stay long in print. It is today a much sought-after collector's item. Copies can occasionally be found in used bookstores or on the shelves of aging baby boomers, right next to the *I Ching* and *The Sacred Mushroom and the Cross*.

But in the late Sixties, it was still possible to imagine that the old cultural conditioning had finally come to its last days. What had begun with the civil rights movement as a challenge to America to live up to its ideals of equality and brotherhood had broadened into a much deeper challenge to the entire culture. Not just national and international politics, but the very foundations of Western consciousness, were seriously under review. The assumptions of the old culture, its belief in logic and rationality, its commitment to science and technology, its faith in a material reality really "out there," its artistic affirmations and religious creeds—all were brought into question.

The merely political disruptions of 1967 and 1968 had their origins in the alienation of many of the baby boom generation from their parents' world. Not knowing any other world, or where to turn, or what to do, drop-outs by the thousands wandered off in search of that something other. The most famous gathering was in San Francisco in the summer of '67, called by the press "the Summer of Love." There the media discovered the hippie phenomenon and celebrated and reported it across the land. Don McNeil makes the argument that, in fact, the "hippie" began on the day that the California laws against LSD went into effect, October 6, 1966. On that afternoon, "a group of colorful kids" came together in Tompkins Square Park for "A Psychedelic Celebration" of love. The press was there, too, and beamed the news of a new phenomenon across the land.

The colorful kids, however, did not intend to create a new category into which colorful-kids-trying-to-escape-categories could be placed.

They were trying to find a way to be human outside of such restricting structures. The "hippie" label simply created another structure to escape from. At the end of the media-saturated "Summer of Love," with the fading of the last notes of Scott MacKenzie's Top 40 call to go to San Francisco and "be sure to wear some flowers in your hair," a group of colorful kids decided to end the sham. On October 6, 1967, exactly one year later, they declared "Hippie, devoted son of mass media" to be dead, and they staged an elaborate funeral, hoping against all experience to rescue some sense of their individuality. Their handbill, passed out to announce the event, says it all:

MEDIA CREATED THE HIPPIE WITH YOUR HUNGRY CONSENT. BE SOMEBODY. CAREERS ARE TO BE HAD FOR THE ENTERPRISING HIPPIE. DEATH OF HIPPIE END. FINISHED HIPPYEE GONE GOODBYE HEHPPEE DEATH DEATH HIPPEE. EXORCISE HAIGHT ASHBURY. CIRCLE THE ASHBURY. FREE THE BOUNDARIES. OPEN EXORCISE. YOU ARE FREE. WE ARE FREE. DO NOT BE RECREATED. BELIEVE ONLY IN YOUR OWN INCARNATE SPIRIT. BIRTH OF FREE MAN. FREE SAN FRANCISCO. INDEPENDENCE. FREE AMERICANS. BIRTH. DO NOT BE BOUGHT WITH A PICTURE, A PHRASE. DO NOT BE CAPTURED IN WORDS. THE CITY IS OURS. YOU ARE ARE ARE. TAKE WHAT IS YOURS. THE BOUNDARIES ARE DOWN. SAN FRANCISCO IS FREE NOW FREE THE TRUTH IS OUT OUT OUT.

But, of course, the funeral itself became just another media event, sending out the words and pictures once again, reinforcing them as stereotype even more solidly. "Hippie" may have died that fall in San Francisco, but it was another two years before the news reached the world and another ten before it was buried.

For San Francisco was not the only place that "hippie" was to be found; it was only the most televised. In cities in every state, similarly lost kids, weekend hippies and the week-long kind, gathered in downtown parks to share their latest drugs and songs and stories, and to be together waiting to see what would happen next.

The assumptions behind much of this counterculture activity were never explicitly stated in any hippie manifesto. At most, they were vaguely understood. But one of the prevalent assumptions was one with a deep history. This was the belief that the old culture did not need to be confronted and overcome, because the old militaristic metaphors were as much a part of the old mentality as the military itself. Instead, the counterculture proposed the creation of an alternative way of life. Why wait? Just do it. Just be there now. As Thoreau had said, why should honest people not simply withdraw from the evils of the established culture, "and not wait till they constitute a majority of one, before they suffer the right to prevail through them. I think that it is enough if they have God on their side without waiting for that other one."

Come-outers, such as Thoreau and the hippies of the counterculture, had long been an integral part of the life of American culture. Every period of religious awakening had its own version of those who, feeling righteousness stirring within them, had refused any further allegiance to the old structures and had instead turned on, tuned in, and dropped out. The first successful British colony in the New World, that of the Pilgrims at Plymouth, had been founded by men and women who were followers of Thomas Brown, himself a separatist. Brown had argued in 1581 in a book titled *Reformation Without Tarrying for Any* that the reformers of his day should not wait until they constituted a majority in England before establishing themselves in communities dedicated to the right ways of worshiping and living together. When these separatists had been unable to sustain their separate communities, they had fled to Holland and then to America. The hippies of the counterculture possessed rock-ribbed ancestors.

But even these Pilgrim ancestors of the drop-outs of the Sixties had ancient ancestors of their own. When the children of Israel turned their backs on Egypt and headed out into the wilderness in search of some distant, undefined Promised Land, they set in motion a pattern of behavior that continued in cycles of awakening to propel Western culture westward. They were the first come-outers, but every movement away from structure, be it political, or social, or spiritual, was the offspring of those first pioneers. The Europeans who turned their backs on the Old World from the seventeenth century to the present, those Asians who left China and Vietnam and Korea behind, those Africans torn unwillingly from their former homes—all suffered the same experience of losing a secure identity and heading into a wilderness to be confronted with the dilemma of rediscovering a self. The metaphor of transformation, the central symbol of Christian piety, was the energy at the heart of the American errand into the wilderness.

From the perspective of Norman O. Brown's symbolic reading of history, this coming out from the structures of the past was itself but a symbol, a type, of the need to come out from the cage of literalism and throw one's rational self into the wilderness of the unknown subliminal self. This antinomian escape from arminian structure is a liberty that can never totally be won but must be constantly defended. If the Promised Land is ever to be gained, pioneers have to keep alive the tradition of breaking out of Egypt. As the Chief said of McMurphy, the "thing he was fighting, you couldn't whip it for good. All you could do was keep on whipping it, till you couldn't come out any more and somebody else had to take your place."

In 1967, as teenagers and college students dropped out and joined what seemed to be a national tribe of the great unwashed, unorganized hippie scene, urban and rural communes throughout the nation tried to provide places where the great undoing of the old culture could take place and a new counterculture could emerge.

The urban hippies were the most visible. But the rural dropouts perhaps provided better examples of what the disruption in the culture was all about. Ray Mungo's *Total Loss Farm* is only one of many books describing one of these communes. But it is a good representation of the theme.

Mungo had begun his public career as the student editor of the *Boston University News*. Active in the antiwar and antidraft movement, he had made national waves when in an editorial in the *BU News* he called for the impeachment of Lyndon Johnson. From there he went on to found the Liberation News Service, a service like the Associated Press that provided antiwar, civil rights, counterculture, and other movement news to media outlets around the country. The story of this operation is well told in his book *Famous Long Ago: My Life and Hard Times with the Liberation News Service*. This stint in radical politics ended badly, with bitter factions competing for control, midnight raids, lawsuits, and finally the suicide of friend and fellow radical Marshall Bloom.

The pattern was a familiar one: Mungo moved from an innocent liberalism to more radical politics and then broke from politics altogether to pursue other routes to utopia. He woke up, he wrote in 1968, to find that "the movement had become my enemy; the movement was not flowers and doves and spontaneity, but another vicious system, the seed of a heartless bureaucracy, a minority party vying for power rather than peace. It was then that we put away the schedule for the revolution, gathered together our dear ones and all our resources, and set off to Vermont in search of the New Age." Does it need to be mentioned that he took along his dope and the books of Henry David Thoreau?

The self that Mungo and his friends sought to lose was the old self of the world. They had followed that highway as far as they could, and, with a powerful kick from psychedelics, had decided to pull off to a side road and then leave the car behind. Their farm in Vermont was merely a launching pad for a new and undefined beginning. "We are," he wrote, "the last life on the planet; it is for us to launch the New Age, to grow up to be men and women of earth, and free of the walking dead who precede us and make it to morning." Mungo's immediate inspiration was Thoreau, whom he quotes liberally throughout his text, but behind Thoreau was an even longer tradition of generations turning their backs on the structures of the old world in the faith that, as Thoreau said, "the sun is but a morning star."

The chronicler of this movement, as Wolfe was the chronicler of the escapades of Kesey and his Merry Pranksters, was the cartoonist Robert Crumb. To find the action of the Sixties, one needs to look at the politics, but as Kesey and Mungo said, the old political games were themselves still only games. To find the heart of the Sixties, one needs to turn from the events of the world to the events of the soul. But these are not available, so instead we look for the artistic expression of the underlying energies of the psyche, that is, to rock music. There the force can be felt as nowhere else. But a book like the one you are holding is verbal; it speaks from a mind to minds, in the fallen realm of the rational. It is an attempt to create a new structure of verbal meaning by which the rational mind can begin to come to grips with and, I confess, exercise some control over the raw emotions that rock puts forth. And so a bridge is needed, an art form neither fully emotional nor paralyzingly intellectual, a middle ground of expression.

Robert Crumb published his first *Zap Comix* in 1967 in San Francisco at the height of the enthusiasm. Zap No. 0 begins with a four-page, twenty-six-panel story titled "Meatball." In the first panel, two fat American slobs, Mrs. Yahootie and Mrs. Knish, are having a terrible fight in a New Jersey dime store when suddenly Mrs. Yahootie gets hit by a mysterious meatball. The angry, alienated nobody is converted by this experience into a happy, well-adjusted, famous celebrity though she is "still just Mom to the kids." Soon, other random people are hit by meatballs and transformed, then more and more people are hit until the smoggy Tuesday in Los Angeles when it rains meatballs for fifteen minutes: "There was rioting and looting and dancing in the streets and a lot of giggling. Cops busted heads but they couldn't stop what happened. After that the incidents of meatballs tapered off."

Zap Comix is not exactly "A Narrative of Surprising Conversions" or "The Distinguishing Marks of a Work of the Spirit of God," but the similarity to Jonathan Edwards's famous descriptions of the Great Awakenings of 1735 and 1741 cannot be dismissed. Like the falling meatballs, the grace of God was a random event that came down occasionally from heaven, transforming alienated, unhappy sinners into saints. And at certain seasons, for reasons beyond their understanding, grace was shed down on them in torrents, transforming hundreds and thousands and combining individual experiences of awakening into a "Great Awakening." And in both Great Awakenings, that of the mid-1700s and that of the 1960s, there were few in the first excited reaction who asked if the conversions were the real thing or a sham.

In the second story, a one pager called "Sky-Hi Comics" with "good

2. An early Crumb published in *Yellow Dog*, 1, #2, 1968. Courtesy of Robert Crumb.

ol' Bill Ding," a straight square-headed, coat-and-tie character is count-
ing his pay and looking forward to a hot date when three little gizmos
drop out of the sky and sing a song in his ear urging him to turn on,
tune in, and drop out. Instead, he crushes them with his foot. Later,
alone in a bar, stood up by his date, sick of the rat race, he regrets his
mistake and wishes he had dropped out. Suddenly, a "wild man," a caricature African with a bone around his neck, a grass skirt, thick lips, and
a huge earring, runs up to him, arms outstretched, and says, "Don't be
scared. Gimme some skin, baby. It's nevah too late mah man." Ding
shakes his hand and happily says, "This is the beginning of a new life
for me."

So there it is. As in other Crumb comics, uptight, repressed Whiteman, alienated from his natural self, caught up in the horrors of the rat
race, clinging to the literal and the rational sense of control, is introduced to nature, to the other side, to sex and dope, by his black alter
ego. As with Baldwin, for Crumb the black man serves as a symbol to
the white of the sensual side of his own consciousness so long despised
and repressed. One of my favorite Crumb comics, titled "Whiteman—a
story of civilization in crisis," shows Whiteman "on the verge of a nervous breakdown! He's a real product of the Great Depression." In the
first half of the comic, Whiteman is trying to repress "my real self deep
inside. . . . The raging lustful beast that craves only one thing . . . SEX!"
The depiction shows a drooling, wild-eyed maniac mouthing "I'm a bad
ass. I'm so virile. I read Playboy." But he gets a grip on himself, remind-
ing himself that he is an American, a citizen of the United States, a citi-

zen on the go. This stance, however, is hard to maintain. So on the commute home, after almost being overcome in a traffic jam by the illicit passion to "KILL," he stops off for a drink to help him get back in control. Leaving the bar late at night, he runs in terror from a crowd of black kids who catch him, pull down his pants, and "em-bare-ass" him.

In the climactic panel, in the middle of the last page, after a tearful Whiteman asks how they could do this to him, one of the big-lipped caricature black kids says to Whiteman, "You jis' a NIGGER like evva body else. No more! No less, mutha." They then invite Whiteman to "join the parade." One says to him, "C'mon nigger! Yo' got music in you' soul! Remember?" He doesn't, of course, but in the final panel, to Whiteman's wondering if he should, the cartoonist asks, "Will Whiteman join the parade?" and he answers his own question on the bottom, "Oh, eventually."

In other comics, Crumb makes it clear that this joining the parade is a return to the natural, uninhibited self. In his full-length comic masterpiece, "Whiteman Meets Bigfoot," the role of the black is played by a female Bigfoot whom Whiteman, the "lovable honkey," meets while camping in Oregon. He returns to nature with her, discovers the joys of the body and the ease of returning to a primitive existence in the woods. His hair grows long and wild until he looks like "one of those hippies." But he makes the mistake of returning with Bigfoot to civilization, thus setting up the classic confrontation between his responsibility to the world and his family, and his socially irresponsible desire to return to nature. Caught on the horns of this dilemma, unable to decide what is right by rational deliberation, he is saved when Bigfoot herself grabs him and carries him off to the woods, where they live happily ever after.

Drugs, of course, play an important part in most of these comics as a chemical means to the natural end. Just as Emerson had suggested that the poet can stimulate the divine perception with artificial means, which "is the reason why bards love wine, mead, narcotics, coffee, tea, opium, the fumes of sandalwood and tobacco, or whatever other procurers of animal exhilaration," so Crumb's happy hippies smoke dope, drop acid, and wallow in ecstatic bliss. On the inside of the last page of *Zap Comix* No. 0, a not entirely satiric ad says in big letters, "HELP BUILD A BETTER AMERICA! NOW YOU DON'T NEED A SHRINK TO FLUSH OUT KARMIC CONGESTION! GET STONED!" The how-to-smoke-a-joint lesson promises, "When the miracle molecules hit the center of the brain, you will find yourself in a new world."

Crumb's credo is that of the pure artist: he wants to present the truth as he sees it, not as he thinks it ought to be, nor even as he thinks he ought to think it, but truth as it most honestly appears. In the Fifties, the Beat junkie William Burroughs published *Naked Lunch,* a book Allen

3. "You Jis a Nigger." From *Whiteman: A Story of Civilization in Crisis.*
Courtesy of Robert Crumb.

Ginsberg referred to as a "reality sandwich." Crumb's equivalent statement was his *Naked Laundry*, in which he stands naked on the cover,
his scrawny body and his fat wife fully revealed in their grungy back
yard, underwear hanging on the line, warts and zits and fat all there in
gross detail. And, in a similar vein, his comics are full of sick and twisted
images, sexual perversions, and unwholesome, politically incorrect desires. Like Kesey's Merry Pranksters on "Furthur," he is letting it all
hang out, faithful to the romantic belief that there is a truth, a reality,
happening—and that truth, not some superficial human construction, is
what needs to be revealed. Brought up as an ultra-believing Catholic,
he rejected that dogma and came to the realization that "the truth about
reality is actually something beyond our comprehension. Nobody knows
the truth. It's something to be curious, not dogmatic, about."

The danger Crumb sees is not a letting out of some neo-orthodox
demon of the soul but the accepting of some inferior, intermediate truth
and believing it. The truth may be "beyond comprehension," but that
does not mean we should settle for some institutionalized rituals of the
world. To do so would be to accept the lies of the illusions of the world.
It would be stopping in the wilderness, out of Egypt but only partway
to Canaan. It would be an abandonment of the artist's calling to keep
revealing, to keep peeling away the layers of lies, to try to get, if not all
the way, then as far as one's talents make possible. Crumb is a true heir
to the Puritan minister Cotton Mather so admired who refused to accept "seemings" in place of the real thing. "I have to keep poking fun
at myself," Crumb says, "and anything else I might be tempted to take
too seriously."

He is the true iconoclast, rejecting all icons because, at bottom, he
believes that somewhere out there "beyond comprehension" there is a
truth. You can take the boy out of the church, but you can't take the
church out of the boy. Attacked by feminists for his often-brutal depiction of women as sex objects, Crumb makes no apologies. Between the
choice of conforming to someone's political ideology or remaining true
to himself, he does not hesitate, regardless of the cost. His depictions of
blacks and Jews are as politically incorrect as his depictions of women.
To follow some party line, to be politically correct, would be to surrender to some human construct of what ought to be. What puts Crumb in
the tradition of antinomian seekers from the Old Testament through the
Reformation to the nineteenth-century romantics, is his belief in pursuing the depths of the self over and against any political construction of
the world. As Emerson said, "Truth is handsomer than the affectation
of love."

Like Crumb's comics, other underground comics such as Gilbert
Shelton's "Fabulous Furry Freak Brothers," Willy Murphy's astonishing

4. "Men are such fools." Crumb's Dharma Bum terrified by "seemings." Courtesy of Robert Crumb.

satires of straight and not-so-straight life, and many others celebrated the hippie life of sex and dope and rock 'n' roll. But their celebration always had a satiric double edge, mocking the affectations of hip culture and radical politics in the same series in which traditional uptight "Amerika" is spoofed. The very use of humor points to the possibility of a point of view from which one can view the folly of the world in all its dimensions. Just as Ram Dass, after losing all of his worldly identities, realizes that he has found a calm center, an "I" outside of the identities of the world, so Crumb and Murphy and Shelton resist the temptation to embrace some worldly ideology and to push political propaganda. Instead, they take the artist's stance of truthfully watching themselves watch themselves and reporting on the absurdity of all that they see.

In doing all this, they spread the sense that a place exists outside the constructs of the world, some Promised Land across the wilderness from Egypt, from which mountaintop they can laugh at the world and let it, as Crumb's Mr. Natural says, "go sit on a tack." These comics were important because they managed to communicate to a great extent the underlying ideas of the many intersecting movements of the era. For the high school and college dropouts who flocked to San Francisco and the East Village or who took to the woods of Oregon and Vermont, these comics provided an accessible form of communication that told them, among other things, that they were part of a larger movement and not alone. For the kids still in high school wondering what this hippie business was all about, the comics were a window into this other point of view, a window that showed them that the world presented by their high school government teachers was not their only choice. From the 1967 Summer of Love to the end of the decade, the same underlying forces that had caused the original upheavals continued to send kids out of their traditional structure into this new paradigm.

The Woodstock Festival of August 1969, has become for good or ill the most important symbol of the height of the counterculture. And symbol, more than anything else, it was. As Norman O. Brown had said, the material world is only a type, a symbolic projection, a play. All the types of the world point to anti-types behind the veil. One can report on Woodstock as a huge orgy of sex and drugs and rock 'n' roll, as indeed it was. But to ignore its symbolic importance is to miss what was really going on.

In an essay published in 1969, Andrew Kopkind saw clearly that the recently concluded concert had deep cultural significance. Begun by a group of hip entrepreneurs eager both to celebrate the new lifestyle and to make a profit, Woodstock presented from the start the problem of trying to unleash the new energies while exercising enough control to make a profit. That they were able to create an enormous, and enormously complicated, event and still retain the image of laid-back indifference to the world was part of the reason that they succeeded in attracting all of the tribes of the many movements and thousands of the independents.

Woodstock was, says Kopkind, "the exhilaration of a generation's arrival at its own campsite." This is where all the ideas of the romantic awakening were called upon to prove themselves. No one, said Kopkind, "had ever seen a 'society' so free of repression. Everyone swam nude in the lake. Balling was easier than getting breakfast." Here there were no cops, no laws, no rules, and everything was available for the asking. Woodstock was the historical child of the events of medieval Muenster, a complete antinomian freedom. It was, said John Sebastian from the stage, "a mind fucker of all time." More sophisticated but no less enthusiastic, Jerry Garcia called it "a Biblical, epical scene."

The fitting comparison is not simply to Muenster, that original summer of love back in 1538, but to each of its later descendants in American history. The Great Awakening of 1741 was filled with huge crowds gathering together not simply to listen to speakers but to celebrate the birth of new communities of faith. The second Great Awakening of the early 1800s had as its symbolic moment of affirmation the famous Cane Ridge revivals in Kentucky in 1801, when thousands gathered at revival campgrounds for several days of antinomian excess. Thomas Jefferson, the incurable rationalist, had predicted that the new states would be temples of classical learning and intellectual achievement. His model for them was Athens, and he believed that if religion still survived, it would be in a benevolent liberal form such as Unitarianism. He was not prepared for the enthusiastic outpouring of pure emotion, the barking and the shouting and the falling down in fits, that so frightened the defenders of reason and order.

The movie made of the Woodstock concert itself is the best testimony to the details of this awakening's biggest revival. From the very beginning, the movie's emphasis is on the confirmation of a new culture in this massive coming together, a culture based on the elimination of repression. In it, the return to a state of nature is found to be, not demonic as their elders had warned, but grace itself. "I'm gonna tell my father," laughed one young celebrant to the camera, "Ha ha, I fooled you. I'm alive."

The image throughout is of the innocence of the return to Eden. Naked children play happily across the stage. Young adults frolic in the nude like happy campers at the lake. To the mesmerizing rhythm of the drums, strangers in the crowd get down into the slipping and sliding primal experience of the mud.

Even the music pushed the themes. Ritual celebrations of community flowed from the stage: "We are doing it," "We are a we." But there were also the reminders of why "we" were different and what "we" were trying to do with that. Sly Stone, in his magnificent performance of "I Want to Take You Higher," did just that, with his music, with his movements, with his costume. He asked the huge crowd to join in singing along with him, and when only a murmur arose in response, he gave them a gentle lecture. "Most of us," he reminded the half a million people listening in the dark, "need approval from our neighbors before we'll let it all hang down." But, he continued, we no longer have to look around for "approval"; we no longer have to worry about whether our behavior is right or wrong, old fashioned or hip. Singing together, he said, "is not a fashion; it's a feeling. And if it felt good then, it'll feel good now." Turn off the logical, fearful, analytical brain that looks around for social approval; if it feels good, do it! And that is the way, sang Stone: "I want to take you higher."

To let go of the rational, analytical self, and to accept one's essential original self as it felt itself to be: that was the goal of freedom. To escape from the centuries of social conditioning and return to the natural self buried under all the debris of culture: that is the Golden Fleece that romantics and mystics continually seek. The chorus of Joni Mitchell's song "Woodstock" put this as clearly as anything:

> We are stardust, we are golden,
> And we've got to get ourselves back to the garden.

"We," our "selves," are golden. At our core, "we" are not evil, not demonic, not some neo-orthodox vision of original sin. Underneath whatever thorny layers may have been added by culture, by parents, by ministers, by media, awaits the pure and perfect heart at the core of consciousness. There, if we can only reach back into ourselves, we should be able to break through that 1/30th-of-a-second wall that consciousness creates and return to the garden, where we will walk again with God.

4

Fourth, No Discovery—

I

"finally on our own"

WHEN HE FINALLY BROKE OUT OF THE WARD AND HEADED BACK
toward home, the Chief remembered "taking huge strides as I ran,
seeming to step and float a long ways before my next foot struck the
earth. I felt like I was flying. Free." And he knew where he was going:
"back to the country around the gorge again, just to bring some of it
clear in my mind. I been away a long time." Returning home to the
garden of his youth, the Chief was returning to the place where he could
be himself again, his natural, original Native American self. This was
how the revelers at Woodstock felt, that having escaped from the combine, they had to "get back to the land and set our souls free."

But in his flight toward freedom, the Chief was also headed for the
same fate as the dog. The "young, gangly mongrel" so "took with the
beauty of the night" had followed the wild geese as they crossed the full
moon and headed toward the highway and the same spot of pavement
as an oncoming car. So Kesey has the Chief tell us that in his triumphant
moment of liberation at the very end of the book, he headed "in the
direction I remembered seeing the dog go, toward the highway." The
expedition for the golden fleece began with an excited rush, but it soon
stumbled. On every front, in politics, in civil rights, in music, in drugs,
in religion, instead of some new revelation, demons arose on every side,
as if the land beyond the borders were not the romantics' garden but
the Puritans' howling wilderness after all.

The romantic quest for freedom, necessary as it is to break the bonds
of Egyptian tyranny, always involves a risk. In Scripture, the generation
of Israel that escaped from Pharaoh did not make it to the Promised
Land. Even Moses died still on the eastern bank of the Jordan—on
Mount Pisgah, in sight but still out of reach of Canaan. Of the original
escapees, only Caleb and Joshua crossed over. Of the others, Scripture
proclaims, "Their carcasses fell in the wilderness." The alternative to

155

the prison of arminian structure is the antinomian wilderness, a place full of both promise and danger. We live in structure for a reason. Culture exists for a reason. Human intellect evolved for a reason. We are naked apes without it. To throw structure aside and release the aboriginal self could be a return to a nature that is loving and benign, but it could also be a descent into a jungle of madness and death. The original self may well be as divine as the romantics hope, but it might also be as evil as what the orthodox fear. To head back through the long dark tunnel of consciousness involves a risk, for we cannot be sure of the nature of whatever light we think we see at the other end.

In 1957, in his famous essay "The White Negro," Norman Mailer had rebelled against the conformist Fifties with a call for a return to the primal self despite whatever risks might be entailed. As a child of the Fifties, a Beat and not a flower child, he had not imagined that the primal self would be a happy baby playing in a garden; far from it. Fully accepting that the consequence would be to release the demonic at the heart of human nature, he had nevertheless proposed that "every social restraint and category be removed." This escape from social structure and return to primal nature "would return us to ourselves, at no matter what price in individual violence."

Even James Baldwin, who hated Mailer's essay for its portrayal of blacks as somehow the symbol of this original primitive passion, agreed that under the constructs of our historically constituted identities lies a demonic passion that must first be confessed. But he and Mailer were both over thirty when the Sixties hit. They were both products of neo-orthodox assumptions about the nature of human consciousness. They both believed, though they did not use this explicitly religious language, in original sin. To enter the wilderness risks the danger that the neo-orthodox analysis of mind might be right, that what will be found there might not be the Garden of Eden but a consuming terror.

Unlike the older Beats, baby boomers like Kesey embraced the escape from structure primarily as an exhilarating adventure across the frontier, albeit a breathless heart-pounding one. They saw the changing of the times only as a positive liberation from the horrors of the past. The lesson of the dog's fate on the highway is subtle and easily overlooked in the heady rush of freedom. This was it. Crosby, Stills, and Nash, on their eponymous 1969 album caught this spirit beautifully in their song "Wooden Ships." In it, the wooden sailing vessels, propelled by nature's freely blowing winds, become the Woodstock generation itself "sailing away from this foreign land." The robotic members of the old combine become "silver people on the shoreline" who must be left behind to suffer the consequences of their own dehumanization:

Horror grips us as we watch you die.
All we can do is echo your anguished cry.
We are leaving . . .
You don't need us.

For Crosby, Stills, and Nash, even the killing of four students at Kent State became a symbol of this break. Despite its theme, "Ohio" is an upbeat song. The meaning of that tragic event for the rock band was that "We're finally on our own," a liberation that was, as the song claims, a "long time coming," and "should have happened long ago." To these radicals, May 4, 1970, was, as Sam Adams had said on the morning of the Battle of Lexington and Concord, "a glorious dawn."

But the belief that there is a promised land and that it can eventually be reached was hard to maintain. The search for the garden, whether inside the self or beyond the borders of "AmeriKKKan" culture, proved difficult, the garden itself elusive, and the discovery of the golden fleece continually delayed. Like the original Children of Israel, these trekkers found, once they had left Egypt behind, that in the desert they were beset by demons and flying serpents. And the Promised Land was nowhere to be found.

Discounting those Israelites who longed to return to the leeks and onions and fleshpots of Egypt, the failure of the original wilderness sojourn came in two different ways, both of which were repeated in the Sixties. Of those who bravely held to the original determination to break on through to another side, many broke through only to find instead of a flood of mystical love that the desert wilderness was death. Many let go of the old constructs of society and mind, went mad, and never recovered either in Old Egypt or in Canaan. Even worse, much worse, were those who went mad in a more subtle way, by falling to idolatry and embracing a new Egypt. These were the ones who adopted some new belief and then fell into the trap of believing those "seemings." They mistook the mirages of the desert for Canaan and then fell to worshipping their own idolatrous illusions.

In this, too, the Sixties generation carried out the example of its Puritan predecessors. At the end of the 1600s, by the time of the Salem witch trials, the grandchildren of the original Puritans had come to believe not in the possibility of grace but in the certainty of it, not in God but in the church of God, not in their sinfulness and their need to be transformed but in their own sanctimonious virtue. Self-righteous prigs like Cotton Mather ceased to think of themselves as sinners in the wilderness praying for salvation and instead came to think of themselves as saints at ease in Zion in the Promised Land of milk and honey. The ministers who knew better preached angrily against this idolatry. Solomon

Stoddard warned his congregation that those church members "addicted to morality and religion are serving their lusts therein. The most orderly natural men do live an unGodly life." But taken with the illusion of their own sanctification, they refused to hear him. They embraced a new worldliness, a new Egyptian idolatry, and forgot the reality of the Fear of God that had sent them out of Egypt in the first place.

II

Stumbling at the threshold

As the Sixties had opened on the high moral hopes of the civil rights crusade, so the civil rights movement, with its promise of striking a direct moral blow at the heart of evil and achieving quick passage to Canaan, became the first to stumble. A crusade that had begun in the churches hoping to touch the hearts of sinners and convert them to the kingdom of love found itself instead sidetracked into the dirty alleys of power politics. The effort to change America's racist heart spent itself instead in the effort to change America's racist laws, as if the Jim Crow laws of the South were the cause and not just another symptom of the real problem. With this change, what had been a struggle for the reformation of the heart became instead another worldly display of the wheeling and dealing of politics.

By 1965, after the death of Kennedy and the passage of the Civil Rights Acts that ended legal segregation throughout Dixie, the civil rights movement began to turn ever more surely away from its Christian origins and its nonviolent tactics. The expulsion of whites from SNCC, the Student Non-Violent Coordinating Committee, had been only the beginning of a transformation of that organization from one advocating Christian love to one angrily demanding "black power." Just as black America had been several years ahead of its white counterpart in the initial romantic rebellion against complacency, so it was ahead of white America when its search for a romantic ethic of love uncovered instead a well of anger and violence.

The image of Christian righteousness so carefully cultivated by King and his lieutenants could barely survive against the anger of the slogan "Burn, baby, burn." That anger filtered back down from Watts and Detroit until what had begun as a clear moral confrontation between good and evil was no longer quite so clear. Martin Luther King's continued call for a moral regeneration began to sound not just archaic but irrelevant and problematic. Even the old hymns that had done so much to touch the heart of the nation lost their spiritual significance and came to be heard, not as speaking the universal language of religion, but instead as a coded discourse used to talk power to the state. Ultimately, King himself, before he died, was denounced by radicals black and white as an "Uncle Tom."

In 1965, the last nonviolent crusade of the civil rights movement began in Selma, Alabama, after a black youth named Jimmy Lee Jackson was killed during a voter registration drive. King's SCLC and the more radical SNCC were working together in the effort, and they determined, despite the refusal of Governor George Wallace to grant a permit, to march from Selma to the state capital at Montgomery in protest. Crossing out of Selma across the Edmund Pettus Bridge, the marchers were stopped and driven back by Sheriff Jim Clark and the Alabama state police using tear gas, horses, and clubs. King sent out a call for help, and two days later thousands of marchers from across the country, eager to take a stand for righteousness, once again attempted to march across the bridge. This time, when the troopers ordered them to stop, the leaders at the head of the march knelt in prayer and then turned around and marched back. It may have been a pragmatic, even a wise thing to do, but in the effort to define an absolute moral confrontation between right and wrong, it was not King's finest hour.

A month later, when the march was finally resumed and thousands made the five-day trek to the state capital, the tension between the increasingly militant SNCC workers and King's older Christian ministers was as much the story as the march itself. SNCC seized the opportunity to organize blacks in Loundes County, where an eighty percent black majority was still denied access to the ballot box. The symbol they chose for the new political organization they were building was a black panther. It was the culmination of Stokely Carmichael's rise to power in SNCC. That, along with the growing prominence of Malcolm X, signaled the distinct shift in the civil rights movements from an emphasis on morality to an emphasis on black nationalism that would, the following summer, result in SNCC's kicking out its white members.

In June of 1966, just after Carmichael ousted John Lewis as the head of SNCC, James Meredith, the first black man to attend the University of Alabama, was gunned down as he attempted to march alone from Memphis, Tennessee, to Jackson, Mississippi, on what he called a "march against fear." One of the early heroes of the struggle for freedom, acting alone in an effort that was as foolhardy as it was brave, Meredith was shot in the back by a cowardly racist. Here was a perfect opportunity for the faltering civil rights movement to seize once again the moral high ground and to present itself to the American public as the champion of the traditional American values of Christian self-reliance and virtue.

Martin Luther King immediately announced his determination to continue the interrupted march, to walk from the place where Meredith had been so brutally ambushed to Jackson. He would pick up Meredith's flag and carry it proudly, reaffirming the principles of nonviolence and Christian forbearance in which both he and Meredith believed.

Stokely Carmichael, then the new head of SNCC, also announced his intention to join King on the march. But Carmichael was more interested in asserting his own brand of black nationalism as a rallying cry for poor blacks than he was in sending any message of Christian love to the majority white population. From the start, he and King clashed over tactics and over rhetoric. This was the march on which Carmichael introduced SNCC's new slogan, "Black Power." The increasingly militant marchers, with their raised fists and their chants of "Black Power," attracted the attention of the media nationwide. They also attracted the attention of the state police, there to guard the marchers and prevent further bloodshed. A confrontation was inevitable. The enduring images of the marchers finally driven out of their campsite by baton-swinging state troopers amid angry shouts of "Black Power," raised fists, and threats of counterviolence dragged the movement down from the pedestal of universal human rights into the muddy politics of group empowerment.

Nor was this an isolated example. In 1965 and 1966, first in Watts and then in the streets of northern ghettos, black frustration, unfettered by any Christian call for love, exploded in violence. In 1967, federal troops had to be parachuted into Detroit as the city burned. Then, after Martin Luther King was assassinated in April of 1968, every urban black community in America exploded in rage. By the time King died, his dream of a nonviolent social revolution, based on the principles of Christian love, was already a relic of the past. His killing merely served to provide a concrete symbol of that death. The year 1968 was filled with such symbols.

In the spirit of the time, this further disintegration of the old American pieties, with their lies and hypocrisies, was welcomed. Having left Egypt behind, the radicals, both black and white, were eager to expose the old myths, to clear the ground for whatever new dispensation might follow. America's promise of democracy, they said, had been nothing but a fraud from the start, a self-serving oligarchy built on the backs of slaves and the oppression of Native Americans. Washington and Jefferson were slaveholders, the first Thanksgiving a celebration of genocide. No good could come from anything they did or said. American history would have to be retold from the start.

White radicals, hurt by being kicked out of SNCC but forced to acknowledge the truth in the charge that all whites carried the disease that had infected their racist culture, turned their guilt into self-abasement.

Like penitents at confession, they searched their souls and their history for evidence of sin, and they confessed freely. It was a part of the whole rejection of who they had been, a purging of their former sins. The rejection of King's Christian nationalism and the development of black nationalism in its place seemed truly revolutionary. Malcolm X and Stokely Carmichael and others pointed out the parallel between their struggle and the struggles of Third World peoples against Western colonialism. That oppressed peoples should need to organize and build their communities seemed a necessary step toward true revolutionary change. So went the rationale.

But black nationalism proved to be less a stepping-stone toward more universal revolutionary goals that white radicals could share than an end in itself. And the white radicals who cheered it on were often left looking foolish. In 1966, when I was working as a teenager in the Boston ghetto at a black summer school run by the state, I went out one night with some black friends to hear a black nationalist speaker, Louis Farrakhan, then a young minister of the Roxbury temple of the Black Muslims. Surrounded by steely-eyed Fruit of Islam bodyguards, he flamboyantly denounced all white devils with a passion and an anger that caused my friends to whisper to me not to worry, they'd protect me if anything happened. In the front row, a white guy, wearing working-class clothes and long unkempt hair, cheered him on. When Farrakhan denounced white people as agents of the devil, this white guy, seemingly unaware of the irony, leapt to his feet and shouted "Right on, brother!" Around me, the black people, gesturing toward him, poked each other in the ribs and rolled their eyes. Like Jerry Rubin, he seemed to believe that having long hair had made him a "nigger" too. But the identification with the community he so badly wanted was not shared.

The sense of righteous community briefly created by the moral authority of the civil rights movement began to come apart in other ways, too. In 1966, a group of women within SNCC posted a series of challenges to what they felt were chauvinist attitudes among the male leadership of the group. Not only did they point out several specific instances in which women were treated as second-class members of SNCC, but they also tied their protest to the very criticisms that SNCC was raising against white racism. "Assumptions of male superiority," they wrote, "are as widespread and deep-rooted and every much as crippling to women as the assumptions of white supremacy are to the Negro." They were tired of oppression and ready to resist. Carmichael, however, did not see the connection as clearly as he saw the connection between American racism and Western colonialism. His public response was to declare that, as far as he was concerned, the only position for women in SNCC was "prone."

The white radicals were no better. After being met with boos and catcalls for raising the question of the role of woman at the 1968 SDS convention, one feminist wrote, "If radical men can be so easily provoked into acting like rednecks, what can we expect from others?" Following SNCC's example, these other interest groups began to realize that they too needed to organize on their own behalf, as SNCC had on behalf of black males. If the civil rights crusade were not after all a universal rights crusade, then other groups—women, Hispanics, gays—would also need to organize to assert their groups' interests. As the old order lay dying, what was beginning to emerge was not a new order but disorder. Nor was the civil rights crusade the only one that stumbled and fell in the wilderness. But once again, it served as a model for the rest.

III

"anarchy, desolation, and chaos"

The Haight-Ashbury community that had flourished so famously during the 1967 "Summer of Love" was, by the fall of the year—when "hippie" was given its funeral—already turning into something having little to do with love. Marijuana and hash had been slowly replaced by harder drugs and the original flower children replaced by harder druggies. The attempt to discover a quick communal route to the Kingdom of Freedom was also faltering. As Chester Anderson observed, "Rape was as common as bullshit on Haight Street."

Lewis Yablonsky's 1968 *The Hippie Trip* catalogues the decline and fall of several communes, all spiraling downwards in the same basic pattern. The established residents of the Haight-Ashbury area, many of whom were Hispanic and African American, turned out not to be the symbols of a benevolent human nature. A Puerto Rican youth named Frank admitted to Yablonsky that he had been hassling some teenage hippie girls in his neighborhood, and on one occasion he and his gang had raped one. According to Yablonsky, "several of the young hippie boys . . . angrily, in violation of their avowed love ethic, threatened Frank with a beating if he repeated his attack on their women. Frank got his boys. They came to the apartment where the youths were staying, and when they were refused entrance they promptly battered the old door down. In the melee that followed, Frank slashed Al with a switchblade knife across the cheek." The snake in the garden was alive and well. But the presence of the snake in 1967 did little to diminish the allure of the garden. After all, the revolution had just begun. A few individual incidents like this could not by themselves dispel the dream.

But over time, the nightmares began to accumulate and then over-whelm the dreamers.

For the "young colorful kids" who felt robbed of their freedom and forced into the "hippie" identity by the press, to say nothing of those repelled by the violence that was overtaking the Haight, there was still the promise of getting back to the land and setting one's soul free. But that promise was not always fulfilled. Yablonsky includes in *The Hippie Trip* a report on Morningstar, a particularly disastrous commune begun just north of San Francisco in the summer of '67. His initial impression of "bad vibrations" is soon borne out by his conversations with several of the people there and his own observations. The owner of the land, a folk singer named Lew Gottlieb, had simply thrown open his ranch to all who wanted an escape from the oppression of the city and then re-treated to his own space. The chaos that resulted proved that it was not the urban environment that was responsible for the breakdown of the Haight-Ashbury community.

Without leadership, without organization, without any central unify-ing structure, the people who wandered in and out behaved like ordi-nary people: they made a mess of things. Yablonsky writes of picking up one dirty four-year-old girl who was wandering around crying. He picked her up and hugged her only to discover "that the child smelled badly from urine and feces." Her mother, he was told, "was out in the woods freaked out on acid." The girl looked at Yablonsky and said sim-ply, "I'm lonely."

Into that "anarchy, human desolation, and chaos" at Morningstar pushed an additional element. Thugs from the city had discovered the place and moved in, successfully taking over and controlling one of the buildings. In the historic pattern, the void of anarchy was being filled by the fist of tyranny. According to one of the people Yablonsky inter-viewed,

> There's a spade cat here named Mystery who threatens everyone with as-sault. He along with about ten or fifteen other Negroes from Fillmore liter-ally believe the Diggers' invitation posted in their Black Free Store and decided to come to Morningstar. They have no concept at all or belief in the hippie philosophy. They're all up here drinking wine and messing around. Last night all hell almost broke loose. There are some real bigoted hippies here who actually use expressions like "The niggers should be put back in slavery."

The hell that did break loose, Yablonsky discovered, involved not just threats but physical violence and rape. Gottlieb had simply assumed that to create a space in which people could be free and do their own thing would, in romantic fashion, allow the flowers to emerge from under the asphalt of human civilization. Instead, demons broke through the crust. As Yablonsky's interviewee said, "It is a heavy undertaking to open up an atmosphere for freedom for people."

Joan Didion saw it coming. But as a prophet of neo-orthodox cynicism, she also expected it and would have seen it whether it occurred or not. Her collection of essays *Slouching Towards Bethlehem* is a neo-orthodox interpretation of the Sixties, a warning against the dangers of a naive romanticism. There is, she argues in essay after essay, no substance to the dreams that propel Americans forward. Those dreams, whether of the middle-class traditional variety or the newer, radical vision, are equally idolatrous illusions; here is no Promised Land but only chaos.

The entire first section of the book, "Dreamers of the Golden Dream," emphasizes not the emptiness at the hippie core of Sixties romanticism nor even the lunatic fringe of Sixties radicalism, but the emptiness at the very heart of mainstream American culture itself. Her first dreamer, Lucille Miller, came from the plains to the "empty California sun" in search of "the dream," which for her was upper-middle-class respectability. Failing to find it with her husband, she burned him alive in a Volkswagen Bug, collected the insurance, and then set out to try again, pursuing a dream she had learned not from her fundamentalist parents but from the movies of the late 1930s, themselves dream images of what the good life could be. Didion notes with horror that Americans had become so disconnected from reality, living on illusions created by illusions, that here we could see how "the dream was teaching the dreamers how to live."

Didion's essay on John Wayne continues this theme, not in the critical style of the first essay, but as a personal confession. For here, Didion acknowledges her own susceptibility to illusions. When she was a child, she writes, she would go to the Officers Club to look at the artificial blue rain behind the bar, and she would go to the movies. There she met John Wayne, born Marion Morrison, and fell in love not with Morrison but with John Wayne, the artificial father figure. This is the Wayne who "looked like a man," who embodied the old American ethos of rugged individualism and patriarchal authority. She confesses that "deep in my heart where the artificial rain forever falls," she is still enamored of that dream. She knows on an intellectual level that it is "just" a dream, that it has no credibility and no substance. She is fully aware of the feminist critique of the socially constructed myths of masculine authority and female dependency. But despite all that, still she can't deny its emotional hold, even on her. The American—no, the human—propensity to believe in unsubstantiated beliefs, in idolatry, is her theme: "I have as much trouble as the next person with illusion and reality."

After picturing Joan Baez, the queen of the pacifist folk music scene, as something of an airhead, Didion shows more respect for Comrade Laski, another deluded dreamer, but a dreamer who exerts every ounce of his will and intellect to hold his dream together. Unlike the let-it-all-hang-out romantics of the counterculture, this old dogmatic lefty, "General Secretary of the Communist Party U.S.A. (Marxist Leninist), a splinter group of Stalinists-Maoists," self-consciously strives to create structure out of chaos. Revolution for him is not an antinomian repudiation of structure; it is a means to get from an inferior structure to what he believes will be a more solid one. Didion recognizes his compulsion as her own, a fear of chaos, a terror of the void. "I know something about dread myself," she admits, "and appreciate the elaborate systems with which some people manage to fill the void, appreciate all the opiates of the people, whether they are as accessible as alcohol and heroin and promiscuity or as hard to come by as faith in God or history." As Solomon Stoddard had preached, even those addicted to morality and religion or revolution are merely serving their lusts therein.

But Laski, with his authoritarian arminian anality, is not a significant Sixties type. For that Didion looks to the reclusive billionaire Howard Hughes, a man driven, she says, by the compulsion for absolute individual autonomy. He is the final secular product of American antinomianism, the capitalist equivalent of the libertarian hippie. He buys Las Vegas, she explains, not because he is driven by the need for control or for money but because he wants to be able to get a sandwich or a haircut any time of day or night without being subject to any external control. This is Protestant individualism carried to an extreme, but it is also, says Didion, the American dream, "absolute personal freedom, mobility, privacy." That it is a socially destructive dream she has no doubts, and that is what so frightens her about the counterculture of the Sixties. Though it had not yet happened when Didion wrote her essay, Hughes's descent into madness in his later years only bore out her point that to step outside of accepted communal structure in pursuit of individual dreams leads inevitably to the pit.

The essay that gets to the heart of her book, the title essay, is a report on the Haight-Ashbury scene in the 1967 Summer of Love. The center of the culture was not holding; nothing was. Vandals, she reports, couldn't even spell the four-letter words they scrawled on the walls. And the results of the social hemorrhage of the dreams of the suburban middle class ended up on the streets of San Francisco. The teenagers she finds to interview are not the articulate Ken Keseys and Timothy Learys. They are reform school dropouts like Max, who wears bells and an Indian headband and has no use for Freudian hang-ups. He also has no use for relationships, possessions, social conventions, drug laws, or taboos. He has, in fact, no beliefs about anything. He just "does his thing." To Didion, Max personifies emptiness.

Even the mystical core of hippie happiness, tripping on LSD, is for Didion an empty event. She refuses offers of LSD or even marijuana, confessing herself too neurotic to take the risk, but she sits there in the living room with pen and pad in hand, while Max, Sharon, and some friends all drop acid. And what did she observe? "During the next four hours a window banged once in Barbara's room, and about five-thirty some children had a fight on the street. A curtain billowed in the afternoon wind. A cat scratched a beagle in Sharon's lap. Except for the sitar music on the stereo there was no other sound or movement until seven thirty, when Max said 'wow!' " In short, nothing.

That something might in fact have been happening out of sight of Didion's visual perception does not seem to have occurred to her. No mention is made of the inner experience of the kids around her. No mention is even made of the possibility that the LSD experience is an internal one. Didion clings to the literal and external, looking for something to happen in the world she thinks of as real. She can't trip, or even smoke, because she fears too much the chaos that she suspects awaits if she lets down her defenses. So afraid is she of letting go that she can't even admit that there might be something other going on. One can't help thinking that the sight that dominated those kids' trips that afternoon was one neurotic middle-class writer nervously chain-smoking cigarettes, crossing and uncrossing her legs, walking back and forth from the couch to the window, staring at them, and writing frantically in her little book, stubbing out one cigarette, nervously lighting another. No wonder Max said "wow."

But to Didion, the emptiness of the afternoon was the message. For even if phony social conventions cannot be ultimately justified, they do provide a kind of social glue that holds society together. They represent a set of conventions, albeit artificial, that people over many centuries have agreed to agree to live by if only to prevent much worse results. Arminian rules do serve a purpose. The structures of law and belief were formed over centuries of human experience. Some of them, as the Marxists say, reflect little more than the efforts of powerful elites to hold onto worldly power. But some of them arose as constructive responses to the chaos of war, anarchy, famine, epidemics, economic collapse, loneliness, confusion, fear, and tyranny. Without those structures, we might once again find ourselves at the mercy of any of those ancient enemies. In the mass of confused, inarticulate kids wandering the country in 1967, Didion sees not the beginning of the Age of Aquarius but the possibility of the beginnings of fascism. For her, the wilderness is not a cleansed land awaiting the coming of God's grace; it is a state of nature full of natural savages waiting for a leader.

What she literally sees, she tells us, is "an army of children waiting to be given the word," waiting for some leader to come along and fill their voids with a sense of purpose and meaning. Chester Anderson and Peter Berg seemed to be two of those would-be leaders. Didion quotes from Anderson's communiqués, with their calls to action, and follows Berg's attempts to stir up political fervor among the stoned-out kids watching a Grateful Dead concert in Golden Gate Park. The media, she says, are so caught up in their rebels-without-a-cause paradigm that they fail to see the political implications. But Didion finds a psychiatrist who spells it out and puts it all in historical context: "It's a social movement, quint-essentially romantic, the kind that recurs in times of real social crisis. The themes are always the same. A return to innocence. The invocation of an earlier authority and control. The mysteries of the blood. An itch for the transcendental, a purification. Right there you've got the ways that romanticism historically ends up in trouble, lends itself to authoritarianism."

For Didion, San Francisco, 1967, threatened to be a repeat of Germany's Weimar Republic, 1927, or a foreshadowing of anarchy—the lack of order that would later lead to the Taliban's takeover of Afghanistan, a social vacuum in which the seeds of fascism are nurtured. Like Camille Paglia several decades later, she argues that the romantic return to the self, while temporarily liberating, ultimately ends up in decadence and chthonian chaos as the structures disintegrate and humanity's true self rises like some long-penned-up beast from the immoral depths of consciousness.

There are, she says, two kinds of morality. On one hand, we have the social codes she calls "wagon-train morality," a historically constructed set of rules we agree to follow that are pragmatic and have no claim to any absolute legitimacy. On the other hand, we have the appeal to the knowable good, the belief that we humans can know right from wrong and act upon that knowledge. This latter approach, she says, is a seductive illusion. To believe that one knows the right is to believe that what one believes is the truth. "There is some sinister hysteria out here in the air tonight, some hint of the monstrous perversion to which any human idea can come. 'I followed my own conscience.' 'I did what I thought was right.' How many madmen have said it and meant it?"

That Martin Luther King then becomes one of the "fashionable madmen" who are leading the nation into disaster is an implication she does not have to spell out. That the leaders of the antiwar movement are also moving that way, along with the politicians and generals who believe that Vietnam is a righteous cause, is also left unsaid. It didn't have to be said. Didion is by no means a product of the Sixties. She was over thirty, after all.

IV

"the Angels are the cops!"

After the success of Woodstock as an event and as a symbol, promoters on the West Coast set out to have a "Woodstock West" to prove, as Mick Jagger said, that they "could do it too." The site finally chosen for this concert was the old Altamont Speedway outside San Francisco. This too was to be a massive gathering in which the Western tribes of the counterculture would assemble and celebrate love and music together. Woodstock had shown, so the wisdom went, that the very power of rock music, when combined with the liberating effect of hallucinogenic drugs, could create true community. Like the revivals of the Great Awakenings, like the mayhem at Cane Ridge, their gathering, so they believed, would bring down fire from heaven and ignite the earth. In the process, they would rock the old world to pieces and create a new American community of love.

Since no police would be needed, none were there. But as a precaution for the musicians, who often had a difficult time dealing with enthusiastic fans, the Hell's Angels were promised beer if they would "watch the stage." After the fact, the stupidity of this was apparent. But at the time, given the context, it seemed to make sense. There was even a precedent for it. In *Electric Kool-Aid Acid Test,* Wolfe had noted that, strangely enough, the organizers of the march against the Oakland Army Base were using the Hell's Angels to ride shotgun. And in the book, Kesey's ability to bring the notoriously violent Hell's Angels into his "movie" and to befriend them was seen as one of the most daring and dangerous stunts he pulled.

For where the hippies liked to play at being rebels who crossed the line of what society approved, the Hell's Angels were truly already out there, real outlaws who had burned whatever bridges they might have had to suburbia. They really were bad. The organizers of the Altamont concert did not anticipate the Angels' violent reactions when they felt their bikes threatened; nor did they anticipate the bloody way in which members of the outlaw group would enforce their version of the law. Perhaps the hippies at Altamont were too caught up in their paradigm of benevolent humanity to see evil when it stared them in the face. Perhaps the entrepreneurs arranging the concert saw only a cheap source of crowd control. It hardly matters.

The most significant event, the one that signified Altamont, if not the entire Sixties, was the stabbing to death of an eighteen-year-old black youth in front of the stage, the whole scene caught by the movie cameras soon after Mick Jagger finished singing "Sympathy for the Devil." But this murder by the Hell's Angels was only part of the Altamont story. Repeated beatings administered by the Angels to nonviolent members of the crowd who merely got in their way are captured in the movie *Gimme Shelter.* By the time the concert was over, three other people were dead, two (like Kesey's young mongrel) run over by cars and the fourth drowned in a mud puddle. In addition, according to Sol Stern, "Over 100 people had their heads bloodied or ribs cracked or were otherwise pummeled and violated by the Hells Angels," and "a reported 700—there were more likely thousands—people were treated at the site for nightmarishly bad acid trips." Marty Balin of the Jefferson Airplane was knocked unconscious while on the stage playing, and Denise Jewkes of the Ace of Cups, who was pregnant at the time, was hit by an empty beer bottle and ended up with a fractured skull.

Stern saw the significance of the event in its proper context. Having ventured beyond the borders of civilization, the counterculture was testing the state of nature to see, as Thoreau had said, if it were "mean" or ultimately benevolent.

> By mid-morning everything seemed up for grabs. There was not a uniform in sight. If there was to be any order or law, it would have to come out of the massive community that had gathered so suddenly. As the sun moved toward the official noon starting time and the tension and expectation increased, only a mythical political category such as the State of Nature seemed to apply. The normal restraints and structures were gone—there were only the people, and the drugs and the music to come and the feeling of incredible energy already beginning to radiate from the empty stage.

But as nature abhors a vacuum, the antinomian moment could not last. For a brief second, said Stern, "it was pure ecstasy." Then, "we went over the edge. Ugliness and meanness erupted all around, all at once." A fight broke out near the front of the crowd as a grotesquely fat man, entirely nude, struggled through the crowd toward the stage. The Angels, seeing this coming, leaped off their seats into the crowd with their pool cues swinging. A man who attempted to help the guy was beaten to the ground. The crowd let it happen. "The Angels are the cops! The unspoken thought chilled me. The State of Nature had been short lived, and now we had law and order of sorts. But the Angel cops had no jail to take people to and no judge or jury to try them. So for the rest of the afternoon, if the Angels decided you broke the law, they did only what they do best—wiped you out, making certain you didn't do it again."

In *Gimme Shelter,* Mick Jagger's ineffectual entreaties throughout the night to the crowd, to the Angels, to everyone to stop the fighting come across as desperation. He sang, he danced, he poured out all of his famous energy in the hope that somehow the music, the scene, the spirit of his performance would capture the attention and energy that surged through the crowd and that he, by his own willful energy, could control the monster unleashed in front of him. It must have been terrifying. "Why are we fighting? Why are we fighting?" he pleaded, to no avail. The man who had in this music claimed "sympathy for the Devil" now stood in the middle of Satanic madness wondering where it had all come from.

When Sonny "I'm not no peace creep by any sense of the word" Barger, the leader of the Angels, came on stage and grabbed the microphone, he was wearing an enormous animal headdress, as pure a pagan symbol of evil as ever dreamed up by any Puritan on the old New England frontier. And he did what Jagger had not been able to do. His presence, his power, his energy captured the attention of the crowd. "In their primitive way and without talking much about it," wrote Stern, "the Angels were so together that less than 100 of them were able to take over and intimidate a crowd of close to a half-million people." Here was one parallel to Hitler.

To listen to the pleas of Mick Jagger and the rationalizations of the other musicians about what was happening is to realize how easily anarchy yields to tyranny. When told of the chaos as he arrives, Jerry Garcia's response to real evil is to mumble impotently, "Oh, bummer." Even worse, Grace Slick grabs the microphone at one point and tries to persuade the crowd that willful submission to the control exercised by the Angels would be to everyone's good. "People get weird," she explained, "and you need people like the Angels to keep people in line, but the Angels also—you know—you don't bust people in the head for nothing. So both sides are . . . uh . . ." What? She never got a chance to say. The Angels continued to beat people, and the crowd continued to resist.

If the hope had been that the use of dope could somehow release not the hate and fear but the love that is dormant in every human soul, then Altamont disproved the lesson of Woodstock. Some romantic survivors of the Sixties still believe that the problem was not in human nature, but in the nature of the chemicals in the drugs at Altamont, or the capitalist motivations of the promoters—anything but the self. The whole Sixties counterculture revolution was premised on the faith that the self was basically good and that to lay it out and open could only produce joy. But Altamont was not the only evidence that the self revealed by the use of drugs was far from Adam or Eve in the Garden.

V

"Bubba's limitations"

One of my souvenirs of that age, fading fast, is a T-shirt promoting an underground comic called the "Forty year old hippy." The character on the T-shirt, who looks closer to eighty than forty, is popping a pill and saying, "200 trips and they've all been bummers. But I ain't giving up."

In *Electric Kool-Aid Acid Test,* Wolfe chronicles the adventures of one Charles Augustus Owsley, not the inventor but one of the early entrepreneurs of LSD production. Owsley acid was a well-known brand name, one that stood for a high-quality trip, and at two to three dollars a tab, young Owsley soon became very, very rich—rich enough to sponsor the Grateful Dead and take them from free concerts in Golden Gate Park to international fame. But before they all got there, they had already been on some other long strange trips.

Richard Alpert, before he became Baba Ram Dass, may have been, as he tells it, relatively calm as he watched his numerous identities appear and then disappear before him while he tripped on acid. But for many other trippers without the sophistication of the Harvard professor, the loss of self was a terrifying experience, a death as real as any. Many who dropped acid expecting colors and lights and groovy tunes instead found themselves in a life-and-death struggle to maintain their sanity, as the reality they had always known and taken for granted dissolved like mist around them.

In his attempt to get inside the Sixties, Wolfe never quite gets inside this aspect of the acid experience. But through Owsley, he does make a good effort to understand it from a safe distance. Owsley, who certainly had plenty of experience of what his own products produced, finally went a tab too far. According to Wolfe, Owsley while on a deep acid trip "got caught in the whirlpool, spun out of his gourd." He went back through time to the beginning of the evolution of his own cells, and then into his cells until "the whole world was coming to pieces molecule by molecule now and swimming like grease bubbles in a cup of coffee, disappearing into the intergalactic ooze and gasses all around—including his own body. He lost his skin, his skeleton, his pulmonary veins—sneaking out into the ooze like eels, they are, reeking phosphorous, his neural ganglia—unraveling like hot worms and wiggling down the galactic drain, his whole substance dissolving into gaseous nothingness until finally he was down to one cell."

Wolfe describes him scrambling out of the bushes and bursting into one of the acid tests at dawn, lurching and groping and screaming, "Survival!" The master chemist himself had gone over the edge, fallen through the rotten covering over the pit of hell, and discovered the terror of the void. He had fought his way back eventually, and now he had to warn Kesey, "Taking LSD in a monster group like this gets too many forces going, too much amok energy, causing very freaky and destructive things to happen." But others discovered that same terror without the excuse of a monster crowd to blame.

Earlier in the book, while Furthur was heading out on its sojourn to turn on the American heartland and to uncover the hidden depths of the self, Wolfe tells us of one young tripper, who as the bus was careening down the highway dropped acid, wore no clothes, slept with everyone, and while no one noticed in that whacked-out context, went completely around the bend. "Stark Naked" they called her, and when they got to Larry McMurtry's house in his suburban Texas neighborhood, she ran off the bus, still naked, and grabbed his son, thinking the boy her own lost child. But her loss of connection to the reality everyone else shared was not half as horrifying as the conclusion. They left "Stark Naked" in a Texas mental hospital under the care of some Texan Nurse Ratched, and then after the steel gates had clanked shut on her, perhaps forever, they blithely returned to the road.

Morality, it must be understood, belongs to the context of the dominant culture. To allow oneself to be stopped by morality is to always stay within the borders of that culture, encaged by the rules already laid down. Furthur's trip was to get beyond those borders, so Stark Naked's loss was simply part of the price that had to be paid for freedom. Kesey's Pranksters were bound and determined not to be like the little boy found crying at the street corner, who responded, when asked why, that he was running away from home but that his parents wouldn't let him cross the street. To escape from the cage of social conditioning required a willingness to cross the street, even if that meant breaking some moral code.

Nor was Stark Naked the only Merry Prankster who paid a price. The perception of the illusory nature of the truths of the world, when not replaced by some higher perception, produces paranoia. If everything is false, nothing can be trusted. Nothing is what it seems; the wilderness is full of mirages. No one is really telling the truth. If infinite layers of belief underlie belief under belief, then no solid rock exists on which to stand. The ground is always shifting, always dissolving, always falling away. In *Electric Kool-Aid Acid Test,* Sandy succumbs to paranoia. Too much acid and DMT. He finds himself literally on the bus but emotionally off it. He is not in sync with the group. He has fears he cannot express. Ostracized for taking unauthorized acid, he begins to see the implicit hierarchy of the tribe he has joined, and he wonders what else he has missed. When the other members of the trip try to stage a ceremony to calm him and soothe his fears, he instead gets the impression that they might be taking him off to eat him, and he panics.

Such acid panics were not uncommon. Alpert, before he had shed his old Professor Richard Alpert persona at Harvard, identified what he considered the five main reasons for acid panic. These were: (1) "Cognitive, the terror of the loss of rational control," (2) "Social, the terror of doing something shameful or ludicrous," (3) "Psychological, the terror of finding out something about yourself you do not want to face," (4) "Cultural, the terror of discovering the painful truth about the institutions with which one is identified; of seeing through the tribal shams," (5) "Ontological Addiction, the terror of finding a realm of experience so pleasurable that one will not want to return." Together, he said, these all can be equated with the fear of death, for the loss of identity is the death of the self. When "the construct of the identity is found to be an illusion," there is then only the void, at least until rebirth: "To have courage to walk through this hell brings the transcendence that lies beyond."

Police departments in every major city in America learned to deal with paranoia freak-outs as best they could. A friend of mine, a big southern boy from Tennessee, was wrestled to the pavement as he ran down the center of Massachusetts Avenue in his underwear, screaming at the top of his lungs. The cops wrapped him in a blanket and took him to a police station, where they shot him up with thorazine. Soon thereafter he dropped out of Harvard and went to India, where he learned Sanskrit and where, he claimed, God came to him, right into his ear. Today he's a tenured professor.

5. "May I see your id." From *The Kingdom of Heaven is Within You Comix,* 1969. Courtesy of John Thompson.

Not all were so blessed. Instead of a community of love where all are in sync, together, back home, Owsley on acid sank into his own consciousness but did not find the one big essential I. Instead, he and untold numbers of other trippers found one hundred million separate aloneness terrors. Owsley's discovery of the primal urge for individual survival was not exactly the Promised Land that Leary, Alpert, or any of the many other acid gurus had prophesied. It was more like the moment of McMurphy's defeat, when he cried out with a "sound of cornered-animal fear of hate and surrender and defiance" that was like the sound of an animal torn apart by the dogs "when he doesn't care about anything anymore but himself and his dying." Owsley's experience was not singular. Many lonely trippers lost it completely. Some never came back. Others came back and vowed never to cross that frontier again, never to look back but to cling to arminian structure as if it were life itself.

The disintegration of the socially constructed self under the influence of LSD was a psychedelic escape from Egypt and an entry into the wilderness. A few, like Alpert and Leary, claimed to find in that chaos something upon which a new more authentic self could be established. Others learned that in the multitude of dreams there are many illusions, that none of the gods of the world could be trusted; and they therefore clung to terror as their Puritan ancestors had clung to the Fear of God. Still others, having tasted of the terror of the void outside the text, returned as Didion had to their texts, knowing them at that point to be only texts, but determined to cling to them regardless.

A few, like Ram Dass, came back, and then returned, and then came back again, like mountain climbers in the Himalayas, carrying news back about what they had seen and experienced. Some of these tried to make sense of their experience, to put it into context. Some even found ways to incorporate their experience into belief structures either as old as Zen or as new as their own invention. Ram Dass never quite surrendered to the idolatry of embracing any particular structure. It has always been one of his attractions that he has remained aware of himself as playing the part of playing the part of a Jewish academic pretending to be some weirdo Eastern holy man. Such playful distancing helped keep him from the unholy error, the original sin, of believing in his own beliefs. Occasionally he got carried away, but he was always able to return and confess the "egg on my beard," as he once put it.

Others have not been so strong. Franklin Jones, a.k.a. Bubba Free John, a.k.a. Adi Da, was one of many self-styled gurus who sprung up like psilocybin mushrooms after the reign of the Sixties. According to his own community's explanation,

Bubba Free John was born Franklin Jones, in Long Island, New York on November 3, 1939. From birth he enjoyed the condition of enlightenment or God-consciousness, thus, he is one of those rare beings known in traditional literature as a Siddha, or one who is born into the world already spiritually complete. During the first twenty years of his life, Bubba's natural condition of illumination was gradually undermined by the conventions of the world, and he was forced to embark on a thirteen-year odyssey to regain his state of enlightenment. In September, 1970, Bubba Free John permanently realized the Condition into which he had been born.

Like many other such gurus, Bubba was able to gather a community around himself and his teachings. The Dawn Horse Communion—still going strong today, with headquarters in San Francisco and an ashram in Northern California—produced books, pamphlets, movies, and the cult of Bubba. The message of the cult was the ancient promise of antinomian liberation from the law and participation in transcendent ecstasy. When you are able, writes Bubba, "to think God, to act God, to make the Divine the present Condition of the world, to live in that Siddi or power, to live that light, to be full . . . you cease to be concerned for the taboos of men, and their rules, their seeking." Then you are free, free of shame, free to be embarrassed, free to be. Life in the ashram was a series of Pentecostal showerings in which, in one example, "nearly everyone in the room began one at a time to sing ecstatically, crazily, about God. We were all clapping and shouting, praising God. It was just nonsense singing, ecstatic singing, happy singing."

But even letting oneself go free to enjoy the absolute abandonment of antinomian ecstasy in the security of the ashram, and inviting others to join the bliss, was not enough for the enlightened one. Sensing a responsibility to let the world know that the spirit had again been made flesh and dwelt among them, Bubba Free John undertook a pilgrimage to India in 1973 to allow his guru, Swami Muktananda, to acknowledge him. Like a faithful Boswell, Bubba's devotee Jerry Sheinfeld, another Jewish boy from Boston, went along as an aide and a reporter. His account of the trip was published by the Dawn Horse ashram under the title "Bubba Free John in India." It is a fascinating book.

Bubba Free John proceeds in the book to visit his guru, confident of the reception the old man will accord him. The God present in the older Indian guru would recognize the same God in the younger American version, and there would be an instantaneous explosion. But it didn't quite turn out that way. When "Bubba" Free John finally has a private meeting with "Baba" Muktananda, a Professor Jain translating, the moment of recognition never occurs. According to Sheinfeld's account, "The meeting was very intense. I felt nervous. Bubba gave Professor Jain a copy of the questions, and he kept one for himself. The questions aren't important here, but Baba misinterpreted the entire purpose of the meeting. He further had no idea of what Bubba was talking about when he asked for Baba's acknowledgment of his ultimate realization. At one time during the meeting I wanted to punch Baba in the mouth for the way he was communicating his assumptions of Bubba's limitations."

The two Americans left as quickly as they could. But Bubba was not daunted. The meeting had instead freed him, Bubba, from his assumption that the older man was "realized" enough to recognize him. He saw, Sheinfeld said, that the Indian was "only another seeker who misunderstood reality and created separation in subtle ways." Indeed, with the need to be acknowledged broken, Bubba declared himself "now able to function as guru without the involvement with any living gurus." And so he returned to California and the adoration of his Ashram of devotees. Today he is Adi Da, the head of a New Age spiritual empire to rival that of Oral Roberts, balding and more Buddha-like every day.

Both Owsley's terror and Franklin Jones's illusions make evident the difficulty of finding any Promised Land. Indeed, of the two of them, Owsley in his terror was a lot closer to the truth. Jones had simply traded one socially constructed fiction for another. He undoubtedly once had the same kind of disorienting, disintegrating experience that Owsley had. And from that he reconstructed a new identity, a new belief system, a new community. Like the born-again converts of the First Great Awakening, he really believed his new identity to be a piece of the living God.

Once in February in Harvard Square, with a twenty-degree wind whipping old newspapers across the frozen slush, I watched a small group of Hari Krishna devotees singing and chanting for anyone who would stop long enough to drop a few coins in their cup. Despite the weather and the wind, the kids were wearing the thin cotton wraps worn by Hindus in tropical India. They did have, it seemed, several layers of long underwear and sweaters on underneath their summer sarongs, but the clash of cultures made a significant statement. Forms that evolved in the cultural and meteorological context of tropical India do not transfer well to New England winters. Out of the emptiness, out of the need to wear something, they had chosen clothes presenting an image that could only make people shiver as they rushed by. They themselves must have wondered how they had gotten to that point.

In Kurt Vonnegut's *Cat's Cradle*, another Sixties book that generated a vast cult readership, a canny old Negro named Lionel Johnson (or as the locals pronounce it, Bokonon) and his companion are cast up on an extremely poor island in the West Indies. They do what they can to try to help the people, but they soon find they cannot do much. So they provide the people not with food or money or housing, but with that which people need most, a story by which they can lead meaningful lives. By a flip of the coin, McCabe becomes the evil ruler in the castle and Bokonon becomes the hunted holy man hiding out in the jungle. This elaborately staged play gives the people a drama in which they can all participate. The penalty for hiding the holy saint is death on the hook, and everyone on the island is a secret Bokononist hiding his or her hero, learning his cynical lessons, and denying it to the authorities when they came knocking on the door. This works well until tragedy strikes: both McCabe and Johnson forget that they are only playacting. They forget that it is all a drama staged to distract the people from their hunger and fear, "McCabe knowing the agony of the tyrant and Bokonon knowing the agony of the saint. They both became for all practical purposes, insane." And then people really did start dying on the hook.

To forget the fear that one does not really know and to begin to believe in one's own beliefs: this was the original Fall from grace in the Garden of Eden. When Adam and Eve ate of the fruit of the tree of knowledge, they came to believe that they were as gods and their beliefs were in fact the truth. The old Puritan's prayer was telling: Lord, give me not seemings, but keep this fear alive in my heart.

Note that the prayer was not to end the agony of not knowing. This would be too much to ask. Instead, that old Puritan prayed that he might avoid the very real human danger of beginning to believe in his own beliefs, to keep alive the Fear of God. To realize that one is a fake does not guarantee that any new persona is really new. As James Baldwin said, "The roles that we construct are constructed because we feel that they will help us to survive and also, of course, because they fulfill something in our personalities; one does not therefore cease playing a role simply because one has begun to understand it. All roles are dangerous."

Legions of Bubbas, gurus, "children of god" of all stripes returned to the world to do what they imagined as God's calling, empowered by the idolatry of believing that finally they had escaped from the cage of constructed consciousness, faced the wilderness, and been granted a vision of the truth outside of the cages of all constructed consciousness, like so many of American evangelicals in the past. Even when, like Gary Snyder tucking his long hair up under his cap and leaving his earring in the car, they were tempted to return to the old TV-watching, beef-eating American way, they resisted the old constructions and held tight to their new beliefs, clinging, as Gary Snyder depicts to their new vision, "To the real work, To/ What is to be done."

VI

"They are all fucking crazy"

To do what is to be done assumes a stance in the real world of politics. It assumes a knowledge of what is to be done, a confident knowledge willing to stand up against the past. Martin Luther King, with his faith in God, had the courage to stand up when few others dared. Bolstered by his historical faith, quoting the God of Jesus, Jacob, and Abraham and the revelations of the Bible, he had risked the charge of anarchy and antinomianism. His was a stand outside of the law of his immediate era but well within the law of a larger historical tradition. He was not alone. He had, as he said, "cosmic companionship." Like King, Alpert also believed that he was stepping outside of the structure of his culture but doing so within the structure of older traditions of belief.

So these intrepid travelers had the courage to head out into the wilderness, leaving Egypt behind, confident that they were not entirely crazy or alone. But the trip into the wilderness is a trip outside of the structures of the accepted boundaries of belief and behavior into that territory we call madness. However necessary the break from Egypt was, it was also necessary that the wilderness should swallow up refugees before they could reach their Promised Land.

Like SNCC, Students for a Democratic Society (SDS) also changed from its earlier incarnation as a social reform movement calling for participatory democracy and a return to traditional American values of justice and equality. The main New Left student organization had begun in the image of the civil rights crusade challenging white Americans, as King had said in '63, to live up to the words of their creed. But this too changed; in the middle Sixties, SDS became a militantly confrontational group, and after 1968, it tripped out on its own illusions of itself as a violent revolutionary front.

In its early years, SDS had been a militant reform movement of the left committed to the notion that America could be saved. Tom Hayden, the author of the Port Huron Statement, was typical of this early group. He began his political career in the civil rights movement and was beaten and jailed while organizing for SNCC in Mississippi. At that time, his politics were like those of most of the liberal left, more reformist than radical and committed to the liberal notion that human beings can take control of the forces that surround them rationally. "We must," he said in 1962, "have a try at bringing society under human control." These early radicals were also mainstream, clean, sober, drug-free, and as committed to the work ethic as any Puritan.

By 1966, with the expulsion of white radicals from SNCC and the growth of black nationalism, it was finally evident that, as the blacks had said, America's problem was not in the South, nor was it a black problem. The problem was back home, in the suburban North, in white America. The civil rights movement's criticism of the South expanded to become a criticism of the entire country, South and North, redneck and liberal. So SDS and other groups on the left turned their attention to the heart of their own communities. And as they did, the horror of Vietnam seemed to prove that the most damning criticisms of the country were correct. America, they discovered, was not a basically decent country that needed to correct some serious mistakes. It was instead "Amerikkka," a country run by racists, war profiteers, and imperialists. The war, as one SDS leader said, is what "has provided the razor, the terrifying sharp cutting edge that has finally severed the last vestige of illusion that morality and democracy are the guiding principles of American foreign policy."

For many, the accumulated lessons of the civil rights movement and the Vietnam war and the apparent emptiness of America's TV-saturated, consumption-obsessed culture were that America was not the champion of righteousness but the very Devil. For the liberals of the early Sixties, the assumption had been that a basically decent America had made mistakes and that these needed to be fixed. For the radicals of the New Left, as for James Baldwin, such innocence was no longer tolerable. There comes a time when the child of an abusive parent realizes that Daddy is a beast, even though he is Daddy, and turns all the fierce love with which he had once clung to him into hate.

More than anything else, the war in Vietnam forced white radicals to step up their demands and to militarize both their language and their tactics. Just as black nationalism had splintered any hope the civil rights movement might have had of communicating effectively to the majority population, so Vietnam created a split between the old liberals and their more radical children. To the radicals, Vietnam proved that the old liberals like McNamara were lost in a mad delusion. One cannot communicate reasonably with madmen; one can only confront them, either to force them to see their own madness or to stop them with force. From 1966 to 1968, as the war escalated and the draft took more and more young men, and as the lies of the politicians poured out across the land and the television news showed the nightly horror of napalm bombs and body bags, the radicals grew more and more alienated. Like acid freaks off on some paranoid tangent, many began to follow their fears outside of the old structures of belief into strange new territories. In this, they became the mirror image of the Cold Warriors whose fears led them step by logical step into the insanity of Vietnam.

The split in SDS was social and geographical as well as political. A younger group, less Eastern, less intellectual, less Old Left, was taking over. For these younger radicals, many of them from the Midwest, moral outrage over the war and racism were more important than careful political analysis. When an attempt was made to draft a new Port Huron Statement to reflect this antinomian, almost frontier, spirit, the very effort was denounced as irrelevant "statementism." They were, according to SDS historian Kirkpatrick Sales, "more thoroughly anti-American than the early SDSers had been." One of these, Texan Jeff Sherol, felt this personally and defined his commitment in religious terms. "In Texas," he said, "to join SDS meant breaking with your family, it meant being cut off. It was like in early Rome joining a Christian sect, and the break was so much more total." The attack on "statementism," in its radical move beyond words, thus pointed in two directions at once, back to St. Paul's "The letter killeth but the spirit giveth life" as well as forward to postmodernism's dismissal of words as having no essential content.

But just as important in the growing radicalization of the New Left was the stridency of opposition among the not-so-silent majority of the population. The majority of Americans, not members of the baby-boom generation but veterans of earlier decades, had long since, through the bitterness of the Depression and the horror of World War II, confirmed allegiance to a United States of America that created the conformist culture of the Fifties. Their belief system was under attack. They knew it and they reacted accordingly. Where the liberals and radicals had once hoped that the country might turn to them, they found instead a growing conservatism that they were unable to overcome. And their frustration drove them further and further toward the edge.

The radicals' response to this, and to the growing escalation of the Vietnam war, was to move steadily and surely from persuasion to confrontation, to thinking of themselves as changing the system from within, to challenging the system from without. With this came a sense that they were no longer working to help liberate others but were now fighting to liberate themselves. They went from seeing themselves as having a social responsibility to help others, basically an elitist and patronizing stance, to identifying themselves as part of the community that needed to break free. During the early days of SDS, the organization had never been able to come to an agreement on just how to confront the draft. Now they threw themselves into draft resistance. This move from liberal strategizing to action was in many ways similar to the transformation induced by the use of drugs. And increasingly, the use of drugs became part of the SDS rebellion as the politicos joined the freaks. Rational considerations had kept them from crossing the line of legal respectability before; now they found themselves no longer caring what the media and the folks back home in Texas thought. One student, after the 1967 antidraft riots at Madison, defined tear gas as the drug that changed his life: "There is simply a total change of consciousness. Nothing matters but eyes and nose and throat. It has an absolution, an ability to take over one's whole being that is shocking at the same time and puzzling afterward."

The year 1968, in many ways the climactic year of the Sixties, brought all these forces to a head. Senator Eugene McCarthy, an antiwar Democrat, had announced that he would challenge Johnson for the Democratic nomination. Many SDSers, not ready for the radical direction SDS was heading, and many not-quite-yet-hippies took the opportunity to give working-within-the-system liberalism one more chance. They went "clean for Gene," shaving their beards and hiding their dope, and threw themselves into traditional political campaigning. As if to humiliate the Pentagon in its assurances that the war was being won, that the United States was in control, the Vietcong launched a nationwide offensive at the end of January that took the American military entirely by surprise. The Tet offensive was so massive and so widespread, endangering even the American embassy in Saigon, that it proved that the American government was either lying or ignorant. Many Americans, including many who supported the war, no longer had the stomach to continue. Money and volunteers poured into the McCarthy campaign. In the conservative state of New Hampshire, working-class Democrats told the students knocking on their doors that they couldn't understand what we were doing over there, that if we couldn't win—and it looked like we couldn't—then we ought to get out. For a brief period, electoral politics seemed to work. McCarthy came within a few percentage points of beating President Johnson in New Hampshire's Democratic primary. The handwriting was on the wall.

Robert Kennedy, who had previously pledged his support for Johnson's re-election, read the handwriting and jumped into the race, bringing with him a lot of old Kennedy New Frontiersmen and seasoned White House hands. When, just before the Wisconsin Primary, LBJ avoided an embarrassing defeat by withdrawing his name from consideration and announcing he would not be a candidate for re-election, it was possible to believe that democratic politics could work, that the country could return liberal Democrats to power, and that the war policies of the Johnson administration could be brought to an end within the system.

The announcement of Johnson's withdrawal came on March 31. A few days later, on April 4, Martin Luther King was shot dead in Memphis, and the black ghettos of the nation exploded. The army had to be called out to protect the capital as large sections of Washington D.C., among many other cities, burned. On April 25, in protest against the university's taking of neighborhood housing to build a gym, Columbia SDS began a traumatic takeover of campus buildings, a confrontation that captured the nation's headlines and ended up in battles with the police. At the end of May, McCarthy defeated Kennedy in the Oregon primary, hurting Kennedy's chances to defeat Vice President Hubert Humphrey, who had picked up LBJ's flag as the one Democratic candidate who supported the war. A week later, in Los Angeles, after defeating McCarthy in the California primary, Robert Kennedy was killed, shot in the head in the hotel ballroom just after he gave his victory speech. Kennedy's delegates divided between McCarthy and Humphrey, giving the vice president the majority he needed. The opportunity for an antiwar candidate to get elected was over. And the Democratic convention was still two months away.

I was there that summer, in the middle of it all. Having taken off a year between high school and college I had enlisted at 17 in the merchant marines for adventure but paid off after six months in the South Pacific when the ship I was on began loading cargo for Vietnam. Instead, I joined the McCarthy campaign, went "clean for Gene," and ended up in New Hampshire, and in Oregon, and I was in Los Angeles the night Bobby Kennedy died. Later I would be in Chicago for that fiasco, at first in the McCarthy offices, then in the convention itself, and finally on the streets. I still remember the sense of an impending apocalypse, a snowball rolling ever faster downhill, gathering momentum and waiting for the crash. When we left Chicago, we headed north into Canada. There, for a while, we felt safe.

During the turmoil of that chaotic summer, SDS also lurched into lunacy. After King was shot, a young white lawyer named Bernardine Dohrn joined the rioters in Times Square and discovered that she "really dug it," that here was real "urban guerrilla warfare." On June 14, declaring herself a "revolutionary communist," she got herself elected to the national board of SDS. At the same time, at Columbia, a New York sophomore, Mark Rudd, was making a name for himself as the spokesman of the radicals taking over the campus. Asked at one press conference if the university didn't have some redeeming features that were worth saving, Rudd had no answer. To him, and to many of the new breed of SDSers, the university, and with it the nation, was so complicit and compromised that even radical restructuring could not save it. Even the most radical sorts of reform were still, as they liked to say, nothing more than shuffling the deck chairs on the *Titanic*. To them, according to Kirkpatrick Sales, "the evils in America had become the evils of America."

In August of 1968, the militants of SDS were joined in Chicago by enraged workers from the defeated McCarthy campaign and by angry students from the city to confront the Democratic party, the war machine, and the police. For several days, with the TV cameras trained on the convention and the city, Americans watched open warfare on the streets of Chicago as angry mobs and angry police bashed it out. I had gone to Chicago still part of the system, as an aide to the McCarthy delegation, but I ended up on the streets. To many Americans at the end of that summer, with the war raging out of control, the body count climbing, the cities burning, the campuses taken over by radicals, the president giving up, the pitched battles in the streets of Chicago, it seemed like the country was falling apart. And it was.

But the centrifugal forces tearing the country into pieces were also tearing SDS apart. Old leftists of the kind represented by Joan Didion's Comrade Laski, doctrinaire ideologues of the Marxist-Leninist camp, had been slowly organizing among those SDS radicals who were wary of the anarchist nihilism of the likes of Bernardine Dohrn and Mark Rudd. The Progressive Labor Party, or PL, was made up of disciplined Maoists who cut their hair short, wore conventional clothes, and dreamed of what they called a "student-worker alliance" that would build a working-class movement along traditional Marxist lines. They saw riots like the one in Chicago not only as unproductive but as a barrier to reaching out to working-class whites. Stylistically and ideologically, they had little in common with the wild SDSers. But they found SDS to be very fertile ground for recruiting members, and their presence within the organization slowly grew.

At the June 1969, SDS convention, the two sides of SDS openly clashed and then split. The Dohrn and Rudd radicals issued a lengthy position paper at the start of the convention, outlining a course of action they believed would attract a majority of the SDS delegates. They took their name from a line in Bob Dylan's "Subterranean Homesick Blues" that went, "You don't need a weatherman to know which way the wind blows."

If PL represented the attempt of the logical, rational side of consciousness to be in control, then the Weatherman faction of SDS was announcing that it did not believe in control or science. They didn't need Lenin, or Marx, or Mao, or the PL central committee in New York, to tell them which way the wind was blowing. They knew; they just knew. It was the old battle of nature versus structure, of the heart against the head. The Nurse Ratcheds of PL, disciplined, organized, logical to a fault, and clean, challenged the unshaven Weathermen anarchists who had no doctrine other than their own emotional outrage. The Weathermen were out there with Jerry Rubin and the other radical freaks beyond the rational structures of even communist politics. They were following their emotions, blowing with the wind. Like George Bush decades later, they trusted their gut.

The Weatherman faction represented the anarchistic element of SDS; PL represented a radical need for discipline and order. Andrew Kopkind's article "The Real SDS Stands Up" in *Hard Times* captured much of the spirit of this convention. It was a fight between "personal liberation and political mobilization." On one hand, "the SDS people seem intuitively to recognize the variety of insurgency in the US . . . they feel a bond with the insurgents and try to fit their politics to a wide range of needs." They were, in short, pragmatic, loose, going with the flow and ready to change, whichever way the political wind blew—trying to escape structure. The PL faction, on the other hand, were rigidly ideological, committed to a system and a structure. According to Kopkind, "PL peoples a Tolkien middle-earth of Marxist-Leninist hobbits and orcs, and speaks in a runic tongue intelligible only to such creatures. It is all completely consistent and utterly logical within its own confines."

Among the specifics of the Weatherman manifesto was an emotional sympathy for a Third World or revolutionary struggle against "Amerikan imperialism." PL, on the other hand, actually opposed the Vietcong because the VC followed the Russian Communist Party line, which these dogmatic Maoists considered revisionist and unorthodox. For this, the Weathermen attacked them. PL also opposed black nationalist movements in the U.S. Their ideology called for a working-class struggle built strictly along class lines, not racial ones. As far as they were concerned, the Black Panther Party's call for black power simply aided the bourgeoisie by dividing up the working class along artificial lines of skin color. The Weathermen were particularly scornful of this privileging of ideology over race. Their politics was an emotional stand supporting all oppressed who were fighting back, regardless of the niceties of Marxist theory and all that other logic-chopping statementism shit, or so they would say.

One of the wilder moments of the convention came when Black Panther Chaka Walls addressed the crowd and attacked PL for its stand against black power. As if to emphasize his sympathy with oppressed people's struggling against oppression, he announced loudly that his group also supported "pussy power." The room erupted in a rage. According to Sales, "Walls paused: we've got some Puritans in the crowd, he went on, apparently misunderstanding the source of the audience's discomfort."

But then again, perhaps not. The audience *was* Puritan, and its Puritan sensibilities had indeed been offended, not because of the use of the obscene word "pussy," but because of the obscene disrespect for women the use of that term implied. SDS had always been Puritan in its demand for moral and political purity now: Freedom Now! End the War Now! Reformation Without Tarrying for Any Now! The antinomian perfectionism that was one legacy of Puritanism was exactly this refusal to accept the fallen world with all its faults, this faith that a utopian society could be built and that evil in all its forms, racism, sexism, classism, all of the evil isms of the universe, could be banished by acts of will by the righteous few. The first English settlers of the wilderness had been motivated by just such passion. The revolutionaries of the War of Independence, too, had believed that they could break from a corrupt old England and create a virtuous republic. The democratic reform movements of the 1830s and 40s, leading up to the Civil War, had been built upon a romantic belief in human knowledge of the divine, the faith that we the people can know the truth and act upon it and become as our Father in Heaven, perfect. Emerson had seen the patterns of American history clearly. There are always, he said prophetically, "the establishment and the movement." The establishment represents power and status and a fear of change. The spirit that challenges fear is the spirit of life, and when it is expressed in the world, it is an "extravagance of faith." According to Emerson,

> This way of thinking, falling on Roman times, made Stoic philosophers; falling on despotic times, made patriot Catos and Brutuses; falling on superstitious times, made prophets and apostles; on popish times, made Protestants and ascetic monks; preachers of faith against preachers of works; on prelatical times, made Puritans and Quakers; and falling on Unitarian and commercial times, makes the [Transcendentalism] which we know.

And falling on the fearful, conservative Fifties times, it made the extravagant forms of faith which characterized the Sixties.

This spirit of Puritanism, defined as faith that a pure moral perfectionism was not just a possibility but a necessity, is what Chaka Walls offended. As a Black Panther, he cared not for the moral reformation of the world but for the more narrow interests of his community. The Panthers and the Weathermen, though allied, spoke different languages. Panther Jewell Cook took the microphone from Walls but did little to restore revolutionary solidarity when he repeated Stokely Carmichael's infamous claim that the only position for women in the movement was prone.

After the split, PL failed to capture the allegiance of the campus radicals, to say nothing of working-class Americans; and under their dogmatic leadership, the organization splintered away. The Weathermen, however, went on for several years as an underground army determined to "bring the war home," to disrupt the nation, and to force the war-makers to divert resources from their imperialist adventures overseas to face the enemy within. To this end, they organized themselves into a tightly disciplined army of the few and the faithful. Living together, working together, fighting together, sleeping together, they imagined themselves as a profoundly revolutionary force that would bring down every aspect of the old society. Individualism was the first to go. Members were not allowed even to go for a walk without permission. Reading a book in a quiet room required a group decision to hash out all the political implications. Under the slogan "Smash monogamy," the Weatherman collective banned one-on-one sexual relationships, requiring even married members of the group to break up with their partners in favor of open sex, free of relationships. This was all done under the notion of "attacking our programmed bourgeois roles." There is a lot in white Americans, said Klonsky, that "we have to fight, and beat out of them, and beat out of ourselves." Even Cotton Mather never went so far as to advocate conversion by "beating" sin out of people.

In all of this, the Weathermen in effect had given up on the possibility of actually creating a mass movement. The army of student radicals was no longer with them. As one ex-SDSer sneered, "You don't need a rectal thermometer to know who the assholes are." But they carried on nonetheless, following their illusions to their illogical ends, truly outside the context of belief shared even by their fellow radicals—in a fairly clinical sense, truly insane.

The most infamous moments of their existence were the "Days of Rage" in October, 1969, planned as a spontaneous outburst of revolutionary violence held on the second anniversary of Che Guevera's death. Instead of the thousands of kids hoped for, at most six hundred radicals showed up for the event. But that was enough. Helmeted and armed with sticks and metal pipes, they ran through the streets of downtown Chicago smashing windows, setting small fires, busting up parked cars. The Chicago police, already veterans of street fighting, were waiting and ready for them.

It was a strange moment. One working-class Chicago kid who got mixed up in the riot said it quite clearly: "They are all fucking crazy." Tom Hayden, obviously not a part of any of this, analyzed it more academically. They were, he said, "more structured and artificial because in their heads they were part of the third world. They were alienated from their own roots."

But at the same time they were, in the tradition of earlier awakenings, the extreme manifestation of the breaking away from the structures of culture, both their politics and in their persons. They had gone so far outside Egypt that they were lost in the wilderness, over the border, so far into their illusion that they were no longer aware how far off on a tangent they had gone. They believed in their beliefs, fully and completely, without doubts. They were giving in completely to their emotional side and not allowing rational doubts to restrain them. As one Weather Pamphlet expressed it, "We're moving, dancing, fucking, doing dope, knowing our bodies as part of our lives, becoming animals again after centuries of repression and uptightness."

Nor did it end with the failure of the Days of Rage. Even the deaths of three of their members, when their homemade bombs blew up their Greenwich Village townhouse, didn't stop them. In 1970, they helped Timothy Leary escape from the California prison where he was serving time for marijuana possession, an ounce having been found in his daughter's underwear when he was crossing back into the U.S. from Mexico. With help from his rescuers, Leary issued a statement that ties together several of the insanities and expresses the extremes to which the movements of the decade had descended. For Leary, this was a "revolutionary war" and he had been liberated by the underground from a POW camp. Nor was this simply another battle of interest groups. It was a cosmic struggle, he wrote, "world-wide ecological religious warfare. Life against death":

> I declare that World War III is now being waged by short-haired robots whose deliberate aim is to destroy the complex web of free wild life by the imposition of mechanical order. Listen. There is no compromise with a machine. You cannot talk peace and love to a humanoid robot whose every Federal Bureaucratic impulse is soulless, heartless, lifeless, loveless.
> Resist spiritually, stay high . . . praise God . . . love life . . .
> Blow the mechanical mind with Holy Acid . . . dose them . . . dose them.
> Resist physically, robot agents who threaten life must be disarmed, disabled, disconnected by force. . . . Arm yourselves and shoot to live . . . Life is never violent. To shoot a genocidal robot policeman in the defense of life is a sacred act.

Soon after issuing this proclamation, Leary fled the country.

VII

"to humble thee, and to prove thee, and to know what is in thine heart."

For the baby boomers still into traditional politics, and for others willing to give the system one last try, the spring and summer of 1968, with LBJ's dramatic withdrawal from the race, was a reawakening of the spirit of the early Sixties. It was as if they had discovered all over again that hope that Egypt could be reformed from within. The pattern of that spring's politics recapitulated the pattern of the decade, moving from cynical despair to cautious hope to excitement.

But after winning the California primary on June 6, less than two months after King's death, Bobby Kennedy made a victory statement to his cheering supporters and then was killed as he turned to leave the ballroom. From there it was downhill all the way to the disastrous August Democratic convention in Chicago. When Kennedy was killed, what slight chance McCarthy might have had was also killed.

The money certainly knew it. As soon as the news of the assassination got out, Gene McCarthy's line of credit dried up. There were no more funds in the bank even to pay the meager salaries of his staff. The campaign released its workers and told them to try to make it home to wherever they had come from as best they could on their own.

I was one of those workers abandoned to their own devices. Having gone clean for Gene in New Hampshire, I had been sent to Oregon to work in the Democratic primary there, where we beat Robert Kennedy. Skipping an appointment with the Portland city court system, where I was expected to pay my time for the crime of jaywalking, I had been flown to Los Angeles to help leaflet shopping centers and even a demolition derby in a last-minute effort to beat Kennedy in California too. Instead, McCarthy got beaten, and at the demolition derby, so did I. After election night, I was forced to put my duffel on my shoulder and, with two friends from Boston, to hitchhike back and face what would happen in Chicago.

It was a long trip. We went up the coast and spent several weeks in San Francisco enjoying what remained of the psychedelic theater, then hitchhiked East from the Promised Land backwards into the American wilderness. In Winnemucca, Nevada, I was arrested on "suspicion" by a cop out of central casting with Cool Hand Luke reflector sunglasses and a badge that came out of a Wheaties box.

"Suspicion of what?" I asked him.

"Just suspicion," he said. And I knew better than to argue. Instead, I spent two nights in jail, just wondering what was going to happen next.

After leaving Egypt, the children of Israel expected to have to cross a wilderness in order to reach their Zion, but they did not expect forty years of trial and tribulation. They did not expect that the whole generation that left Egypt would perish in that wilderness. As even their new age of hope unraveled and was undone, they cried unto the Lord, why did thou lead us these forty years in the wilderness? His answer: "To humble thee, and to prove thee, to know what was in thine heart."

5

Fifth, No Crew—

I

"Southeast Asian Birmingham"

IN 1968, ONLY MICHAEL HERR, JOURNALIST AND AUTHOR OF THE WAR'S most mind-blown book, fully comprehended the extent to which the war in Vietnam was, as he put it in *Dispatches,* "at the other extreme of the same theater." Whether they dropped out and blew their minds with acid or dropped out and blew their minds in combat, thousands of baby boomers, hawks and doves, rich and poor, radicals and right-wingers, blacks and whites, boldly marched outside of structure only to be overwhelmed, their corpses left to rot in the wilderness. Herr's genius was to realize that Vietnam and the rebellions back home "had run power off the same circuit for so long that they didn't even have to fuse." The war, which at the time seemed to divide the baby-boom generation into antiwar rebels and pro-war patriots, was in the final analysis a bummer of an acid trip for both groups, a bloodier Altamont but with the same lesson.

The pattern that here repeats itself is the same tale told in a dozen different forms. In the beginning, in the innocence of youth, the first act is the awakening from fear to the possibility of action in the world. No longer mere abstractions mired in paradox and complexity, evil and righteousness become clear and distinct realities, as real and immediate as death on the highway. Pessimism is thrown off; childish insecurities are cast aside; the call of the trumpet is answered. The world no longer seems so large or complex or beyond comprehension that some degree of human control cannot, as Emerson said, "bring it into conformity with the pure idea in the mind." The liberal hope reborn is that we humans can seize control of our lives, that we do not have to let ourselves be kicked around like so many hapless victims of an angry God.

Having found an essential reality, a solid rock in the shifting relativistic fog, we can, said these innocents, begin that first act; we can change the world. We can do it—YES WE CAN! Thus youth ever marches into battle. As Melville said of another American war,

> So they gayly go to fight,
> Chatting left and laughing right.

But something went amiss on the road to victory. In the second act, certainty was lost, the leader shot dead and no one was sure by whom or why. Then the path disappeared into a jungle that was rapidly disappearing into swamp. But the search for the golden fleece was not abandoned; instead, it assumed a more radical form. At this point, as the clear trail begins to get lost in the swamp, the choice is to hold back and stay clean and in control or to plunge on into the primeval ooze, ready to face whatever comes. If the second choice is taken, then what started as a brave adventure becomes instead a holy cause in which the entire self must be committed and from which there can be no retreat. At last, one's comrades fall, and then the self, exposed and alone, realizes that it too no longer has a mission, or a ship, or a crew, realizes finally that it too all along has been ensnared in a massive sham. And then the self, no longer lured by the illusion of being in control, abandons everything, lets go, and lets it happen, in a final mad orgiastic frenzy before collapsing in exhaustion after the tryst.

That first, heady freedom of the quest was a crusade to make right a world that was out of joint, to return it to the ideals presented by the best of structure. The awakened children of the early sixties pursued victory in the name of the values their culture had taught them to believe, to do what was "right," to awaken from their neo-orthodox stagnation and to bravely head across that New Frontier. King and Kennedy's trumpets echoed the notes they had been taught, the ideals they believed America stood for; and so they gave themselves happily to the cause. After all—Melville again—

> All wars are boyish and are fought by boys
> The champions and enthusiasts of the state.

The second act was the loss of that innocent enthusiasm, and with that loss, the revelation that all the best values of the state were but the compromised and corrupt manipulations of the combine. The third act, then, was a return to nature, an escape from the combine with all of its lies and meaningless rules.

But what happens if the return to nature turns out to be not a tiptoe through the tulips but a descent into dangerous jungle, after all? What happens if reality turns out to be not the love of the Garden of Eden but a mean old bitch right out of the Old Testament? What if the reality we think we know and can trust turns out to be but a virtual-reality sham, a veil of symbols within which we are held suspended over the void?

When folk singer Phil Ochs rhymed "Sailing over to Vietnam" with "Southeast Asian Birmingham," he had brought together symbolically the two leading political events of the decade. Not long after, SNCC's 1966 position paper on Vietnam reinforced the point: "The murder of Samuel Young in Tuskeegee, Alabama, is no different than the murder of peasants in Vietnam." Just as the expulsion of white liberals from SNCC brought a knee up into the liberal American groin, the Vietnam War forced even the most stubbornly patriotic liberals to wonder at what pass the trail had been lost. What were we doing, and why? Was Vietnam merely a political blunder, correctable at the next election? Or was it the symptom of a much more profound disease?

Bill Ehrhart, like many other grunts, went through exactly that transition. Starting out as a gung-ho enlistee in the Marines, he got to Vietnam only to find that things were not as he had been led to believe. After a while, he said in PBS's "Vietnam: A Television History," "you began to realize, this was crazy, this was nuts." But survival depended upon keeping alert to the immediate reality and not letting doubts intrude; so, he said, you had to "keep your thoughts well within the immediate environment you were dealing with." But even within that fortress, the doubts got through. "I increasingly began to have the feeling," said Ehrhart, "I was a redcoat. It was one of the most staggering realizations of my life. To suddenly understand I wasn't a hero. I wasn't a good guy. I wasn't handing out candy and cigarettes to the kids in the French villages. Somehow I had come to believe that I was everything I had believed was evil." To imagine oneself comfortably the hero of one movie, and then to have the scenes suddenly shift and to realize that one is playing the bad guy in a different movie, was mind-blowing. Ehrhart's first reaction, like the reaction of millions of baby boomers back home, having turned on and tuned in, was to drop out, actually to desert and end up "disappearing into the world somewhere."

Others, of course, many of them REMFs (rear echelon mother-fuckers) or officers who flew air-conditioned bombers high above the battle, never made that transition; instead, they continued to believe in the liberal dreams of Camelot, the New Frontier, and the fight to save the world from tyranny. But for the young grunts suddenly thrown out of the American illusion into the jungle wilderness, the transition was brutal.

In a line Herr throws off almost as an aside, he tells of a young grunt who "had mailed a gook ear home to his girl and could not understand now why she had stopped writing to him." Why? Why did he do it? Why didn't he understand?

Because he had crossed over into a different reality and didn't know it.

Vietnam was more than a different country in a different corner of the world, more than a different culture. It was so far beyond the American combine, so outside its rules and assumptions, that this grunt might as well have lost his mind tripping. He had slid, bit by bit, into this other realm without realizing how different he had become. He had entered his trip without realizing he was tripping. Within that new context, the gook ear had meaning. He forgot what the ear would mean back home when Suzie opened her package in front of her folks on the front porch of their home in suburban Omaha.

That kid had, by most clinical definitions, gone crazy, over the edge, around the bend, freaked out. For to be crazy is to live with other assumptions and beliefs than those of the majority. He might not have planned to drop out, but he was as far from the world he'd left behind as any spaced-out hippie. But was he really crazy?

From Suzie's perspective, of course he was. To cut off a human ear is barbarous enough, but to mail it home as some sort of grotesque souvenir can only be the act of a person no longer aware of what society deems decent and right and good. Such a person no longer lives in the same reality as his family and friends left behind. He has gone what we call crazy.

But from the perspective of his fellow grunts, hardly at all. To go alone into insanity is to go mad and know it. But when a whole community shares a new perception, it becomes all too easy never to doubt, perhaps never even becoming aware of the change that has taken place, like the gradual graying into middle age.

But what about the ear from our perspective? Which reality was more real? That of suburban Omaha? Or that of Vietnam with its bitter life-and-death struggle for survival? Or both? Or neither? Is the peace and prosperity of suburban America reality or sham? Is the grim struggle for survival in which predators rip off their victims' ears a closer approximation of what's really going on behind the veil?

The point is that the artificial reality of suburban Omaha is a world we can live with, plastics and all, thank you very much. The elemental struggle for survival may be the ultimate reality upon which our security and prosperity rest. But we don't want to see it. We buy our meat in plastic packages neatly trimmed, not off the bloody floor of the slaughterhouse. We ignore the pollution our cars and lawn mowers pump into the air, just as we pump our gas without worrying about protecting oil supply lines in the desert sheikdoms that keep us pumping. We buy shoes made by children chained to factories in China and Bangladesh. We let our white blood cells engage in life-and-death struggles with alien invaders of our very bodies while we lie on the beach enjoying the serenity of life. We repress our fears, pushing them below what Freud called the censor, thinking they are therefore out of mind. We flush our excrement away out of smell and out of sight. It is a part of nature we'd rather not return to. But as the bumper stickers say, "Shit happens."

Vietnam was all that and more. The generals kept promising a light at the end of the tunnel. Some boys believed them and entered into that long dark tunnel full of foolish courage and hope.

II

"Down at the Crossroads"

From the very beginning Herr makes it clear that Vietnam, for all of its horrifying reality, was also a state of mind, both literal history and typological symbolism. *Dispatches* begins with a sharp intake of breath, a "Breathing In," which isn't let go until the final chapter, "Breathing Out." Between those two moments is a long strange trip. On the first page, Herr describes an old yellowing map of Vietnam that hung on the wall of his hotel room, a relic of the French colonial past, labeled "current" but totally irrelevant with its quaint old colonial names, "Annam," "Tonkin," and "Cochinchina." By late '67, when he wrote this piece, "even the most detailed maps didn't reveal much anymore; reading them was like trying to read the faces of the Vietnamese, and that was like trying to read the wind. We knew that the uses of most information were flexible, different pieces of ground told different stories to different people." In the strange light of Vietnam, the old certainties shifted and dissolved like mist. What once had seemed certain no longer even seemed possible. The Vietnamese jungle was a wilderness literally and typologically, as uncertain and terrifying as any psychedelic trip into the heart of darkness.

The Vietnamese themselves knew all this. After all the generations of war and shifting allegiances and cultural conflict, they had become natural deconstructionists, simple and essential on the outside, complex and multilayered within. Nguyen Cao Ky, the playboy pilot who eventually became president of the Republic of South Vietnam, tried to warn us. In 1965, in an article in *Life*, he said, "You should never believe a Vietnamese. He's not like you. He's an Asiatic. The Vietnamese of today has seen too much dishonesty, too much maneuvering, and he doesn't believe in anything anymore. He automatically thinks he's got to camouflage himself. He doesn't dare tell the truth anymore because too often it brings him unhappiness. What's the point of telling the truth?"

Herr saw all this, but the brave young grunts "chatting left and laughing right" were made of sterner stuff. Like the innocent American doughboys who sailed to France in World War I to straighten them out "over there," like the Kennedy New Frontiersmen in 1961, they were a happy band of brothers, men with a mission. At the end of his first week in country, Herr was taken along by an enthusiastic young officer who delighted in showing off to everyone how they had not just defoliated but totally flattened the thousands of acres of the Ho Bo Woods. This kid was really into the effort, completely gung-ho. "It seemed to be keeping him young," wrote Herr. "His enthusiasm made you feel that even the letters he wrote home were full of it." Herr describes another soldier, a LURP (a long-range reconnaissance patrol), who had been the only survivor of a VC ambush back in '65. He was on his third tour of duty, the world back home having proved too straight for him. He did drugs by the handful, and he "wore a gold earring and a headband torn from a piece of camouflage parachute material, and since no one was about to tell him to get his hair cut, it fell below his shoulders, covering a thick purple scar." He was the "other extreme of the same theater" that Herr had seen just a few weeks before in San Francisco, where counter-culture dropouts were into a heart-of-darkness trip. As in that other extreme of the theater, Herr was terrified to discover that a glance into such freaked-out eyes "was like looking into the floor of an ocean."

Like the Merry Pranksters, the grunts were also in sync on their own bus, going further. "They were," wrote Herr, "wired into their listening posts out around the camp, into each other, into themselves." With a line directly out of Kesey's book, Robert Mason says in *Chickenhawk*, another in-your-face revelation of the Vietnam experience from the bottom up, "Never trust a grunt." Even the music spoke to them in the particularity of their moment. Johnny Cash's "I Fell into a Burning Ring of Fire" took on its own significance in Vietnam, as did the Beatles' "Magical Mystery Tour," "coming to take you away, dying to take you away . . ." It all made sense within their context, and they clung tightly to that, needing, as Ehrhart said, to be as much in control as possible, which meant tightening the new context around them and holding on tight as they passed from one reality and broke on through to the other side. "All those faces," wrote Herr. "Sometimes it was like looking into faces at a rock concert, locked in, the event had them." Ironically, the grunts drifted into this space with their fingers on their triggers and their senses totally alert. Yet for all that, they never saw it coming.

"I got to hate surprises," says Herr, "control freak at the crossroads. If you were one of those people who always thought they had to know what was coming next, the war could cream you." Robert Johnson's old blues number, "Crossroads," repeated as one of the great rock 'n' roll classics, was more than appropriate:

> Down at the crossroads
> Fell down on my knees
> Asked the Lord above "Have mercy
> Save poor Bob if you please."

Just as the music had progressed from the sentimental clarity of folk to the insanity of rock, so in Vietnam "one place or another it was always going on, rock around the clock." It took a little while, but Herr got to the point where he realized every time he got on a chopper or went out on patrol with a group of grunts, "I must be out of my fucking mind." And he was.

This was the moment of conflict, the crossing over, the crossroads between the old security and the revealed insanity. The African-American literary critic Henry Louis Gates has identified the crossroads as a limit where two worlds meet. It is at the crossroads that Bob makes his deal with the Devil. In *Mystery Train,* his classic study of rock 'n' roll and American culture, Greil Marcus explains that Sixties rock had its roots in Robert Johnson's Delta blues, but that Johnson's Delta blues had its roots in the old New England Puritan experience of the human battleground in which the hope for divine grace confronted the reality of evil. "The dreams and fears of the Puritans, those gloomy old men," he writes, "are at the source of our attempts to make sense out of the contradictions between the American idea of paradise and the doomed facts of our history." This is where Americans began, searching hopefully for God in the New World wilderness but finding instead only their own inherent demonism, the devil that lurks at the crossroads of the mind. Says Marcus, "As they panicked at their failures, the devil was all they saw," and what became their ultimately unbearable curse was "the impossibility of reconciling the facts of evil with the beauty of the world." This was Johnson's legacy, rock 'n' roll's legacy, America's legacy. Vietnam was but another example of the old typological pattern unfolding.

So why was Herr there in Vietnam? Why was the U.S. there? Why are any of us anywhere? What humps us through the night? Below the official lies and the reluctant draftees who "had" to be there, somewhere in the recesses below understanding, at that crossroads, wrote Herr, "the mythic tracks intersected from the lowest John Wayne wet-dream to the most aggravated soldier poet fantasy." We all have our reasons why we think we believe. We all have our hopes and dreams, our cities on a hill. But in fact no one really knows. On one side is our dream of divine possibility; on the other, Satan's leering sneer, that abyss of uncertainty, of unknowing, of the terror of the void. What we think we know and affirm is always confronted by the terror that we don't. We exist in the illusion of our beliefs, in a bubble that curves back upon itself and only occasionally allows a glimpse through the illusion to the emptiness beyond.

To go where the action is provides perhaps the possibility of breaking through that veil, as Ahab tried to, to strike at that hidden force that propels us to our fates. But even then, being there doesn't tell the tale: "The information isn't frozen," wrote Herr, "you are." That is, the brain cannot compute. Instead, it stores up as much as it can and lets it out bit by bit later, sometimes much later, to be absorbed but never understood. Vietnam was about "locking into a role" and discovering that instead of watching other people locked into their roles, your own role was the one being watched. Shades of Ken Kesey—when Herr tried to go out on one patrol, he got shuffled from officer to officer until one sergeant warned him, "This ain't the fucking movies over here, you know?"

For Herr, and for most of the Americans over there, Vietnam provided a peeling back of the movie screen. For some, it was a slow but dawning revelation that Jason was a sham; for others, the truth arrived in a quick, horrid rush. In the PBS documentary "Vietnam: A TV History," Private Charles "Tex" Sabatier narrates the story of how he got shot in the back trying to rescue a buddy while they were out on patrol. He remembers being hit and falling forward in the mud and suddenly thinking, "How did I get here? I started thinking for the first time, what the hell is Communism?" and there he was, about to die to stop it. Until that moment, he had lived in the old movie. Herr tells the story of another grunt suffering the terrors of reality withdrawal: "First letter I got from my old man was all about how proud he was that I'm here and how we have this duty to, you know, I don't fucking know, whatever . . . and it really made me feel great. Shit, my father hardly said good morning to me before. Well I've been here eight months now, and when I get home I'm gonna have all I can do to keep from killing that cocksucker . . ."

Here we see the basic division of the generations that was one of the marks of the Sixties. The old man still believed in an older corporate faith. The movie running in his head was an old black-and-white from World War II, with Hitler overrunning Europe, Vietnam as Czechoslovakia, Munich prevented from happening again. In that movie, Americans were a beleaguered people working hard together to survive the Depression and keep food on the table and democracy alive. His son, brought up on John Wayne movies and taught to believe in them, had headed out to accomplish his father's dream. But the dream was popped, the lie exposed, the horror under the surface revealed. The movie's inspiring fantasy, the John Wayne wetdream, was lost.

The fathers back home couldn't understand their kids, whether in San Francisco or Vietnam. They believed too strongly and clung to their old beliefs as if for survival itself. Threatened by the destruction of the world they knew, the damn hippies in the streets, the blacks protesting and rioting everywhere, the commies making their moves abroad, they did what they had been conditioned to do. They closed ranks and fought back. If the enemy was chaos and irrationality, then logic and reason were the tools to fight with: the hard reality of firepower and technology, of bombs and bullets. McNamara, Kennedy's whiz-kid liberal, who kept coming up with technological fixes for the war, was the perfect representative of his overly logical generation. Herr says of CIA spook "Blowtorch" Komer, another such literalist, that if "William Blake had reported to him that he'd seen angels in the trees, Komer would have tried to talk him out of it. Failing there, he'd have ordered defoliation."

Such men were, as Baldwin had said of Northern liberals, "innocent." They were, in effect, playing their roles as handed to them by history, never questioning, never doubting. Herr says of them, "Mostly they were that innocent and about that conscious." Vietnam was for them a kind of jihad, a holy war, a defense of America's traditional way of life, a culture that in their eyes didn't need justifying. It was the rock upon which they stood. To understand why they were there would take an unraveling of all of human history.

According to Herr's account, most "mission intellectuals" liked 1954, the end of the French Indochina war, as their date for the beginning of it all. To go back as far as World War II or the Japanese occupation, wrote Herr, made you practically "a historical visionary." But Herr insists that the history lies deeper than that: "Might as well say that Vietnam was where the Trail of Tears was headed all along. . . . Might as well lay it on the proto-Gringos who found the New England woods too raw and empty for their peace and filled them up with their own imported devils."

III

Holy terror

For us Americans at least, those "proto-Gringos," the Puritans, set in motion the patterns of the movies that continue to hump us through the night. If they filled the New England woods with devils, it was because they were projecting onto the howling wilderness around them the howling terrors they felt in the wilderness of their own dark souls. Theirs was not some romantic belief in the goodness of the human heart or the nobility of the savage self within. Far from it. They looked at themselves with a ruthless stare that left no illusion standing: so they saw not peace but a sword, not a civilized garden but a howling waste. This terror, which they named the Fear of God, shook them more profoundly than even the fear of death. And the only thing they had to live for, the only thing that kept them forcing themselves grimly onward into the New England winter, was the hope that if they forced themselves to be destroyed, to be crucified, in that holy terror, then out of their crucifixion might arise some regenerated spirit that would replace the desert wastes of their existence, a new heaven and new earth. The holy terror stood in stark contrast to their image of a kingdom of God to come; America for them was the crossroads between Egypt and the Promised Land.

Some did imagine that such an experience in fact had come to them: this feeling rose at first in 1741, in the Great Awakening. And sixty years later, after the Revolution had proven God's blessings on the new nation, the Second Great Awakening seemed to renew the blessing. Out of that came the belief that theirs was the one redeemed community, the one true Zion. That theirs was the Kingdom of God, and that it had to be built in the face of Satan's desperate opposition, was proven to them again and again, as Satan seemed to stir up enemies in opposition. It was against these enemies that the new nation defined itself and certified its holiness. One reads in the sermons of the American Revolution a conviction that America is the New Israel and England the reincarnation of the evil nation of Egypt. Samuel Sherwood's "The Church's Flight into the Wilderness," preached in 1774, rallied the colonists against the British, calling the Americans the children of light at war against the children of darkness. It has, he proclaimed,

> been the constant aim and design of the dragon, sometimes called the beast, and the serpent Satan, and the Devil, to erect a scheme of absolute despotism and tyranny on earth, and involve all mankind in slavery and bondage—, and so prevent their having that liberty and freedom which the Son of God came from heaven to procure for, and bestow on them.

Out of a hundred a fifty years of such preaching was created the cosmic duality of our righteous identity fighting back against a worldwide despotism that would destroy our freedom. The American Children of Light then have a cosmic mission, not just to defend liberty and freedom from the beast, but more:

It is to be hoped that the dragon will be wholly consumed and destroyed that the seat and foundation of all tyranny, persecution, and oppression, may be forever demolished; that horns, whether civil or ecclesiastical, may be knocked off from the beast, and his head receive a deadly wound, and his jaws be effectually broken; that peace, liberty, and righteousness might universally prevail; that salvation and strength might come to Zion; and the kingdom of our God, and the power of his Christ might be established to all the ends of the earth.

When David Riesman, as quoted in in Halberstam's *Best and the Brightest,* warned the Kennedy liberals about the dangers of stirring up the sleeping demons of the invisible world, they reacted to him as if he had professed a belief in witches. But it was he who understood that despite the hopes of the Enlightenment and the French Revolution, Reason is not and never has been God. Reason, as Benjamin Franklin joked, merely comes up with rationalizations to justify anything the appetite desires. These appetites are both biological and cultural. We individuals each have our unique contingencies of reinforcement. But as members of historically constituted cultural groups, we also have a certain degree of what Northrop Frye calls "mythological conditioning." Or, as Erik Erikson has written, "Psycho-social identity . . . also has a psycho-historical side, and suggests the study of how life histories are inextricably interwoven with history." We are all socially and biologically constructed and unaware of the visions that hump us through the night.

Americans, all strangers in a strange land who left their ancestral homes for a new one in the wilderness, have always wrestled with the question of identity, torn between allegiance to a new American identity and a profound doubt as to its legitimacy, between their utopian dreams and their satanic fears. In periods in which the national identity is undergoing severe questioning, its defenders rise up in holy war to protect what little they have. Thus was born the need for an enemy against which an emergent American identity could define itself. In the nineteenth century, the Pope, that Whore of Babylon, became that other. So did the Mormons, those seemingly degenerate heretics who carried the metaphor too far, too literally, as if the Jews had been right after all and Zion but a geographical place on the map, not a spiritual Kingdom "within you."

Thus American culture grew and developed, defining its new self against the opposition to it. By his opposition, said Cotton Mather, Satan proves the new American Zion to be God's Kingdom. If to Protestant Americans, the Catholics and the Mormons were outside the new identity they were creating, then, as James Baldwin has shown, blacks too were an alien "other," profoundly symbolic of that dark "other" within the self. So also to the North were the Southern whites, who tried to imagine not a new Israel but a new feudalism. Even more than these, who had at least taken on the trappings of Christianity, the Indians were seen as the very type of satanic barbarism, the original Canaanites who stood in the way of the Children of Israel establishing their New-World Zion. Later, in World War I, long after the Indians had been defeated, the wilderness conquered, and no opposition left against which the American nation could define itself, that devout Presbyterian, Woodrow Wilson, called upon the nation to return to Europe to fight the Hun in order to make the world "safe for democracy." It was an echo of the old cry, the old American manifest destiny that we be the agents for destroying a Satanic tyranny and establishing the kingdom of God "to all the ends of the earth." After World War II, with the Hun finally crushed, Soviet communism assumed the role of the beast that was determined to spread its tyranny across the world and destroy the children of light and freedom.

With the Soviet "evil empire" defeated, we now have another one— terrorists and Islamic fundamentalists—a monolithic centrally organized attempt to take over the world, an axis of evil as bad as any that Satan had launched against us before. Al Quaeda became for George Bush and Dick Cheney the new evil empire that was trying to "erect a scheme of absolute despotism and tyranny on earth" against which we must define ourselves as truly the Children of God. Especially for Bush, that born-again Texan, the need to confirm his identity must have been strong.

So Herr was right. The Vietnam War had to be seen in a larger context, as part of a cold war between East and West. But the Cold War itself had to be seen, in the American imagination, as part of a cosmic struggle between the children of light and the children of darkness. For us Americans, the war had begun in the New England woods, in the needs of a people who had left behind old identities to define new ones. The enemy of this definition was their own self-doubts, their own internal fears; and they projected those terrors onto the wilderness and its inhabitants. If beneath the artificially constructed layers of what we call the self lies no essential reality but only an infinite upon infinite regression of layers, then the void opens up within us as a bottomless terror. This is the wilderness, the forest primeval, the rank and steaming jungle onto which we Americans have often projected both our greatest hopes and our greatest fears. The grunts in Vietnam routinely referred to VC territory as "Indian country."

Which opens up one other element in this conundrum. In a parenthetical aside a few pages later, Herr uses the phrase "regeneration through violence" as part of his attempt to explain the psychohistorical dynamics of the struggle. A few years later, Richard Slotkin, taking his cue from Herr, makes that phrase the title of an important academic book that argues that all of American culture, up to and including the Vietnam War, is an example of an ancient need born in the Puritan imagination to seek regeneration through violence. Slotkin, a Jew who admitted to me little understanding of Christian typology, argues that the phrase and the concept originated in the Indian captivity narratives, most notably the narrative of the captivity of Mary Rowlandson, which, he shows, had been very popular in the colonial era. He even argues that the Christian revivals of the Great Awakening owed their power to the popularity of the imagery of these captivity narratives. But he got it backward. For the captivity narratives drew their power from the fact that regeneration through violence had been the central image of Christianity for the sixteen hundred years since the crucifixion and was already well established in the Christian imagination when the Puritans arrived in New England.

In this tradition, the descent into the void, that wilderness of darkness beyond the borders of structure, was the typological equivalent of the crucifixion, the experience that led sinners out of bondage in Egypt to regenerate vision and salvation. On many levels, then, the war in Vietnam was a holy war, a war both to save humanity from the beast and to experience a collective and an individual regeneration through violence. Not that anyone had to know it. History does not work that way. As Mailer said, you never know what vision humps you through the night.

The defense of identity can be analyzed in the specific terms of the historically constructed identity being upheld. But one can glean some universal aspects by stepping back from the specific content and looking at the process. To defend an identity is an act of anality, a defense of order and structure. It is Nurse Ratched fighting against insanity and chaos and trying to establish orderliness, cleanliness, sanity. It is the fight against the dark chaos of the soul, the fight each thinking rational human being wages every day in order to hold it all together, to stay sane.

James Baldwin had said that white people feared blacks not because of any actual threat coming from black people but because of the symbolism of black people. To whites, said Baldwin, the black skin represented sensuality and death, both forces that threatened to destroy the orderliness, indeed the very sanity, that kept civilization together. Phil Ochs's connection of Vietnam and Birmingham was more than a cute rhyme. It established a continuity of purpose. Just as black people back home in the U.S. were seen as a threat to rational order, so the eruption of rebellion in places like Vietnam seemed also to upset the orderliness of the world. Tie that local rebellion to the spread of a worldwide tyranny out to destroy "peace, liberty, and righteousness," and the war in Vietnam becomes a holy crusade. "Charlie," the grunts' name for the Viet Cong, was nothing less than Satan's latest tool to destroy America. You have to give this much to the hawks: while the liberal doves were protesting that Vietnam was just a local civil war with no cosmic meaning beyond the borders of that tiny, insignificant country, the conservatives saw the world in a larger symbolic realm. With their faith in the literal, their belief in the goodness of political motivation and the possibility of enlightened reason to control events, the liberals were the innocents.

James Baldwin had also said in *The Fire Next Time* that to black Americans, whites "seemed to be the slightly mad victims of their own brainwashing." Blacks, who had specific identity problems of their own, could not understand, he wrote, why white Americans were "mesmerized by Russia." However evil communism may have been, and however great a military threat, the fear of Russia seemed far out of proportion to the actual danger, making the Cold War more a pathological than a military condition. A young Al Gore, years before he became a U.S. senator or vice president of the United States, wrote to his father during the Vietnam conflict, "We do have inveterate antipathy for Communism—paranoia as I like to put it. My own belief is that this form of psychological ailment—in this case a national madness—leads the victim to actually create the thing which is feared the most." With this, Gore showed that he was even then a step beyond the Kennedy liberals like his father or the Arkansas liberal who would later be his boss.

IV

"Firepower freaks"

Herr was also well aware of that larger symbolic realm. He knew that even the rational liberals were reacting not to the rationalizations on their tongues but to the hidden fantasies that humped them through the night. The spooks who first got us into Vietnam, he said, were "not exactly soldiers, not even advisors yet, but Irregulars, working in remote places with little direct authority, acting out their fantasies with more freedom than most men ever know." But the fantasies of the educated spooks gave way by '65 and '66: "The romance of spooking started to fall away like dead meat from a bone." Just as the gentle highs of marijuana had been taken over by LSD and the sentimental romances of the folk music scene had been drowned out by electric rock, the McNamara fantasies of limited counterinsurgency and controlled engagement were overtaken by wilder, more emotional, uncontrollable passions. Says

Herr, "The war passed along, this time into the hands of firepower freaks out to eat the country whole." Stanley Karnow, quoting *Tiger Force,* a recent book on Vietnam, said, "The operation degenerated into a nightmare as the U.S. grunts 'ignored the rules of war. They went berserk.'"

In letting their fears, however rationalized, rouse them to action, the best and the brightest who got us into Vietnam, intellectual whiz kids though they were, were following their hearts as surely as any let-it-all-hang-out hippie. The grunts they sent to Vietnam rode their wave through the tube. Back in the more cautious Fifties, President Eisenhower had warned against getting involved in a ground war in Asia. He had kept the U.S. out of the French indochina war, rejecting all appeals to send troops and turning down John Foster Dulles's request to use the atom bomb to lift the siege of Dien Bien Phu. Ike was of a generation well aware of the dangers of following one's heart instead of ones head. Emotional appeals, either from the left or from the right, had little impact on him. His cool detachment would not be seen again until the election of Barack Obama.

But after 1964, Vietnam, like the Sixties themselves, became a letting go. The Kennedy New Frontiersmen felt little respect for the cautious advice of those elder statesmen back in civilized society. Their determination to cross the frontier into the wilderness only increased after they felt the call to justify the legacy of their martyred leader. However Eastern and provincial they may in fact have been, they had from the start imagined themselves as daring cowboys unafraid to confront the enemy—high noon at the Khe Sanh corral. Their soldiers, from the Green Berets on down, caught their spirit and let it all hang out. They went more than a few tokes over the line. They shut out whatever rational doubts might have held them back and rode their emotions through the tunnel made by their breaking waves. Perhaps the trauma of Kennedy's death unlocked the last barrier and let the emotions flow. Whatever the reason, the young president's advisors, his successors, and his children seemed blinded by their own tears and unable to hear the voice of caution. Emotion took over. Where Ego had been, the Id had come to be. Describing his response to an utterly logical explanation of a friend's death in combat at the height of the war, Robert Mason in *Chickenhawk* says, "We all looked at Sherman. Of course he was right. But nobody wanted to be rational. It was so . . . out of place."

So the pattern of Vietnam was the pattern of the American Sixties. In the beginning was a belief that Camelot could be created by rational people acting justly, doing the right thing for the right reason. But right reason gave way to the raw emotion that was always waiting, as David Riesman had feared, just under the delicate fabric of American life. The early innocence was lost. And those early Sixties optimists were left high and dry, wrote Herr, "the saddest casualties of the Sixties, all the promise of good service on the New Frontier either gone or surviving like the vaguest salvages of a dream, still in love with their dead leader, blown away in his prime and theirs."

The gung-ho guys who took over the crusade, who rode their Cobra Hueys into the heart of the beast like Custer shooting away at Little Big Horn, were nowhere near as sophisticated as the Ivy League spooks they had replaced. Theirs was a cruder instrument and a more mindless motivation. They knew not what they did. Instead, they acted directly out of the deep visions humping them through the Vietnamese night. Herr captures this perfectly in his description of a conversation he had at a bar on the second day of the Tet offensive. This sergeant stood there with a beer in his hand and his eyes open talking but dead asleep on his feet, "responding to some dream conversation far inside his head." It gave Herr, he says, "the creeps." But Herr did not tell the story just to capture a moment in the insanity of the Tet offensive. It was an illustration of how we all hump our way through life: "When I told him about it later, he just laughed and said, 'Shit, That's nothing. I do that all the time.'" So do we all.

To operate out of the mindlessness of an unknown structure, to accept what we know as given and not to question what we are or who we are or why, is the human condition, the curse of the Fall. It is Sin in its most profound hold upon us, our profound unknowing. Yet it is who we are. We imagine we are awake and aware of what we are doing, but in fact we are walking in our sleep. We live in a constructed illusion of sounds we call words, and ideas we think we believe, and sights that at least seem to have reality. Most of the time, the illusion holds. But, as Jonathan Edwards warned in "Sinners in the Hands of an Angry God," "we walk over the pit of hell as on a rotten covering, and there are places in that covering so rotten that they will not bear our weight, and these places are unseen." Experiences can puncture the illusion, like the experience of losing it on drugs. But so can combat. And that is one of the points that Herr reaffirms throughout *Dispatches*, that combat is like tripping at its most ferocious, moments of sheer insanity outside of structure, outside of reason, outside of anything that can even be imagined even by those who have been there.

Language is the first to go. Language, confirms Herr, was, anyway, at its loosest in Vietnam. Ordinary words took on new meanings, and new words were being invented and strung together all the time. Much of language was like the commonly heard phrase "good luck," about which, Herr says, "though I meant it every time I said it, it was meaningless." More meaningful, and more revealing, were the Soldier's Prayer

that came in two versions, the standard GI-issue on a Pentagon-pro-
duced little plastic card and what Herr called the "Revised Standard."
This was not from the combine but from the heart. It couldn't be written down because "it got translated outside of language, into chaos—
screams, begging, promises, threats, sobs, repetitions of holy names
until their throats were cracked and dry." This was only part of the insanity of combat, moments in which young kids "took possession of the
madness that had been waiting there in trust for them for eighteen or
twenty-five or fifty years."

At such moments, the line between the craziness of the psychedelic
madness and combat evaporated. Says Herr:

> Under fire would take you out of your head and your body too, the space
> you'd seen a second ago between subject and object wasn't there any more,
> it banged shut in a fast wash of adrenaline. Amazing, unbelievable, guys
> who'd played a lot of hard sports said they'd never felt anything like it, the
> sudden drop and rocket rush of the hit, the reserves of adrenaline you make
> available to yourself, pumping it up and putting it out until you were lost
> floating in it, not afraid, almost open to clear orgiastic death-by-drowning in
> it, actually relaxed. Unless of course you'd shit your pants or were screaming
> or praying or giving anything at all to the hundred channel panic that blew
> word salad all around you and sometimes clean through you.

To be there was also to experience that same experience, to know how
it felt, to know that what humped them also humped you.

One of the unique qualities of Herr's reporting was his determination
not to cover the headquarters or interview the generals or write about
the broad political/historic sweep of it all, but to get down and dirty with
the grunts in the field, the high school dropouts and street kids who got
drafted and didn't know any better, the kids whose parents didn't have
the right contacts to keep them out. Herr does not deny their horrible
brutality, but neither does he deny their humanity. Instead of making
the war a morality play of virtuous dissenters and murderous soldiers,
he tells how he was forced to surrender the distance between actor and
watcher and to pick up a gun and become a shooter, another one of the
trapped Americans in the Alamo. At a field hospital, he assumed the
role of medic, and after a day of not knowing what he was doing with
people's lives, he ultimately recalled them all, real and imagined, "mo-
tionless figures in a dance, the old dance . . . until I felt that I was just a
dancer too."

The final paragraph of the piece begins, "From outside, we say that
crazy people think they hear voices, but of course inside they really hear
them. (Who's crazy? What's insane?)" As with McMurphy and *Cuckoo's
Nest*, that which had seemed crazy to the old Nurse Ratched, with her

anal, in-control mentality, suddenly appears in a different light. No longer is it "Some of us are sane and others crazy." Suddenly it's "We all dance to an unheard tune, and some of us are called crazy and some sane, but the so-called crazy people are really no crazier than the average asshole out there on the street." If the grunts in Vietnam went crazy, they were only meeting what had been waiting for them anyhow, coiled up for eighteen or twenty-five or fifty years.

V

"dreaded and welcome, balls and bowels"

In "Hell Sucks," the second piece in the book, Herr tells how during the Tet offensive of 1968 "we took a huge collective nervous breakdown." Westmoreland had just come back from Washington, where he had promised that there was light at the end of the tunnel, that the enemy were just about played out, that we had victory within our grasp. Reality told a different story. And what happens when the constructs in one's head are confronted by an external reality that will not conform to the expected paradigm? In this case, "The Mission Council joined hands and passed together through the looking glass." As if to confess that actual control was no longer possible, they accepted the illusion of control as a substitute.

The result was the siege of Khe Sanh, a deliberate attempt to replay the battle of Dien Bien Phu but this time to get it right. At the original battle, the French, after a two-year siege, had finally been forced to surrender. It was the American illusion that superior American firepower and air cover could succeed where the French before them had failed. The rhetoric coming out of the command was geared toward creating the illusion of control, of being in control of everything—anality in action.

But the attempt was doomed from the start. The very scene of the siege saw to that. It was in the highlands, a spooky area at the best of times. According to Herr, "The Puritan belief that Satan dwelt in Nature could have been born here." The issue here, as everywhere in the Sixties, was less the economics or the politics of government, but the nature of Nature itself, whether Satan did dwell there, as the Puritans had said—and their neo-orthodox descendants in the Fifties—or whether, as the romantics proclaimed, Nature is a garden of delight.

Nor was this about the flowers-and-trees nature; it was about human nature, that part at the core of every constructed human consciousness, that original part. Are we noble savages at the core? Or monsters? To find out, one had to step outside of structure, outside of civilization, and return naked to the wild. This, the grunts in Vietnam did. They passed over and left the Victorian niceties of suburban America behind. They became brutal murderers and knew it. "The madness, the bitterness, the horror and doom of it. They were hip to it, and more: they savored it. It was no more insane than most of what was going down." So they accepted their verdict. They even laughed about it and told jokes, revealing, horrifyingly, that they knew how far outside of the circle of acceptability they had slid. Said Herr: "They got savaged a lot and softened a lot, their secret brutalized them and darkened them and very often it made them beautiful. It took no age seasoning or education to teach them where true violence resided."

And into this madness, Herr came not as a conscript forced to endure it but, being a journalist, as a volunteer. The grunts could no more believe he was there by choice than McMurphy could understand how the guys in Ratched's ward could be voluntary and not committed. All of which only raised again the question of who was the craziest. It was a question raised and quickly answered: everybody was equally crazy before the great equalizer of combat. The violence of battle carried even the sanest reporter over the edge into madness. Like LSD, it respected neither high school dropout nor Harvard Ph.D., four-eyed runt nor NFL tackle. Nobody knows why we do what we do, and when all the rationalizations and defenses are down, everyone is equally terrified. In his most explicit comparison, Herr writes of combat and of tripping:

> It came back the same way every time. Dreaded and welcome, balls and bowels turning over together, your senses working like strobes, free-falling all the way down to the essences and then flying out again in a rush to focus, like the first strong twinge of tripping after an infusion of psilocybin, reaching in at the point of calm and springing all the joy and all the dread ever known, ever known by everyone who ever lived, unutterable in its speeding brilliance, touching all the edges and then passing, as though it had all been controlled from outside, by a god or by the moon.

To abandon control completely, to let go and surrender to the hundred-channel word-salad panic, to shit in one's pants, that most infantile of reversions to a state of being back before the most basic symbol of anality—this was what combat and acid were all about. This is where the Vietnam War and the acid freaks back in San Francisco experienced their separate halves of the same theater.

And just as some back home clung to structure and refused to let even the slightest doubt invade their armor, so were there officers in Vietnam of equally heroic stuff. The ones who drove Herr into "mad, helpless rages" were the mindless optimists, "the kind who rejected facts and killed grunts wholesale," who insisted, despite the chaos around them, that everything was "fine," "outstanding," "first rate." For such men, the world was as it had been taught to them, orderly, logical, meaningful, clear. After trying unsuccessfully to interview General Westmoreland, Herr notes, "I came away feeling that I'd just had a conversation with a man who touches a chair and says, 'this is a chair,' who points to a desk and says, 'this is a desk.'" No Freudian symbolism of a woman "balling it as in a dream" for his desk, no sir.

Perhaps the best of all these examples was the brigadier general who began a briefing during the siege of Khe Sanh by declaring, "The sun is up over Khe Sanh by 10 every morning." Asked about the marines, he answered, "I was at Khe Sanh for several hours this morning and I want to tell you that the marines there are *clean.*" Clean? Clean? What did he mean by that? "Yes," he continued, "they're bathing or getting a good wash every other day. They're shaving every day, every single day. Their mood is good, their spirits are fine, morale is excellent and there's a twinkle in their eye."

If, as Herr says, Vietnam was where the Trail of Tears was headed all along, here is the crossroad where the trails intersect. To rid the nation of those dirty savages and to prepare the way in the wilderness for the coming of Christian civilization had become in the nineteenth century the American fixation. The cowboy, John Wayne, on his horse, riding into the wilderness and bringing law and order to the outlaw West was the very symbol of the bringing of anality and self-control to the realms of darkness and chaos. The peasants who fled the structures of Europe and came to the wilderness of America had to learn a new identity. They had to abandon the old one in what must have been an agony of self-destruction and fear. Unable, however, to remain in that wilderness, they had to construct a new identity and affirm it in the face of chaos. They had to become self-made men, first—like Ben Franklin—to make themselves an identity, and then, with that identity, consciously to create out of nothing for the first time in history a nation. Then they had to hold that new nation together and protect it from internal enemies such as the Southern slaveholders who would reestablish a European feudalism. They then had to help it prosper and grow, so that they and their children too could grow, so that their new identity could take root and stand among the identities of the world.

All of this required, on the part of peasants who had never before had to take a bath, a supreme act of anality. The religion that gave them their identity and their courage also gave them the means of repression and self-control. If they could control and repress their own lawless emotions, if they could control and repress the savages of their souls, then the land too could become theirs. And the repression of the heathen savage, with his animal howling and bestial ways, was but a literal counterpart of the spiritual struggle as they had come to understand it. Vietnam was an extension of the same American anality that conquered the West and expelled the Cherokee along the Trail of Tears and forced black people into subservient segregation. It was Nurse Ratched's starched white lab coat hiding her natural breasts. The politicians who begot the war and the officers who organized it were of the Fifties, the old ways, still fighting the old battle against chaos and disorder. Many were shell-shocked WWII vets who had been forced to repress and live with what we now call PTSD. It was part of the fight against nature.

The grunts who were drafted to fight the war, however, were baby boomers, getting stoned and listening to Jimi Hendrix. For them, Vietnam was a letting go and an abandoning of their rational selves to primitive, original nature.

VI

"the need to 'tell it' "

Perhaps the most telling of Herr's chapters is the one called "Colleagues," in which he turns his night flares on his fellow reporters and implicitly on himself. The "dumb, brutal kids" in the field were not the only ones caught acting out movies unaware. The chapter opens with a hypothetical scene from some old World War II movie in which the courageous old reporter is banging out another story on his manual typewriter by the glow of a candle. It is the romantic movie scene, the soldier-poet fantasy, that Herr is confessing sent him into Vietnam.

Like Kesey in *Electric Kool-Aid Acid Test,* Herr uses the metaphor of being in a movie as a way of talking about our living our socially constructed roles. We tend to see not what is really out there in front of us, not "I am," or that which is, but our own internal movies projected outward. Like Adam and Eve after the Fall, we see what we prefer to see, and we prefer what we think ought to be over what is. More often than not, we believe that the world is as we have been taught to believe it is; and therefore that is the world we see, regardless of facts. The generation that came out of the Depression and World War II saw nature as a threat and every external threat as Hitler come again. They needed an enemy to help define the borders of identity; we all do. George Bush really believed that Saddam Hussein had weapons of mass destruction; he needed to. So back in the twentieth century, communism had become that enemy. Never mind that Vietnam had historically always been one nation; never mind that the French colonialists merely subdivided the country into three administrative regions; never mind the history of the Japanese occupation or the temporary division of the country into two military repatriation zones after the war; never mind the Vietnamese Declaration of Independence on September 2, 1945, its words taken from our own declaration; never mind the subsequent French attack on Hanoi and the attempt to recolonize the whole of Vietnam; never mind the Geneva Accords and the international pledge to hold elections that would reunify Vietnam; never mind Eisenhower's confession that the elections had to be cancelled because the Vietnamese were sure to vote for their George Washington, Ho Chi Minh. To Americans in the Fifties, afraid of the satanic beast of communism marching across the globe, the attempt of Ho Chi Minh and his allies to reunify their nation was seen as an extension of the Great Communist Conspiracy to destroy the children of light. The cold war between the East and the West, itself an extension of the cosmic battle between God and Satan, was the cinematic context in which the Vietnamese civil war became a global holy war.

And the cinematic context that sent Michael Herr to Vietnam to "blah blah blah cover the war" was the "soldier-poet fantasy" of the war correspondent, Hemingway in Italy in World War I or Spain during its civil war. "There were those," wrote Herr, "whose madness it was not to know always which war they were actually in, fantasizing privately about other, older wars." That one of Herr's colleagues was Sean Flynn, son of the old silent screen hero Errol Flynn, Captain Blood himself, merely served to thicken the confusion between movie and reality, as if anyone could ever tell them apart anyhow.

But Vietnam was not World War II; it did have its own reality. There is an "I am" outside our merely human texts, and He is a jealous God. Thus it became the responsibility of reporters like Herr to try to escape from their own movies, however impossible that might seem, and tell it. We too easily succumb to the inevitable movies that run in our heads, confess our inability to escape from them and the foolish innocence of even trying. Everything, after all, is a movie; even the attempt to escape from the movie is itself a movie. If there is only an infinite regression of movies, one behind the other, if the realm outside the matrix is but another matrix in an infinite succession of matrices, why bother even trying to escape? Because once you know that it is a movie you are participating in, and not the reality it pretends to be, then comes the voice that demands, as one sergeant did to Herr as he was leaving, "Okay, man, you go on, you go on out of here you cocksucker, but I mean it, You tell it! You tell it, man. If you don't tell it . . ." Call it, if you will, the voice of conscience, the icy insistent sense of something true out beyond the movie, beyond the matrix, that insists upon its own superior reality. If there is a truth, can a subjective constructed self know it?

And can he or she ever tell it? Herr like many of his generation felt at least that he had a responsibility to try.

He returns to his theme at the beginning of the last section of "Colleagues" by "thinking about all the kids who got wiped out by seventeen years of war movies before coming to Vietnam to get wiped out for good." Nor were they alone. The correspondents, too, everyone, was and is caught up in paradigms and constructs that carry us along despite our best intentions and educations and determinations to resist. To the extent we only imagine we are in control, we are, as Herr said of the leathernecks, "getting their pimples shot off for the cameras"—insane. But like the grunts, "the war hadn't done that to them." The war was only one theater of a greater production in which every living human is played like a puppet on a string held over the pit of hell on a thread in the hands of an angry God. We all dance to unheard tunes and live off the energy passed down to us by visions we cannot see that hump us through the night. That is the significance of the quote from Bob Dylan that Herr uses as an epigraph for this section: "Name me someone that's not a parasite / And I'll go out and say a prayer for him."

We are all parasites, living off the structures handed down for us. Not to be a parasite would place us outside of structure, out there in the wilderness, in the darkest heart-of-darkness jungle all alone, in need of all the prayers we can get.

Of "all the grunts tripping out on the war and the substantial number of correspondents who were doing the same thing," a significant subculture emerged, one that stretched from the Mekong Delta to the San Francisco Bay. These were the freaks who had seen outside of structure, who had been to the jungle and tried to keep their eyes open, and to tell it. Not that they really could, because what they had seen was beyond language, beyond even word salad panic. But there they were, trying to say with words what they knew could not begin to be said. It was too awful not to try to tell it.

Herr's correspondent freak exemplar was a young reporter named Page, "a crazy child," someone people talked about as if he were more legend than were made-up lies. "People made him sound crazy and ambitious, like the Sixties Kid, a cold-stone freak in a country where the madness raced up the hills and into the jungles, where everything essential to learning Asia, war, drugs, the whole adventure, was close at hand." He was where "it" was at. He was hit by shrapnel for the first time at Chu Lai in 1965; later, an air strike caught up with him while he was adrift in a boat on the South China Sea. In the States, recuperating between bouts of Vietnam, he got busted with the Doors in New Haven. Back in Vietnam, he continued to mix "the war, history, rock, Eastern religion, his travels, literature," and dope ("Why don't you roll a five-handed joint while I prepare a steamboat for this ugly, filthy roach?").

The Marine officers from the Combat Information Bureau were the antithesis of Page. Where he was McMurphy, they were Nurse Ratched, and the lesser reporters and soldiers the acutes. And the acutes resented, when they were in the bar, the officers' "constant attempts to impose Marine order on our lives there." The reporters didn't like them, and they didn't like reporters. But of all the bunch, Page freaked them the most: "They don't like your hair, Page, and you're a foreigner, and you're insane, and you really spook the shit out of them. . . . They're not sure about a lot of things, but they're sure about you, Page. You're the enemy." He really was "it."

Page got hit again, this time almost fatally, coming out of it with a piece of steel through his brain. He survived, barely, and Herr tells bits and pieces of his slow but bizarrely self-conscious recovery, like the times he would be up staring at himself in the full-length mirror "to survey the wreckage, laughing until tears came, shaking his head and saying, "Ohhhhh, fuck! I mean, just look at that, will you? Page is a fucking hemi-plegic," raising his cane and stumbling back to his chair, collapsing in laughter again." But nothing is as funny to him as the request from a British publisher that he put together a book of war photographs that would once and forever "take the glamour out of war." He couldn't get over the insanity of it. You can't take the glamour out of war, he shouted. "It's like trying to take the glamour out of sex, trying to take the glamour out of the Rolling Stones. . . . The very idea! Ohhh, what a laugh, take the bloody glamour out of bloody war."

Sex, and death, and rock 'n' roll. These were the themes that tied the "glamour" of Vietnam to the "glamour" of the rest of the theater of the Sixties. It was, Herr says at last, his nightmare to realize, after he had returned to the States, that "there'd been nothing happening there that hadn't already existed here, coiled up and waiting, back in the World." In both theaters, the passage out of structure was a passage into a place of such ferocious and terrifying intensity that one couldn't help but love it, despite the terror, despite how hard that was to explain to people who had never been there. He even knew what it was like when some vet suffered a sudden flashback and almost or actually lost it. "We all took a bad flash sooner or later and usually more than once, like old acid backing up, residual psychotic reaction. Certain rock and roll would come in mixed with rapid fire and men screaming." Nothing to worry about, Page said, quoting the Stones, "just your nineteenth nervous breakdown."

This then was the point, that the experience of the baby boomers of the Sixties was all one, all the same breaking through to the other side.

"Out on the street, I couldn't tell the Vietnam veterans from the Rock and Roll veterans. The Sixties had made so many casualties, its war and its music had run off the same circuit for so long they didn't even have to fuse. . . . Freezing and burning and going down into the sucking mud of the culture, hold on tight and move real slow."

To step outside of structure is to step outside of Egypt, which is both a political state and a state of mind. The veterans of the Sixties that Herr refers to had stepped out of both. They crossed over into the wilderness at first eagerly, later with their eyes wide open in horror. But once having stepped out, there could be no turning back. Once one has seen that beyond the orderly boundaries of reality is a blinding light in which everything that once seemed real is melted away, one can never stand on solid earth so comfortably again.

Once one has seen oneself as a behavioral mechanism tossed in the eddies and backwash and onrushing turbulence of history, what can one do but hold on tight and stare awestruck as our ever-falling Babylon hurtles down Abaddon's pit? The war was but one of those highly concentrated points of history in which the breakthrough between literal history and cosmic history, between what Melville called the Horological and Chronological, can be felt. As such, it becomes the symbol, not for some specific sins of economics or politics but for all of history, all of culture. Herr's final line has it right: "Vietnam Vietnam Vietnam, we've all been there."

6

Finally, No Golden Fleece—

I

"the man in the mirror"

THE LIGHT AT THE END OF THE TUNNEL MAY HAVE BEEN THE METAPHOR for Vietnam—for the hawks victory, for the doves a train coming at us. But both were wrong. As Herr showed, the war was but one more symbolic rendering of the escape of consciousness from structure to the wilderness. The light at the end of that long tunnel turned out to be, not victory, not a train, not the Garden of Eden, but the gleam in Charlie Manson's eyes.

Terror manifests itself in many forms, most of them coming not from outside ourselves but from within. The external objects and events that scare us awaken fears slumbering in what Emily Dickinson called the cellars of the mind. The beasts under the bed, the monsters in the night shadows moving behind the trees, are the projections of our internal fears onto the landscape of the world. Enough real evil does exist to sustain our projections, but in the end even the projections are rationalizations, lies we tell ourselves to prevent our having to face the real fear within ourselves. We need external demons to keep the demons in our souls at bay. This, according to Baldwin and Ellison, is the role that blacks had played in white consciousness before the civil rights movement freed them.

By the end of the Sixties, the beliefs of the old military/industrial combine had unraveled. The protective shell had been shattered and thrown away. With our protective social constructs crumbling, all that was left was the state of nature waiting to reveal itself as either friend or fiend. The idyllic suburbia of "Leave it to Beaver" had become a bad joke. John Wayne was no longer there to protect us from the Indians or lead the way to the next watering hole, . . . and, as at Altamont, the hot sun was climbing over the rim of the desert. Out of that desert emerged the very apparition that had always been there coiled up in the heart of the culture. Indians, wolves, monsters under the bed. Commies coming to get us, the Vietcong, "Victor Charley," and finally that other Charley, Charlie Manson.

Joan Didion remembers that in Los Angeles in August, 1969, "everything was unmentionable but nothing was unimaginable. This mystical flirtation with the idea of 'sin'—this sense that it was possible to go too far, and that many people were doing it—was very much with us." She remembered how the first reports came in, garbled, confused, contradictory, and, she wrote, "I also remember this, and wish I did not: I remember that no one was surprised."

"I am the man in the mirror," says Charles Manson. And in that at least he may be right. "Anything you see in me is in you. . . . I am you. . . . And when you can admit that you will be free. I am just a mirror." Nor is that the least that he is right about. And because he was and has since become even more of a symbol, not just of the end of the Sixties, but of the terror that lies at the heart of the darkest cave in consciousness, he compels a more careful study.

Why then is Charlie Manson, as Geraldo Rivera said, "the stuff of a nation's nightmares?" Not for what he did, nor even for what he said. Many others have killed more people more brutally. The answer is because, as Didion foretold, we found in him an icon upon which to project our own latent fears. We took the load off the black man and put it instead on him. No one was surprised because everyone knew the potential was there, in each and all of us. So Manson became a living metaphor of our own latent demons. He became Abaddon, the God of the bottomless pit. We looked into Manson's eyes and saw in those dark caves what we most feared within ourselves, the paranoia of what might happen if you go too far. He was the monster in the wilderness, the shadow in the night forest, the beast said to lurk in the Terra Incognita beyond the edges of the map. By projecting our monsters onto Manson and then locking him up for life, we imagined we had put the beast back in its cage.

If the world is the web we weave to protect us from the void, then Manson's eyes were black holes into that void. This was the downside of freedom; this even more than Altamont was what conservatives had been warning against. Out of their fear of what human beings might come to, they had defended social structures like segregation and argued for the need to preserve order in Vietnam. Because of that, conservative apologists for structure lost their credibility. Their fear of sin had overwhelmed them and frozen them in place. They clung to the slavery of Egypt and denied that there could ever actually be a Promised Land. To have no faith in the future dooms us to stagnation, but of the many thousands of the Children of Israel who followed Moses out of

Egypt, only Joshua and Caleb made it to the Promised Land. Of the rest, "their carcasses rotted in the wilderness."

Charlie Manson was exactly the kind of menace the establishment foresaw and feared in 1517 when Martin Luther had first dared to suggest that truth lay not in the rationalizations of the scholastics but in the subjectivities of the spirit. Such philosophical abstractions are fine for the educated who converse with each other in Latin and, in the final analysis, know what social codes sustain them. But to preach such things to peasants invites anarchy of the wildest sort and leads to such events as the Anabaptist rebellion at Muenster. Even Luther recoiled in horror at the extremes to which those radical Protestants took his ideas. He never imagined that true faith would be achieved here, on earth, in the literal realm of time and space.

The antinomian strain that runs through American culture began in Martin Luther's Reformation with its declaration of "Sola fides," "Faith alone," superior to logic, and with the "Priesthood of all believers"—the belief that anyone might experience the subjective authority of God in the soul. Luther rejected the radicals' application of this to the political worldly realm and blessed the soldiers who slaughtered the enthusiasts of Muenster. But John Calvin, who had married an Anabaptist, constructed a system in Geneva that imagined a new order based upon those few people who could be identified as members of the elect. He dared to believe that a few people could escape the solipsistic maze of human stupidity and break on through to Zion. Upon these rocks would be built a new church and a new society that would be Israel reborn. This is the ideology that founded the American colonies, the faith that the invisible would be made visible within us. This was the legacy of the Radical Reformation of Europe carried to America by the English, the Scots, the Dutch Calvinists, German Anabaptists, Bohemian Husserites, and French Huguenots. No wonder American culture has always produced rebels and outlaws, madmen and saints, who claim to know and speak for God, who claim that they and not the institutional church members are the true elect, truly awakened and truly free.

In 1636, Puritan John Winthrop had seen Charlie Manson in Anne Hutchinson's eyes. Winthrop believed in the possibility of creating on earth Calvin's "Kingdom of Freedom," as his 1629 Arbella Sermon showed, but he also knew full well that not all spirits are divine. The Devil can clothe himself in the robes of righteousness and lead innocent souls astray. Anne Hutchinson's antinomian subjectivity, itself a clear echo of "the enthusiasts and anabaptists" of Muenster, threatened not just patriarchal authority or political stability but human sanity itself. Political and social structures exist to back up mental structures, and in return the collective consciousness of the people helps to sustain the institutions of the state. They need each other: "no Pope, no king." The state backs up the church, and the church provides the beliefs that give us meaning. Once you start taking apart the structures that sustain us, there is no telling what else will fall. There is no telling to what extremes the human mind will go. At Ann Hutchinson's trial, Winthrop proclaimed, *"These disturbances that have come among the Germans have been all grounded on revelations, and so they that have vented them have stirred up their hearers to . . . cut the throats one of another, and these have been the fruits of them, and whether the devil may inspire the same into their hearts I know not. For I am fully persuaded that Mrs. Hutchinson is deluded by the devil."* Manson, too, in following his own revelations, stirred up his hearers, and as a result throats were cut. As Solomon said, "There is nothing new under the sun."

In 1636 Ann Hutchinson was banished from Massachusetts, but the Puritans still ended up falling to their own idolatry. Believing themselves no longer sinners in the wilderness but saints at ease in Zion, they imagined that they knew the truth and thus tried to cement their Israel into place. Eventually another generation rebelled against this idolatry in the name of the living spirit and set out once again in search of the Kingdom of Love. Such awakenings inevitably lead, as they did in 1741 and 1802, to excesses of enthusiasm that threaten not just self-crucifixion but the disintegration of a whole culture.

Romantic periods breed such antinomian excess. The command to follow ones heart wherever it might go very well might lead off the deep end. Camille Paglia has argued that romanticism almost always leads to decadence, that Rousseau with his noble savages was followed by the Marquis de Sade: "The continuum of empathy and emotion leads to sex. Failure to realize that was the Christian error. The continuum of sex leads to sadomasochism. Failure to realize that was the error of the Dionysian Sixties. Dionysus expands identity but crushes individuals. There is no liberal dignity of the person in the Dionysian. The god gives latitude but no civil rights."

The American romantic Ralph Waldo Emerson urged his readers to trust their own intuitions regardless of social conventions or the moral code. "Truth," he wrote, "is handsomer than the affectation of love." Love itself must be rejected "when it pules and whines." At the execution of the religious fanatic John Brown, who had led a raid on Harper's Ferry after God told him to stir up a slave rebellion, Emerson proclaimed his gallows "as glorious as the cross." The somewhat less romantic Nathaniel Hawthorne muttered that no man was ever more justly hanged.

But the antinomian strain is so strong in American culture that despite every return to structure, it survives to rise again. For every attempt to build a Constitution that will contain the excesses of the mob, there is the insistence that a Bill of Rights be included to insure that individualism is allowed to flourish. After all, hadn't the leading conservative, Barry Goldwater himself, said in 1964, "Extremism in the defense of liberty is no vice." The Republican Party today remains torn between a moralistic wing that would pass laws controlling everyone's behavior and a libertarian wing that would abolish many of our laws. Pro-life crusaders torching abortion clinics, Oliver North refusing to obey the laws of Congress, Timothy McVeigh's bombing of the federal building in Oklahoma City, even Bush's dismantling of economic regulations to set the markets free, are as much in the antinomian tradition as Henry David Thoreau and Martin Luther King. Paul Hill, the Presbyterian minister who murdered a doctor who performed abortions, quoted the abolitionist John Brown at his trial. The Unibomber Ted Kazynski and Oklahoma City bomber Timothy McVeigh were two sides of the same coin. In America, even the so-called conservatives have a red streak of antinomianism in their souls.

Charles Manson, then, is in good company. And what makes him an antinomian rather than simply a lawless thug and "mass murdering dog" is that his deeds and words are buttressed by an implicit philosophy. He constructed a belief system and believed it and preached it. Another con man could be easily ignored, but Manson has proven himself faithful to his beliefs. He is not faking them to get out; instead, his refusal to abandon them keeps him locked up tightly in jail.

Manson is fascinating, even mesmerizing, because his voice comes from somewhere else, somewhere faintly recognizable. Emerson said that if you "speak your latent conviction it shall be the universal sense." That is, if you speak the most honest truth of your heart, others will recognize their own most honest truths and listen. Like Malcolm X, and like Emerson himself, Manson meant what he said. Like Malcolm X, he had no formal schooling, but he is sincere; and like Malcolm, his sincerity are his credentials.

II

"I wasn't directing traffic, lady!"

To begin with, and to take care of one of the most persistent misunderstandings about Manson, he was never convicted of killing Sharon Tate or the LaBiancas. He was never even charged, much less convicted, of any of the murders that occurred that August in Los Angeles. The man who prosecuted Manson and put him away makes this quite clear in his book about the trial. In *Helter Skelter,* Vincent Bugliosi goes to great length to describe how he had to put together a circumstantial case in order to convict Manson, not of murder, but of "conspiracy to commit murder." Even Bugliosi admits that Manson had no direct role in the killings. Instead, Bugliosi had to show that Manson somehow directed the killings and then stayed back while his followers got their hands bloody. But the problem was, as Bugliosi admits, "Manson rarely gave direct orders." Indeed, Manson rarely speaks in direct or clear statements. Instead, he is, said interviewer David Felton, "a super acid rap—symbols, parables, gestures, nothing literal, everything enigmatic, resting nowhere, stopping briefly to overturn an idea, stand it on its head, then exploit the paradox." He may never have actually told anyone to commit any of the murders. Bugliosi argued instead that Manson implied what he wanted done and that his followers inferred that intention. The command was never explicitly stated, and to this day Manson insists that his followers misunderstood and took literally what had been only another of his mind games.

Though this mind game ended up in deadly reality, it was not the only such game played at the group's desert hideout. Asked what they did every day at the ranch, Manson told Tom Snyder in a 1981 interview, "We played games,—forgot who we were,—went off into other dimensions." They even had a name for such game-playing, "The Magical Mystery Tour." But not everyone understood it as just a game. As Manson explained it:

> We speed down the highway in a 1958 automobile that won't go but fifty, and an XKE Jaguar goes by, and I state to Clem, "Catch him, Clem, and we'll rob him or steal all of his money," you know. And he says, "What shall we do?" I say, "Hit him on the head with a hammer." We Magical Mystery Tour it.
>
> Then Linda Kasabian gets on the stand and says: "They were going to kill a man, they were going to kill a man in an automobile." To you it seems serious. But like Larry Kramer and I would get on a horse and we would ride over to Wichita, Kansas, and act like cowboys. We make it a game on the ranch.

The particular game that ended up in brutal murder has been described many times, but it bears repeating. That it was believable, even to these uneducated dropouts, tells us as much about where the country stood in 1969 as it does about the particular consciousness of these individuals. What made Manson such a potent symbol was that his mad fantasy could just as easily have been anyone's. Manson, like Vietnam, was where the trail of tears was heading all along.

It begins with the Beatles, and with the Beatles's celebrated White Album, which came out in 1968. While tripping on acid, Manson heard in it, the message that put it all together for him. There would be a war between blacks and whites; whites would lose. Manson and his followers would hide out in the desert when the slaughter took place. When it was over, they would emerge from their hiding places and somehow convince the blacks that they, Manson and his followers, should be made the leaders of this new world.

He got all this not just from his interpretation of the Beatles but also from the Bible. Perhaps his most fascinating connection was to put side by side the Beatles song "Revolution 9" with Revelations 9. Revelations, the final book of the New Testament, has always been the favorite of mystics because its wild apocalyptic imagery so bluntly addresses not the literal but symbolic consciousness. For those who read Scripture not as a moral code of social behavior nor as a literal history book but as a symbolic rendering of a reality out of time and out of mind, the book of Revelations is the proof text. No one can read John's visions of the beasts with the seven heads and seven horns and believe that it is a rational, literal narrative. This is mysticism.

Nevertheless, Manson seems to have taken the literal descriptions and compared them, as so many mystics have done so often in the past, to literal events and persons in his own world. This led him to imagine that the predictions of Scripture were indeed addressed to his times. Revelations 9 begins with the fifth angel being given the key to the bottomless pit. Out of that pit comes, among other things, locusts, "and unto them was given power, as the scorpions of the earth have power." These locusts, Manson reasoned, were insects, bugs. This was a hidden reference to the Beatles. They were ordered not to hurt the grass nor any people "who had not the seal of God on their foreheads." The shapes of these locusts "were like unto horses prepared unto battle." They were the four horsemen of the apocalypse out to wage the battle of Armageddon. And though they had faces of men, says Scripture, "they had hair as the hair of women." Hard as it may be to believe now, the length of the Beatles's hair was a scandal when they first arrived in the U.S. in 1964. The breastplates described in Scripture were their electric guitars; the "sound of their wings . . . as the sound of chariots of many horses running to battle" was their music. Their "tails like unto scorpions" were the cords of their electric guitars, and "the stings in their tails" was their electrified power.

This and more like it convinced Manson that the message was being sent from the Universe to him through the Beatles. So he turned from Scripture to interpret the text of the lyrics of the album itself. There he found a consistent theme lurking between the otherwise cryptic lines and apparently random songs. Only on the surface was it all meaningless and random. Like life itself, it only appeared random to those who had not eyes to see. To Manson, the message was clear: "What do you think it means? It's the battle of Armageddon. It's the end of the world. It was the Beatles' Revolution 9 that turned me on to it. It predicts the overthrow of the establishment. The pit will be opened and that's when it will all come down. A third of all mankind will die."

"Rocky Raccoon" was the song that made the implicit connection to the black revolution. "Coon. You know. That's a word they use for black people," Manson explained to *Rolling Stone* while he was still in jail waiting to be tried. "Blackbird" was a song calling on black people to "rise." "Piggies" was a description of the rich establishment that would be overthrown. And "Helter Skelter" was a description of the battle of Armageddon itself, pure chaos and confusion. But "Revolution 9" was the song that Manson listened to and talked about most. It's a good six minutes of disorganized, disconnected noise, babies crying, machine guns going off, church hymns, car horns, whispered words, football yells, and the repeated chant of "number nine, number nine, number nine." Even more than Revelations 9, it is so freefloating as to allow itself to be interpreted in almost any way the listener wants—or fears. As such, it serves the purpose of much great art: it bypasses the logical mind and zaps straight into the subliminal, allowing a direct flow of associations from the subconscious. Listening to it, Manson was inspired.

Manson's crime, thus, was an act of imaginative literary criticism. Had he been a professor at Berkeley, rather than a hustler on the street, this reading might have won him tenure, a different sort of life term than the one he now serves. Did he believe it literally? How is one to tell? He himself may not have known. Here is where the line between the "real" world of cause-and-effect rational logic and the romantic realm of imagination disappears. Bugliosi, the prosecutor, is all logic and literalism, pure arminianism, pure Nurse Ratched. Rejecting Manson's interpretation of "Helter Skelter" out of hand, he says, "There was a simpler explanation. In England, home of the Beatles, helter skelter is another name for a slide in an amusement park."

But so what? Does it even matter whether Manson knew this? Symbols are always both their literal selves and the things they symbolize. The existence of a literal object does not by itself discredit any symbolic meanings that might be attached to it. Perhaps Manson was thinking along the lines of James Baldwin, with his argument that blacks represent the subconscious and whites conscious rationality. Perhaps Manson's race war between blacks and whites was itself a symbol of the war of the subconscious rising up to take over consciousness, as Norman O. Brown said it must. Manson was asked if he thought the Beatles intended the meanings that he found in their texts. His answer speaks to this very problem of authorial intention: "I think it's a subconscious

thing. I don't know whether they did or not. But it's there. It's an association in the subconscious. This music is bringing on the revolution, the
unorganized overthrow of the establishment. The Beatles know in the
sense that the subconscious knows."

Nor is it clear how Manson's followers understood him. Perhaps, as
he claimed, they took him more literally than he intended. Perhaps they
heard things spoken through him which he never intended to say. It is
clear that at least one of his followers, a girl named Ouish, saw that both
interpretations were possible. She told her friend Barbara Hoyt, "We
all have to go through Helter Skelter. If we don't do it in our heads, we
will have to do it physically. If you don't die in your head, you'll die
when it comes down." Here, the literal and the metaphysical meanings
run on parallel tracks.

Manson's main defense is that his followers, sensing some frustration
that his predicted Armageddon still had not occurred, set out on their
own to get it started, to show the blacks how to do it, and to show the
world their leader. According to Manson, they did it as if to say, "Here,
we want you to see this guy, but [says Manson] I didn't want to be seen."
Just as Lenin, unwilling to wait for history to achieve its inevitable Marxist end, had jump-started the worldwide proletariat revolution in pre-
capitalist Russia, these zealots, utterly taken by Manson's vision, wanted
to bring their revolution quickly to life. After the Tate killings, when
Susan Atkins proudly told him that they had just given him the world,
Manson claims to have shouted, "You dumb fucking cunt, I already had
the world. You just put me back in jail again."

Just as Luther was astonished and then horrified at the literal way in
which the Anabaptists of Muenster tried to put the "Priesthood of all
believers" into practice in the world, so others have been amused and
amazed at the extent to which our innocent American willingness to believe in a literal and material Kingdom Come remains part of our culture. Here too, we Americans are the descendants not of the Lutheran
but of the Calvinist Reformation, heavily tainted by Anabaptist enthusiasm for the coming Kingdom of Zion, here in this world literally, in the
flesh. If Luther came up with the idea of a door, Calvin pushed it open
just a crack, a crack through which poured many of the zealots who had
been looking for a way to break out of the structures in Europe. The
Kingdom of God in America has been the dream of enthusiasts since
long before the nation began. Our antinomians are the ones who took
the words seriously, who took them all the way beyond mere symbolism,
who came to America because they really did believe that here in this
world and in this flesh they might create the Kingdom of Freedom in
which all constructed hypocrisy and pretense were shed and the pure

bliss of essential truth could be had. Gypsy, one of Manson's more articulate followers, put it thus:

> The Dream can be real when you see it, and when you live it. And that's
> what the Beatles are singing about. They're singing it's all a dream, life
> passes by on a screen. They're singing it, but they're still asleep singing it.
> They haven't woken up to the fact that what they're singing about is more
> than a song. They could be living it. . . .
>
> Give up everything and follow me, Christ said, and we have given up a lot
> to follow our dream. There are other communes, but everyone has their old
> lady and their old man. It's just the same old song in different costumes.
> There are no couples here. We are all just one woman and one man. "All
> you need is love." We were the only ones gullible enough to take the Beatles
> seriously. We were the only people stupid enough to believe every word of
> it.

Gypsy uses the word "stupid," but she doesn't mean it in a negative
sense. She means it in the sense of being innocent as babies, as being,
to use a phrase from another Beatles song, "the fool on the hill" whom
everyone laughs at but who sees it all. Here we have a twentieth century
American, like her predecessors, trying to convince worldly skeptics that
in America the mystical promise really can be made flesh.

It must be said that if Manson did not really want his followers to
initiate the race war he called "Helter Skelter," he had the responsibility
to make that perfectly clear—but he didn't. Instead, he allowed ambigu-
ity and uncertainty to proliferate. He stayed within his own circle and
did not take responsibility for the influence he was having in other people's circles. Like the cagey ex-con that he is, he played his cards close
to his own chest. In the world of prison, that ethic works. In the outside
world, a broader definition of responsibility comes into play.

If Manson is to be held responsible for his ambiguous creation of a
scenario that others then brought to life (or death), what is to be said of
anyone who writes a book or a movie or sings a song that inspires others
to go out and live its message? Is Marx to be held personally responsible
for Stalin's massacres? Should Orson Welles have been tried for the
deaths of those people who might have killed themselves when they
mistakenly thought his "War of the Worlds" was a real alien invasion?
Should the creators of violent television shows be jailed if a kid picks up
a gun and imitates what he sees on TV? And what then of the Beatles
themselves? Don't they have some responsibility for what Manson
heard in their music?

If metaphorical obscurity combined with a violent suggestiveness are
criminal activities, then the Old Testament itself deserves to be banned:
the bloody account of the Children of Israel's re-conquest of Canaan,

with whole cities slaughtered and blood flooding up to the horses' thighs. Or the text can be read, as Jonathan Edwards did, as pure metaphor:

> There is no necessity in supposing that the word death, or the Hebrew word so translated, if used in the manner that has been supposed, to have been figurative at all. It does not appear but that this word, in its true and proper meaning might signify perfect misery and sensible destruction, though the word was also applied to signify something more external and visible. There are many words in our language . . . which are applied to signify external things, . . . yet these words do as truly and properly signify other things of a more spiritual, internal nature.

Death, in this typological, symbolic reading of Scripture, thus becomes a signifier of spiritual or ego death, the experience that was said to be a precursor of conversion. Jonah's "death" in the belly of the whale and Christ's death on the cross thus can be read metaphorically as well as literally. Those who misunderstood the spiritual reading and took the words literally have been responsible for millions of deaths over the two thousand years of Christian history. Perhaps this is why Plato wanted to banish all poets from his perfect republic? The Beatles were poets, too, creating images and messages that had repercussions.

Like so many others in the Sixties, the four Beatles followed a familiar progression from innocence to romanticism to decadence and back again. In the innocent early Sixties, they sang naïve teeny-bopper love songs like "I Want to Hold your Hand." As they and the decade aged, they toked deeper into dope, let their hair grow longer, and played music further and further out there. They remained enormously popular because their audience was undergoing the same transition. They evolved along with the baby-boomer population they were playing for. "Sergeant Pepper's Lonely Heart's Club Band," with its Woodstock fun-and-happiness approach to the drug culture, was perfect for 1967. "The White Album," with its faceless cover and its demonic possibilities, spoke to the madness of 1968 and 1969. "Revolution 9" especially was a bonfire in a tinder-dry forest. Its violent associations, provocative noises, and complete incomprehensibility played to the heightened paranoia of the time. As the Stones had sung "Sympathy for the Devil" during the worst moments of Altamont, so the Beatles, by putting together a series of images upon which frightened people could project their worst unconscious fears, had to be at least partially responsible for the chaos that followed. It is perhaps not a coincidence that their next album, "Abbey Road," was a total reversion, a plea to "Get back, Jo Jo / Get back to where you once belonged" and to "Let it be." As David

Felton wrote in *The Mindfuckers*, "I just can't help thinking: If Abbey Road had come out sooner, maybe Sharon Tate would be alive today."

If this is so, then Manson's crime was that he never clearly designated the line between reality and imagination, between the fantasy and the deed, the literal and the symbolic. In that ambiguous realm, he moved from what we consider rational to the irrational. He abandoned all civilized self-control and became the complete antinomian, outside the structures of the legal and the mental law.

At the trial, Manson's followers certainly claimed they were doing his bidding. He had said to them, "Just do what you have to," and they had had a pretty good idea what they thought he meant. Manson's proven presence at the LaBiancas' residence, having driven the killers there, undercuts whatever claim he continues to make that he was an innocent whose followers took it upon themselves entirely on their own to begin the slaughter.

But Manson's repeated claim that he "broke no law of man or God" is not entirely without basis, either. For in the prison world in which he grew up and lived most of his life, people are responsible for their own deeds—period! The act of murder is what is punished, not some vague indirect suggestion by a third party. "I take responsibility for my acts," he insists. "Every man must take responsibility for his acts. We each live within our own circles." To this day, Manson still does not understand how the law can hold him responsible for murders that other people actually committed. His stubborn refusal to confess his guilt, as misguided as it may be, is at the very least an honest statement of his beliefs and not an artful dodge. He really believed it relevant that, as he shouted at Diane Sawyer, "I wasn't directing traffic, lady."

Indeed, that is the heart of the enigma of Manson. That is why back in 1969 and still today, people find something fascinating about him. Bugliosi and other spokesmen for society have tried at times to say that Manson is little more than another two-bit thug, a thief, a pimp, a hustler out for himself, a murderous con filled with uncontrollable rage. It is too neat and too well known a box. More is going on.

Manson's true crime, and the reason he will remain in jail until his death, is that he didn't just blur, he erased, the line between reality and imagination. He crossed over to the other side, completely outside the combine. Most of us are like the little boy crying at the corner because, he sobs, "I want to run away from home, but my parents won't let me cross the street." Manson demonstrated that the street could be crossed, that society's rules and moral codes, even its prohibitions against murder, are artificial constructs and not to be thought essential or absolute. Once the human mind is finally liberated from the rituals and traditions, the taboos and inhibitions, that have bound the web of human culture together, anything becomes possible. To some this is the meaning of freedom. To others, it is the definition of insanity. "Crazy" becomes a label applied to those who don't agree with the consensus. Even Emily Dickinson felt:

'Tis the Majority
In this, as All, prevail—
Assent—and you are sane—
Demur—you're straightway dangerous—
And handled with a Chain—

But the need to break the bonds of the combine's programming requires that occasionally people step outside the bounds of what is allowed and dare the wilderness, at whatever risk. Manson actually told his parole board, "It's so abstract that someone has to carry insanity. Someone's got to be insane. Some one's got to be the bad guy." Looking at the world around him, Manson was not always convinced that he was the only one. Acknowledging the disintegration of the old paradigm and the resulting confusion since the Sixties, he recently remarked, "A long time ago being crazy meant something. Nowadays everybody's crazy."

Individuals have crossed that line before, many times, but what Manson also did, and what he was convicted for, was, like Socrates, corruption of the innocent. He spun the tales that they believed. His imagination created the constructions that they acted upon. Bugliosi could find no evidence that Manson ever said directly that his followers should actually kill anyone. What Bugliosi claims, and what seems believable, is that they believed he wanted them to kill and, freed from the usual inhibitions that would keep middle-class American kids from slaughtering strangers, that they acted out his fantasy and did not need his direct command.

III

"the power of an empty head"

Setting aside as much as possible the horror of the Tate/LaBianca murders, it is instructive to look into Manson's belief system for evidence of why he was believed. According to Bugliosi, part of Manson's charismatic appeal was "his ability to utter basic truisms to the right person at the right time." What were these truisms? Why did they work?

What we find when we do take Manson's own words seriously is that he had managed to absorb much of the developing philosophy of the Sixties. In some way, he was the final extension of the mind's true liberation, of the ideas of the civil rights movement, of the white radicals of SDS, of Timothy Leary and Baba Ram Dass, of Norman O. Brown. What he said seemed to make sense to so many innocents because these same ideas were running all around them. Manson is no intellectual in the conventional sense. He is at best self-educated but not at all bookish, having spent nearly his entire life, from childhood up, behind bars. He has a sharp mind and has paid attention to the world around him. But he never had much opportunity to compare notes or to talk with others about ideas. He was like someone who learned French entirely out of books but never heard the language spoken. When he emerged from prison in 1967, in the Summer of Love, his language and his approach were just bizarre enough to seem to be a part of the multifaceted counterculture. And his beliefs seemed like the culmination of a decade of antinomianism, the logical extension of what had been going down, not just in the Sixties, but also throughout American history.

We can see here why so many people in the counterculture at first embraced Manson as one of their own, why the underground press treated him as a martyr to the cause. By taking on so much of the many strains of the Sixties, "Manson" became a symbol of the hippie freak fighting back against the machine. And the immediate assumption was, as it was when a black man was accused of rape, that this was an obvious frame, that Manson was being made a scapegoat by a crumbling establishment terrified that it was losing control over its children. There were even a few, who had already gone over the edge, who assumed that he was indeed the perpetrator of the crime and congratulated him for striking a blow in a revolutionary war. Bernardine Dohrn of SDS, when she heard the news, said, "Offing those rich pigs with their own forks and knives, and then eating a meal in the same room. Far out! The Weathermen dig Charles Manson." Her husband, Bill Ayres, the same man who caused Barack Obama such heartburn in the 2008 election, claims now that she was being "ironic" and didn't mean this seriously. Jerry Rubin, who had rejected his parents' liberal rationalism for the spontaneous emotions of the crowd, said, "I fell in love with Manson the first time I saw his cherub face and sparkling eyes on TV."

In the romantic revolt of the nineteenth century, Ralph Waldo Emerson had proclaimed the superiority of individual intuition over the corpse-cold tea of rationality and logic, and he had urged himself and others to be totally self-reliant. What if this spirit you trust is from the Devil, not from God, asked his Calvinist aunt, Mary Moody Emerson? "I do not believe it is," he replied, "but if so I will live then from the devil." What is in the self is paramount. It and not the combine must be allowed to direct traffic. Emerson proclaimed that reality exists as consciousness and not as matter; and thus truth is to be sought not in science but in the subjective intuition of each mind. Each of us, he said, if we dig down through the layers of culture and belief that have been accumulating over the millennia, will find a universal consciousness we all share and from which we all come. Therefore, he called on every free person to "speak your latent conviction and it shall be the universal sense."

Walt Whitman read Emerson and was inspired to believe that his heart's truth was indeed this universal truth, that when he said "I" he was both "Walt Whitman, a kosmos," and "of Manhattan the son." He was a specific individual in the material world, but his voice was also a voice that came from the infinite. As such, he was beyond the moral law, beyond even the Victorian era's horror at anything sexual, much less his flaunted homosexuality. He was part and parcel of the universal mind and thus beyond good and evil. A baby in the cradle, two teenagers in the bushes, a suicide lying dead on the floor, were equally innocent in his eyes.

The Sixties have been called neo-transcendental because in many ways the ideology of the era was an echo of the Transcendentalism of Emerson and Whitman's day. Martin Luther King, a Baptist minister, opened the door a crack when he stood up in the name of righteousness against the laws that defended segregation. He was willing to proclaim in the name of God that these laws were immoral. How did he know? He felt it in his heart. But he denied that he was an antinomian. He was after all, a Baptist, in the historic tradition of his namesake, Martin Luther. He spoke from within a historic tradition tied to the morality of the Bible and his Protestant faith. He may have been outside the circle of American law, but he was still well within the circle of Western cultural beliefs. Calvin had once before opened that door a crack, and the result was the Puritan peopling of America. Now through that same door streamed a generation of baby boomers who did not identify with the Baptist tradition, who in fact identified with no tradition, who had no grounding, and thus were truly antinomian and entirely on their own. Norman O. Brown's call to suspend rational common sense and follow the consciousness of the body spoke to these rebels. Timothy Leary and Baba Ram Dass and the psychedelic experience heightened the sense of being outside the normal realms of consciousness and in touch with higher truths. The radicals of SDS attacked American capitalism and militarism and racism and imagined themselves capable of superior insight into the political problems of humankind. Even the grunts in Vietnam stepped outside the combine and gave themselves over almost completely to the wilderness outside the civilized laws they had been brought up to respect.

Into all this, Charles Manson emerged in 1967 and soaked up the ideas then prevalent and articulated them with a voice that commanded attention. One of his followers, Clem, tried to explain that he wasn't brainwashed by Manson but impressed by him: "The words that would come from Manson's mouth would not come from inside him, [they] would come from what I call the Infinite."

Just like Walt Whitman, Manson believes that his "I" was more than the limited ego of one particular small-time hoodlum. When he says "I," he means the same thing that Whitman meant when he began his "Song of Myself" with "I celebrate myself, and sing myself." The initial reaction of most people reading this is, "What a conceited, egocentric ass!" But further reading reveals that his celebration is not of Walt Whitman, "of Manhattan the son," but Walt Whitman, spokesman for the "kosmos." When Walt Whitman the particular human opened his throat, the voice that spoke came from the infinite. His was the "latent conviction" that Emerson proclaimed would be "the universal sense," a voice inside each and every one of us. This voice is presumed to exist not in rational consciousness but in the subconscious, below the petty games we play. Whitman is no dualist, no finite sinful human out of touch with truth. He is a pure romantic, a monist, convinced that what he feels in his heart is one with the falling rain, the blowing clover, the rising sun.

You hear this same conceit in much of Manson's rhetoric and behavior. Where does your music come from, he is asked? His response is to stand up, say "It comes from this," and go into a dance of flinging arms and swinging legs, a whirling dervish of energy. His spirit, he is saying, is the basic spirit from which all life emanates. He taps into that spirit. "I respect the will of God, son," he says to Geraldo Rivera.

"What will is that?"

"The will of God." And then he goes into his dance again, humming and chanting along with it. "Whatever you want to call it. Call it Jesus. Call it Mohammed. Call it Nuclear Mind. Call it Blow the World Up. Call it your heart. Call it whatever you want to call it. It's still music to me. It's there. It's the will of life."

That this will is also his will is implicit in what follows: "They crowd me in," he tells Rivera, "and I've got this little space. I live in the desert. I live in the mountains, man. I'm big. My mind is big, but everyone's trying to crowd me down and push me down and make me something they need me to be. But that's not me."

Manson calls himself Jesus Christ, but, like Emerson, he also says that every man is Jesus Christ. Every man has the original energy within him. "I am everything, man," he says, and he means it. But he does not bother to explain whether the "I" of his discourse is the person, Charles Manson, or the Universal eye that is the will of God. Thus he tells Rivera, "If I could kill about fifty million of you, I might save my trees and my air and my water and my wildlife."

Taking him literally, and hoping for a good soundbite, Rivera responds, "You're going to kill fifty million people?"

Manson's answer is instructive. It shows both what he is trying to say and his inability to communicate it. "I didn't say I would kill anything," he protests. "I'm reaping the head in thought. I'm Jesus Christ whether you want to accept it or not . . . I'm reaping it in thought. It's a thought, a thought." Obviously frustrated, he jabs his fingers at his head to emphasize his point. "Do you see what I'm saying? In other words, the whole world is a thought, and I am in the thought of Peace-on-Earth."

The point is not simply that Manson is speaking metaphorically. He is doing that, but he is also saying that everything is a metaphor, that our very lives, our bodies, our surroundings, are metaphor; that we live in an illusion if we think this material reality is real. Like Emerson and Edwards, he is a philosophical idealist. He believes that what is ultimately real is not matter but consciousness. This whole thing we call reality, or the universe, is an illusion, a dream. What we call God is the dreamer. And our bodies are no more real than are the strange beings that flit through our dreams at night. The whole world is a thought, and each person's perceptions are but a series of thoughts within the framework of the larger thought. As Manson once put it, "Everyone's playing a different game with the thought." All of the many perceptions of this existence are but dreams within a larger dream. This is where Manson is coming from when he says to the court and the straight world, "I don't live in your dream." This is why he says, "You've got my body in a cell . . . but I'm walking in forever, man." In his jail cell he is freer, he claims, to wander among the mountains than if he were struggling to survive in the day-to-day realities of the outside world. To believe that this physical world is the ultimate reality is to be trapped in the illusion. To be aware of the cosmic mind is to be liberated from the illusion.

That is where all the emphasis on life as game-playing becomes important. It is not a question of being brainwashed by the capitalists' game, as the Marxists imagine, but of being brainwashed by any game, capitalist, Marxist, Buddhist, scientific, you name it. All of rational human consciousness is a walking dream from which people need to be awakened. We are each, as Kesey kept saying, trapped in a movie. And the first thing we need is to realize it so that we might try to break out of the movie or, perhaps, enjoy it more fully, more consciously, more completely and honestly.

The key to this notion is the same as the key to most poetry; it is the idea of symbolic consciousness. To realize, as Emerson said, that "we are symbols and we inhabit symbols," is to take the first step out of the common-sense perception of reality and into a transcendent consciousness. Here, Manson sounds eerily like Norman O. Brown, whom he may never have read. But Brown's words were abroad in the Sixties; Manson could have picked them up anywhere. *Rolling Stone*'s article on Manson, written in 1969 and reprinted in *Mindfuckers,* puts quotes by Brown and Manson back to back. "Words are symbols," Manson told *Rolling Stone,* "All I'm doing is jumbling the symbols in your brain. Everything is symbolic. Symbols are just connections in your brain. Even your body is a symbol." In *Love's Body,* Brown writes, "The body is not to be understood literally. Everything is symbolic, everything including the human body." And elsewhere in the book he writes, "To make in ourselves a new consciousness, an erotic sense of reality, is to become conscious of symbolism. Symbolism is mind making connections (correspondences) rather than distinctions (separations)."

Manson saw the world as a symbolic manifestation, not a literal reality. It is an illusion, a mask, and the things within this illusion point beyond themselves to some transcendent presence. Everything from Scripture to sex is a symbolic message from the divine trying to tell us something. We are surrounded by messages we cannot read and locked into game-playing roles we do not understand, all at the mercy of some cosmic game-player.

When Starbuck protests that Moby-Dick is just a whale, Captain Ahab responds, "All visible objects, man, are but as pasteboard masks. But in each event—in the living act, the undoubted deed—there, some unknown but still reasoning thing puts forth the moldings of its features from behind the unreasoning mask. If man will strike, strike through the mask! How can the prisoner reach outside except by thrusting through that wall?" Ahab, awakened to the fact of his being an actor in a greater movie not under his control, cannot enjoy the part, and so determines to make his role that of the rebel who resists his assigned part, a rebellious role he realizes he was fated to play from the beginning of time. It is a paradox.

The Calvinists believed that we are all trapped in predetermined roles over which we have no control; but following Calvin, they imagined a way out. They imagined that if they could crucify their human selves, they might get in touch with the divine. They imagined that a few, a very few, had the fate to escape the cage, and they imagined that they could identify these elect few. This idea of the elect, dead to their old selves and born again to the divine self, expanded in America until it included almost anyone who wanted to belong. In this democratization of spiritual election, we came to imagine the entire nation to be God's nation and we created worldly structures based on that conceit. Yet the original conception remained alive beneath the sham.

So in America we continue to have periods of awakening in which people realize that they have been playing parts that are not divine, that are in fact stupid and gross and evil. They awake from their sleep and determine to break away from the old world with its corruptions and begin anew, to recreate the garden of Eden in a new world. They imagine that their reborn consciousness is the mind of God; and if that is so, it empowers them beyond any imagination.

Throughout the Sixties, this same message was repeated again and again. We are all playing games. We are all stuck in a movie. We are all conditioned to believe in things that are not true. We are all socially constructed, not essential, not in control, but an essential reality, a Zion, does exist outside these texts. Some would replace the old conditioning with new conditioning, a better jail with a kinder jailer. The true children of the Sixties, however, unlike the Marxists in SDS, did not embrace some new Egypt but kept on sojourning toward the Promised Land outside the cages, outside any jail.

This is who Manson said he was, a Christ, the person who had broken through, who was free. Like Randle P.McMurphy, another sort of Christ, he had never been under the control of the combine. In jail, where they did not bother to educate or socialize him, he ironically remained free of all the institutions by which the state brainwashes its other children. He received, as did McMurphy, another kind of conditioning, for sure. But it was different, so he came out different and knew it. He knew it was all a sham, and he believed this insight set him apart, put him on a higher plane.

Rationality, he said, is a false god. It is part of the game-playing of the world. The whole rational logical structure of the world is false, and the people who play its games without realizing it are fools. So he had little respect for the law, for the courts, for the lawyers, for any representative of the establishment. His attack on the law had its parallel in *Love's Body* when Brown quotes Theodor Reik: "The enormous importance attached by criminal justice to the deed as such derives from a cultural phase which is approaching its end." He then adds, "A social order based on the reality principle, a social order which draws the distinction between the wish and the deed, between the criminal and the righteous, is still the kingdom of darkness." The interconnectedness of all things in the realm behind the veil means that everything is dependent upon all, that there is no individual consciousness, hence no individual freedom, and therefore no individual responsibility. To be, as romantics imagine, in the divine consciousness, to participate in the godhead, is to be as Manson said, "inside of you. I'm inside every one of you. It's beyond good and evil."

To be romantic is to imagine that one exists in a realm of perfect Oneness in the garden, not in the fallen world of alienation, duality, and separateness. The Fall, original sin, dualism, and all that belong to the orthodox and neo-orthodox, the over-30s who think themselves still in Egypt or the wilderness, not at ease in Zion in the Promised Land. At its core, the consciousness of the counterculture, so evident at Woodstock, was a belief that we had somehow passed over into the garden and set our souls free, that we had left the fallen world of dualism and sin and passed into a new dispensation in which dualism had been overcome. It is perhaps the highest vision of the oldest American dream, its most powerful inducement, but also its most dangerous delusion.

Emerson's remarkable poem "Brahma" brings this all together— traditional American romanticism, Eastern mysticism, and the transcendence of binaries like good and evil, life and death, killer and killed:

> If the red slayer thinks he slays,
> Or if the slain think he is slain,
> They do not know the subtle ways
> I keep, and pass, and turn again.
>
> Far or forgot to me is near;
> Shadow and sunlight are the same;
> The vanished gods to me appear;
> And one to me are shame and fame.
>
> They reckon ill who leave me out;
> When me they fly, I am the wings;
> I am the doubter and the doubt,
> And I the hymn the Brahmin sings.
>
> The strong gods pine for my abode,
> And pine in vain the sacred seven;
> But thou, meek lover of the good!
> Find me, and turn thy back on heaven.

To find that one mind behind the dualities of life, to find that cosmic center, that essence that Baba Ram Dass also thought he found, is to find a place beyond good and evil. Hence, even heaven is part of a binary. To believe in it is to reveal one's attachment still to the world with its binary consciousness. Manson believed he had found that one mind, tripping away on acid, and hence he had turned his back on all of the false constructs of the language of the world, all of the artificially constructed binaries, including "heaven."

Manson's message then to the hippies he picked up along the road was one they were ready to hear, that the rational world they had dropped out of was false and that new possibilities existed once they broke free of that mindset. "People only love each other in books," he said. "You can't love each other in reality because you're all trapped in books, locked up in wars. You are all locked up in the second world war. . . . I'm trying to unlock that war." As the war raged in Vietnam, with the generals and politicians all projecting Hitler's invasion of Poland onto Ho Chi Minh's push into South Vietnam, this made sense. With segregation still rampant in the South, racism a curse throughout the nation, the cities burning in yearly riots, leaders assassinated, nuclear Armageddon threatened, the need to break away from the old games and enter a new dispensation seemed clear.

Manson's songs are perhaps the best example of this message. "Look at your game girl," the song that Axl Rose made infamous, is Manson trying to convince a young girl that it is all "a mad delusion / living in that confusion / Frustration and doubt / Can you ever live without your game?" So everything she is, is a game, and she needs to realize: "You can tell those lies baby, but you're only fooling you." Every adolescent, every human being, has doubts that reach far into the soul. In the Sixties, a whole generation going through an intense identity crisis faced doubts about the game we had all been taught. Manson's message was not unique, but communicated one-on-one to young, uneducated dropouts, it came across as cosmically original.

One other Manson song, "Ego is a too much thing," also brings down to a basic level a complex idea that was very much part of the mindset of the era. They have placed rationality, your reason, Blake's Urizen, in control, and shoved all the love into the back: "And they call it your subconscious." The computer up front demands to be in control; it demands to be accepted as you. It "makes you want to jump on a band and fight / And you can't stand not to be right." It makes you "afraid you are gonna act like a clown / And you get mad when somebody puts you down." The answer to the problem of ego being a "too much thing" is to lose your ego: "Your certainty turns to doubt / And then you start flipping out / And then you ease on out of your mind."

To lose one's ego is to lose one's common-sense view of the world, to leave rationality behind. Included in all that is whatever social construct one was brought up to believe, be it Mormon Republicanism or Jewish liberalism or Roman Catholicism or scientific atheism. It does not matter. Each and every worldview, conservative or radical, is just another worldview, just another discourse, another game. This anti-rationality therefore lends itself very easily to relativism, to the idea that all belief systems are equally valid, or invalid, but equally whatever value systems are. They are all "just games." Or as Manson once succinctly summed up the spirit of relativism, "Shit's like sugar to flies."

And the games all take place in an illusion in which even the concept of time plays a role. It is part of Manson's whole conception that the normal cause-and-effect relationships in which we all believe, including time, are themselves part of the illusion, part of the fallen world, not the Godhead from which it springs. There is only, he keeps saying, an eternal NOW. In this, he is saying nothing that mystics haven't said since the beginning of time. But in his mouth, the idea has important legal implications. If there is no time, there is no cause and effect; if there is no cause and effect, whatever he might have said was in a separate sphere from whatever his followers might have done. The circumstantial cause-and-effect connections that Bugliosi carefully put together have no meaning. "The idea," said Leslie Van Houghton in a recent cellblock interview, "was to let time disappear. There was no time." Asked by Diane Sawyer what he expected would happen after he told the girls, "You know what to do," Manson answered, "I don't live in anticipation, woman. I live in now."

As a capstone, there is the theory of language. "The Fall is into language," said Brown, and Manson echoed that idea, too. He blamed his conviction on the way the prosecutors "had to use catchy little words to make it into a reality, like 'hippie cult leader.'" In such ways, the illusions with which we live in the world are created and sustained by language. Language is the instrument of the illusion, of the Fall. Said Manson,

> That's what Jesus Christ taught us: words kill. They've filled every living thing with death. His disciples betrayed him by writing it down. Once it was written, it was as dead as a tombstone. . . . They killed him with every word in the New Testament. Every word is another nail in the cross, another betrayal disguised as love. Every word is soaked with his blood. He said, "Go, do thou likewise." He didn't say write it down. The whole fucking system is built on those words—the church, the government, war, the whole death trip. The original sin was to write it down.

If the Fall is into language, as Norman O. Brown had proclaimed, then words are the evil of the world. Words are the tools of deception and control, the way in which the illusion is maintained. They must be used carefully, if at all. Or they must be discredited to liberate people from the illusion that words actually "mean" anything. What, after all, does it even mean to "mean?" It's all just words trying to fool us into believing we know not what. There is no presence in the text.

The way, finally, to escape from the illusion was to surrender the letter and to accept some larger vision. This could be achieved by breaking the hold of language, the letter, which keeps us chained to the illusion of the rational. Once one realizes that words are just sounds and then passes beyond the illusion of inherent meaning or presence in the text, escape becomes possible. In the "Bug Letter," written from his cell, Manson provided an example of this process:

> To write I must slow my mind down. I'm not human in my ways of thought and I don't want to be programmed by schools of thought what man is or what man is not, woman, etc. "Nature" has a balance. I want it like a hunger. I learn a universe in a look, in a flash. I could slow down and spell the word over and over until it hangs in my thought pattern and holds little bits and pieces of power. I try to clear all patterns out of my mind to where I can become a tree or woods, a mountain, a world, a universe. Sparks in my mind become the only pattern I crave.

The pattern here for Manson is one that had been part of the Protestant background for centuries, a death-and-rebirth sequence; it was to be born again. He himself often told the story of his own death-and-rebirth experience in the desert. He even used the scriptural language to define it. About the kids on his ranch, he said, "I turned 'em loose. They became free in their minds. We started a rebirth movement, a rebirth in Jesus Christ. It's a Holy War really." But so ignorant was he of the larger historical framework and its wider influence over so much of American culture that he once charged Jimmy Carter and the religious right with stealing his idea, as if he had thought it up first.

This explains his fixation with death and the need to die. This is the meaning of the song "Cease to Exist" that he wrote for Dennis Wilson and the Beach Boys, which they put out as a mere seduction song, "Cease to Resist." But as so often throughout the history of Christian hermeneutics, the question of literal and metaphorical readings is constantly a problem. To have stated clearly a distinction between the two would have been to embrace another duality. As Emerson said in "Brahma," "Shadow and sunlight are the same." So Manson talked death to his followers, some of whom never did understand that there was even a question of whether he meant literal or spiritual death.

Yet literal death is important as a way of talking about spiritual death. They really cannot be divided. The death of Jesus of Nazareth, the incarnate human on the cross, is a necessary symbol of the spiritual death of the soul that is conversion. We humans love ourselves, our bodies, our existence. We don't want to die. So this fear of death becomes an image or shadow of the greater fear of spiritual death, of eternal death—Said Jonathan Edwards, "To die and know it! This is it. This is the black widow, death." Fear and paranoia thus become a part of the package. When the old Adam starts to die, he panics, trying to hold onto the old consciousness as it disintegrates in his mind, leaving him exposed and naked. When the old certainties disintegrate, anything suddenly becomes possible, absolutely anything. Images of the Devil, of hell, of aliens farming humans for consumption on their home world, you name it. The Beatles's message, then, to "let go and surrender to the void. It is not dying" was a push into a terrifying experience.

To realize that one is only playing a game, and then to watch oneself playing that game, and then to watch oneself watching oneself playing that game, is a terrifying fade back into the infinite upon infinite layers of consciousness until one's mind is, as Jonathan Edwards said, "swallowed up in God." Thus all the emphasis on exposing game-playing that one reads throughout the Sixties finally culminates here. We have all been programmed by the combine. We need to realize that we are programmed, that we don't know why we believe what we believe or do what we do, and we need to escape from those illusions. This is true liberation from all of the games that have been laid down for thousands of years of civilized history.

Growing up in prison, Manson had experienced a different reality, a different world entirely from that on the outside. In prison, little tolerance is shown for the pretensions that so often mark personalities in the outside world. There, each individual is forced back on his or her own final line of defenses, reduced, like the soldiers in Vietnam, to an elemental struggle for survival that has no patience for the petty games that people play. "In the pen you learn this," Manson told one interviewer. "Don't lie. I stand on my own. Not many people in your world can do that. I didn't realize this at that particular time. I didn't realize how weak and mindless you people really are." When he got out, Manson simply did not comprehend that people on the outside really believe their own movies. He had no idea that people actually took their own games seriously. This may partially explain why he allowed the game to get out of hand. At a rare moment in his 1986 parole hearing, when asked if he felt any responsibility for the murders, Manson responded, "Sure, I influenced a lot of people unbeknownst to my own understanding of it. I didn't understand the fears of people outside. I didn't understand the insecurities of people outside. I didn't understand people outside. And a lot of things I said and did affected a lot of people in a lot of different directions. It wasn't intentional. It wasn't with malice aforethought." But a few seconds later, when asked if he also felt remorse, which presumes guilt, Manson sat for a long time in silence before saying, in resignation, "We reach an impasse here, man."

One of Manson's proudest boasts is that he always spoke what he called the "truth": "I walk a real road. I am a real person. I'm not a phony. I don't put on no airs. I say what I think." What he meant by this is that he does not lie, that he insists on telling it as he believes it. In the parole hearing, he knew what the parole officers wanted to hear. He could have lied; he probably could even have lied successfully. He didn't. Asked what he might do if he was let out, would a hustling con have told the parole board, "I'll cheat. I'll steal. I'll do whatever I have to do to survive, and that's a reality"? But even in simple questions, when pressed for a yes or a no, whether he had a family still waiting for him on the outside, he answered, "I can't explain it to you, man. It doesn't have a yes or no." All he has is what is in his mind. For him to give that up, to lie, would be to surrender the void back to the world, which is what society wants. Instead, he says to the court, "I showed you some strength. I haven't surrendered to this by copping out to yours or telling tales or playing weak. . . . You've done everything you can to me, and I'm still here."

This is part of the voice from the Infinite that his follower Clem was drawn to. It was a large part of Manson's appeal for kids trying to escape from a sham suburban world of lies wrapped around lies wrapped around lies. "Manson is the only person I ever met who just tells you the truth and doesn't even understand someone having bad feelings about it," said Gypsy. "It's hard to live with a person who tells the truth all the time. Why? Because lots of time we don't want to hear the truth. Manson knows the truth because he knows nothing; he knows the power of an empty head."

But the ultimate irony is that in knowing the power of an empty head and how to use it, Manson also knew the destructive force of a whole civilization of empty heads all playing mindless games. He preached death to liberate his followers from the games of the old culture, games that were leading to wars, famine, oppression, the destruction of the planet. But the death of the old game-playing ego was only a prelude to the rebirth of the new spirit. Manson wasn't just a tree-shaker; he was also a jelly-maker. Not just another deconstructionist proclaiming the void in all things, he saw the possibility of creating a new essential narrative. And it is in his horrifyingly honest articulation of his solution to humanity's dilemma that he fulfills Joan Didion's darkest paranoid fear, that out of this army of lost children would arise some fascist leader appealing to the cosmic mind inside everyone for which he was the self-appointed spokesman.

"Whoever is going to put order into the world," Manson tried to explain to Geraldo Rivera, "has to stumble across Hitler." Order is the answer to disorder. If the planet is to be saved from the rapacious destruction of human civilization, then, according to Manson, someone needs to "put order into the world." Manson even for a while set up his own organization, ATWA, with its own webpage (www.atwa.com) for this purpose. ATWA stands for Air, Trees, Water, Animals—the life that will be saved when he reorganizes our helter-skelter madness. Asked to explain the swastika he has cut into his forehead, Manson said, "How do you have Peace on Earth? How do you communicate to a whole group of people? You stand up and take the worst fear symbol there is and say, there, now I've got your fear. And your fear is your power and your power is your control. I'm your king of this whole planet. I'm gonna rule this world through ATWA. I want this world cleaned up." But the swastika is more than a symbol of fear. It is also a symbol of Hitler's particular attempt to put order into the world, an order that included each race staying within its own circle. Manson is definitely both anti-Semitic and racist, to say nothing of sexist. He freely admits it. His idea of order is in fact more like that of the pre-war generations with which he identifies than that of the flower children of the Sixties. The older generation had experienced the horror of the Depression and the world war and wanted security. So did Manson. His ideas of social and political order were very old-fashioned. He also admitted that he preferred the music of Frank Sinatra to the mayhem of rock 'n' roll or even the Beatles. He wanted to overcome the chaos around him and restore a sense of order.

Manson once warned his parole board, "If I'm not paroled, and I don't get a chance to get back on top of this dream, you're gonna lose all your money, your farms aren't going to be able to produce. You're gonna win Helter Skelter. You're gonna win your reality." Whether this "I" refers to Manson the man or the universal "I" locked within each of us in the subconsciousness is, as usual, not at all clear. And it makes a difference. But in either case, Helter Skelter is the confusion of a world gone crazy and in need of order. "This dream" is the consciousness of mainstream society that is leading humanity into chaos and suicide. According to Manson, the liberation of the voice of the unconscious collective mind to organize all the individual unconscious minds into one big consciousness can change the dream in such a way as to prevent mankind from destroying the planet.

When Manson argued that his consciousness came from a deeper place "beyond good and evil," he at least conjured up, in the minds of more learned people, a historic parallel. Nietzsche, who used that phrase in a famous book, was also the product of a romantic movement, the culmination of nineteenth-century German mysticism. He was also the son of a Calvinist father. His theory of the Superman who existed outside the merely artificially constructed codes of bourgeois culture inspired the Nazis. Like Nietzsche, Manson saw that the codes of society are artificial, contingent, socially constructed, and thus unworthy of respect. Like Nietzsche, he believed himself capable of freeing himself from them and living on a higher plane. He saw the void, but rather than surrender to it, he believed he had what it took to fill the emptiness with a new and better structure.

Joan Didion was right. At the end of the antinomian Summer of Love, a rough beast was slouching toward Bethlehem, as her book and Yeats had described it. A potential Hitler was organizing his small but faithful army. More importantly, if it hadn't been Manson, it would have been someone else. All of those ideas were out there waiting to be brought together and applied. Romanticism, as Paglia warns, ends in decadence that leads to Fascism. The Sixties themselves, though they began on a note of triumphant liberation, ended up liberating too much too soon. Like the peasants at Muenster in 1535, the counterculture went too far, too fast, not just ahead of society but ahead of itself.

In light of all this, for reporters to harp on the literal facts of "who did what when" during the murders often seems as absurd as showing "Reefer Madness" to high school kids to keep them from smoking pot. Once again, the adults haven't a clue. Until they address Manson's issues, they won't have any credibility either. Someone needs to address these questions in language that people understand. Otherwise, kids will turn to the Mansons among us for their answers. "A lot of the kids," says Manson, "never met anybody who told them the truth. They never had anybody who was truthful to them. You know, they never had anybody that wouldn't lie or snake or play old fake games. So all I did was I was honest with a bunch of kids." That is a powerful indictment of our society.

However appalled one must be by the literal reality of Manson, it is almost impossible not to also take him on the level of symbolic consciousness. "They don't want to ever let me go," he explains, "because they feel secure as long as they've got me locked up in that cell. They feel like, yeah, they've got THE MAN locked up right there in a box." Perhaps this is only literal; or perhaps Manson has taken over the role in society that black people used to play, the symbol of the terrors of the subconscious. We need to keep our rational consciousness safe from the chaos on the other side. So we lock up the subconscious under what Freud called the censor. And through the power of symbolic consciousness, we imagine that by segregating black people, or locking Charlie Manson in a cell, we have the irrational forces of the subconscious under our rational control. We try to keep the conditioning going. We try to make the combine run more smoothly by adjusting everyone's programming so that everyone will think and behave as they should. And yet the secondary meanings are always there. The literal continues to point to the symbolic for anyone able to read between the lines of the text. Even when—perhaps especially when—it is least intended, the ironic meanings bring us up short.

At his last parole hearing, Manson was of course rejected. The parole board went through a long explanation why and listed a series of problems. The final problem, number five, reads like a line from Ken Kesey's *Cuckoo's Nest:* "The prisoner has not completed the necessary programming which is essential to his adjustment and needs additional time to gain such programming."

To which Manson has the final, chilling word, "Can't you see I'm out, man? Can't you see I'm out? Can't you see I'm free?"

7

Jason—Sham—too

I

To say, as historicism does, that all our efforts to grapple mentally with the world are shaped by a frame of reference, and that we do not have any rational basis for choosing between frames of reference, is to suggest that reason is indeed enslaved by (or at least confined within) the particular social and historical context in which it finds itself. And if that is the case, it is difficult to see how rights and the other insights proclaimed by reason can be anything more than mutable social conventions. They evidently cannot be natural or possess any other sort of ultimate foundation. They become, at best, merely agreed upon fictions and their value; if any, becomes merely instrumental, open to negotiation, subject to change.

—Thomas Haskell,
Objectivity is not Neutrality

ROMANTICISM, SO CAMILLE PAGLIA HAS ARGUED, LEADS INEVITABLY TO decadence and anarchy, which invite tyranny to "put order back into the world." Each of the stops on this cycle may well be, in its own way, a truth, a different part of the elephant. But postmodernism's greatest crime, especially from the point of view of the Sixties, is not its exposure of the void in all things but its inability to empower. If there is no presence in any construct or words, there is no place left to stand from which to move the earth.

The Sixties began with a modernist and politically liberal belief in the ability of the head, that symbol of rational self-control, to understand and to know and to act correctly. But reason proved itself to be little more than rationalization. As Franklin had said, "So wonderful a thing it is to be a rational creature because a rational creature can find a reason for anything he has a mind to do." Thus, like the romantics of the nineteenth century, the children of the Sixties rejected the head for a faith in the irrational heart. Rationalism, which had been the tool of the generation that fought the Depression and World War II, was replaced by a romanticism that instead trusted the irrational. For the counterculture hippies and their assorted fellow travelers, Nature became the new

God, and human nature in particular came to be seen, not as some monstrous id to be kept locked up in the subconscious, but as the very spirit of life itself, longing to be free. After centuries of tucking it in, the children of the baby boom decided to let it all hang out, to let the id out of its cage. The liberation of the id would be, said Brown, the resurrection of the body. Essentialism ruled as baby boomers challenged the old absolutes in the name of an epistemology of the heart.

But nature proved to be as elusive as reason; the garden became a swamp and then a jungle. Human culture for centuries had gone back and forth between trusting the head or trusting the heart, from classical to romantic and back again. But the lesson at the end of the Sixties was that neither the head nor the heart can provide the answer. Just as with the economy, the experts cannot organize from above and get it right using their heads, but to let the invisible hand of nature have its sway is as bad, if not worse. "Hell of a life," as Scanlon said in *Cuckoo's Nest.* "Damned if you do and damned if you don't. Puts a man in one confounded bind I'd say."

The cruelest irony of all is that baby boomer George W. Bush's trust in his own gut, a trust that led us into the Iraq War, may be the last gasp of the Sixties romantic legacy, the final evidence that Emersonian self-reliance has its limits. As Tom Ricks said in *Fiasco,* his account of how we blundered into that war, "The first Bush had been shaped by World War II. The second Bush was a product of the 1960s, at times more in sync with the attitudes of sixties radical Jerry Rubin than with those of Winston Churchill." Beyond that embarrassment, all that remained of Sixties essentialism was the constant reminder by an ascendant feminism that arguments from nature, "Biology is destiny" and "Birds of a feather flock together," had been the bulwarks of sexism and racism. McMurphy was, to be sure, a sexist and racist pig. As the Sixties ended in chaos and disillusionment, the romantic liberation of the id came to appear, as that rioter said in the Days of Rage, "all fucking crazy."

With the head discredited and the heart a traitor, we had left only the idea that we are shams, that both head and heart offer only illusions, and that what we or our parents once thought to be sacred truths were nothing more than self-serving narratives. Julie Stephens makes this point in her *Anti-Disciplinary Protest: Sixties Radicalism and Postmodernism.* The radicals of the late Sixties, she says, went beyond essentialism, abandoned any faith that a knowable reality is achievable, and instead "came to the conviction that reality was in essence mythical, amounting to nothing more and nothing less than a series of mediated images." It is all a sham. We, who were once so sure of our righteousness, discovered that "we" is a fabrication, that nothing is as it seems, that we are entrapped in texts we cannot see out of, much less escape from. And, say the deconstructionists, there is nothing outside these texts, no nature outside the combine to find answers in. By the end of the decade, the faith that there is an essential alternative to the sham of social construction was overpowered by a cynical postmodernism that knew that the letter killeth, but had no spirit that giveth life.

Thus did the academic world in the decades after the Sixties embrace a paradoxically rational attack on both the head and the heart. In 1966, a French academic named Jacques Derrida gave a lecture titled "Structure, Sign, and Play in the Discourse of the Human Sciences." Soon thereafter, he published three books, *Writing and Difference, Speech and Phenomena,* and *Of Grammatology.* Although slow to catch on, eventually these led to what came to be called postmodernism, not any one specific philosophy but an umbrella under which many of the intellectual barn-burners could huddle. If nothing else, postmodernist ideas are all antifoundational: they challenge the idea that any foundation exists for any ideas, even their own. They reveal the emptiness, not just in the old words, but in the new ones too, in all words, all beliefs—no presence in any texts.

Postmodernism deems it necessary to "deconstruct" the ruling paradigm, with its rigid male sense of literal material reality. The best way to do this is to demonstrate how all claims to some absolute knowing or Truth are in fact not absolute but socially constructed. If what we claim to know is not grounded in some absolute, essential reality, but is grounded in contingent circumstances, then any claim to absolute Truth is contingent upon the specific circumstances of the perceiver of that Truth. In this case, it is not absolute at all. It is conditional. Thus, all such claims to knowing truth by the old Enlightenment standards of reason and science are discredited. But so is any appeal to nature or intuition. All truth becomes relative, and the foundations of the old Egypt crumble.

This is on one hand liberating. With the traditional discourses discredited, no longer can an authoritarian patriarchal voice look down upon the Anne Hutchinsons of the world and say, "You are wrong." Previously discredited voices can now come to the fore and make their claims, however different, however radical, however strange according to the old rules. No longer can a claim to Truth through access to Scripture or "science" be used to justify slavery, or to keep women subordinate, or to condemn homosexual lifestyles. As the old absolutism disintegrated, freedom would flourish and the previously marginalized groups of society would be empowered.

The heart of Derrida's argument lies in his denial of presence in language. Words have no essential meaning other than that which comes from the context. Taken apart, language reveals not essential meaning but constructions that serve the interests of power. The binary opposites of language, white/black, good/bad, up/down, are artificial constructs, as are all phrases and words. Derrida teases out the meaninglessness of language with a style that is at once playful and impenetrable. Since there is no place to stand, one is forever slipping and sliding around in the text.

The roots of this thinking can be found even in the most essentialist of the writings of the Sixties. The world, as Norman O. Brown said, is the veil we spin to hide the void. In 1965 Brown said he wanted to get the nothingness back into words: "The aim is words with nothing to them; words that point beyond themselves, rather than to themselves; transparencies, empty words, corresponding to the void in things."

In this, Brown foreshadowed postmodern theory. So, in his own way of exposing the void in all things, did Manson. But Brown at least believed that the crucifixion of the ego would be followed by the resurrection of the body, that there is an essential force in the universe that we do have access to in the depths of the self. The postmodernists echoed his exposure of the hollowness of the world without also echoing any possibility of salvation.

The Merovingian, one of the villains of the '90s cult film series *The Matrix,* perfectly epitomizes this type: snooty, arrogant, aristocratic, and French. He understands full well, as he says, that everything is but "contrivances for the sake of appearances." He tells our heroes that "there is only one real truth in the universe, causality," what some today call contingency. When Morpheus, the American romantic, the classic "Magic Negro" who shows the confused white man the way, denies that we are trapped in causality, arguing that everything begins with choice, the Merovingian responds, "Wrong. Choice ees an eellusion created between those weeth power and those weethout. You think you know why you are here. But you do not. You were sent here, and you obeyed." Neo and Morpheus think they are making self-willed choices. They fail to realize how every choice is contingent upon some previous link in the chain of causality. So the arrogant, aristocratic Merovingian proceeds to show them how he can use his power to manipulate people for his own amusement. The belief in contingency is itself self-serving. Tenured professors wring their hands at the unfair contingencies of the world that gave them easy jobs for life at the state's expense. But if the system includes the oppression of adjuncts, well, we are all caught up in the contingencies of life. As the Merovingian explains: "Causality—There is no escape from it. We are forever slaves to it. Our only hope, our only peace is to understand it, to understand why. This is what separates us from them." We cannot, he is saying, escape the text. Instead we must accept it and learn how to manipulate it to our advantage.

II

*And of course it is true that power and wealth within the prison
should be equitably redistributed. But it should be noted that what
is crucial to your survival as a race is not the redistribution of power
and wealth within the prison but rather the destruction of the prison
itself.*

—Ishmael

Once having torn all presence out of the language, postmodernists
have a slippery time trying to find some footing of their own. Zygmunt
Bauman, in a widely reprinted essay on this topic, acknowledges that
causality has undermined all claims to certainty, leaving us with little
more than the circular confession that "choices cannot be disputed by
reference to anything more solid and binding than preference and the
determination to stick to the preferred. The preference for one's own,
communally shared form of life must therefore be immune to the temptation of cultural crusade. Emancipation means acceptance of one's own
contingency as is grounded in recognition of contingency as the suffi-
cient reason to live and to be allowed to live." Thus, McMurphy's freedom to be his own original, essential self, sexist and racist and arrogant
though he is, becomes the ultimate in emancipation. We are each as our
tribal identities shaped us, never more, never less. This is the cage we
cannot escape from: we are who we are, boxed into what Dylan called
"life in the same old cage."

But such group identity, or tribalism, is not the only alternative. One
can also give one's will over to an individual, an inspired leader who
seems to speak with a voice that comes from the Infinite. Deconstruction tears down the old temple where the false gods are worshipped. If
one's original tribal identity is deconstructed, what then? Deconstruction provides no way to find new gods or build new temples to them. It
creates a vacuum, and into that vacuum something must be drawn by
the sheer human need to know and to be. "Something will have the
heart of man," said Jonathan Edwards. "It is impossible it should be
otherwise. And that which a man gives his heart to may be called his
God."

This is not simply the problem that any madman might rise to fill the
void. This is the story of a particular answer to the ancient dilemma.
What is so chilling about it is the dramatic similarity between what Manson had to say and what the deconstructionists today are saying. The
ideas are almost indistinguishable. He too saw the emptiness in all
words and playfully teased all meaningfulness out of them. Then he
stepped into that void and offered himself as Fuhrer.

This, then, from the perspective of the Sixties, is the worst aspect of postmodernism. The means of deconstruction cannot in fact empower. They are the means of discrediting, but they are a universal acid discrediting everything. If everything is socially constructed, that includes even the voices of the previously marginalized. As Richard Rorty says, "The ironist should not be blamed for humiliating but for failing to empower." This ironist position is one that sees the contingent nature of everything, that denies that any one of us has access to any essential reality. This philosophy that discredits as it deconstructs the old patriarchy also applies to the new voices. They too are socially constructed. They are certainly no less valid than the previously dominant voices, but neither are they any more valid. They too are shams and exposed as such. What we are left with is a wilderness of deconstructed voices, an empty waste of lies and illusions. Jason—Sham—too.

If truly essential, a faith stance, or some tribal allegiance, might well be grounded in the universe and be transcendentally true. But if it is merely another contingent human choice, then its contingent ties are more than likely to be expressions of self and self-interest. We love ourselves and love to see ourselves mirrored, even our collective selves. Hence, the result of such a privileging, or faith stance, may well be not a choice based on tradition or logic or aesthetics but on group identity. Thus African-Americans who despise *Huckleberry Finn* for its use of the word "nigger" are accorded a privileged position over those white males who make elaborately rationalizations for continuing to teach the offensive book. Women who would privilege the literary productions of their eighteenth-century sisters over those of the previously privileged white males can now do so. Once any claims to knowing universal truth are discredited, what we have left, as a result, is not objective criteria but group privileging. Such tribalism is at best a momentary winning of recognition, a hollow victory, a castle built on sand. It is the surrender of one's own illegitimate constructed self for someone else's. But it is an acceptance of an admittedly phony constructed position within the world.

This is all the postmodernists have to offer, in the end. They do not believe that such a thing as a universal truth exists, but only the endless collisions of dead atomic matter. To them, it is all a sham, and beyond the sham is nothing but endless void. We must, they say, make the best of the sham. We must equalize, sanitize, and make the best of our cages.

But whatever it is that the philosophers try to establish through reason alone, the historical record suggests that a philosophy or a theology like neo-orthodoxy or postmodernism that stresses absence and denies presence can never empower. To stand up against the powers of the world requires a belief in presence, a belief that one has some power that touches the absolute. For Ken Kesey and the rebels of the Sixties, that power was tied to the idea of nature. So even if the deconstruction-ists are right, and nature is only another social construct, the belief that it exists and is more than just another construct may well be a "foma" (in Vonnegut's term a harmless untruth) without which we cannot proceed.

Before he can awaken from the fog and escape from Nurse Ratched's cage, Chief Bromden has to return to his identity as an Indian with its connection to the land. He stands at the window of the hospital and stares outside, realizing "for the first time that the hospital is out in the country." Up to that point, the point of his awakening, he was so disori-ented and in the fog that he did not even realize the physical location of the building in which he was imprisoned. As he looks out the window, he becomes oriented not just to the geographical land but also to the reality that the land represents, to nature as an essential ground of being from which life can be lived. The dog in the moonlight running around sniffing, rolling, happy just to be alive and to be a dog in the moonlight, is the natural being, just being itself, even if sexist, racist, warts and all. "If dogs run free," sang Bob Dylan, "then why can't we / Across the universe of time?" McMurphy may have been an old-fashioned sexist and even a racist; he may have been a throwback to some discredited vision of independent individualism like that of a nineteenth-century cowboy or robber baron. But he was able freely to be who he was, to be his natural self.

What other choice is there? If there is no essential, known personality or revealed truth, we have the choice only of our phony socially and evolutionarily constructed selves, enslavement to somebody else's phony construct, or the terror of the void. Between those extremes are merely different degrees of neuroticism, of fear and anxiety and doubt and desperate attempts to be who we would be according to some ideo-logical constructs we cannot ultimately justify. The irony is that only with a rejection of this socially constructed model of consciousness, and a turn to romantic essentialism, can true change occur.

For Martin Luther King, it was of first importance that African Americans be freed from what he called the "psychology of servitude." And he knew that this could only be done by shaking off the idea that we are all trapped in our conditioned roles and that there is no essential reality we can turn to. Instead, he argued, we need to feel a part of the creative, essential force that created and runs the universe: "Human progress never rolls on wheels of inevitability but comes through the tireless efforts of men willing to be co-workers with God." Traditional Christian religion was an important part of the civil rights movement; it could not have succeeded without it. True or not, the sense of being at one with God was empowering, just as it had been for Martin Luther back at the time of the Reformation.

6. Jippo the Bear. Even cute Bearzie Wearsies strive to escape the cage. Courtesy of Robert Crumb.

The peasants of Luther's day had suffered from the same profound marginalizing that outcast groups have always felt. They were considered as, and hence thought of themselves as, less than human. Not until Luther introduced the idea that God speaks not through the head but through the heart, not down through the hierarchy but up from the bottom of society, not through reason but through subjective experience, could these people begin to believe that the reality that created and sustains us was available to them too. Not until they were provided with an ideological rationalization that empowered their essential feelings could they begin to emerge from the fog of their oppression. Their sense of empowerment fueled the social wars of the next three centuries, from the Thirty Years' War in Europe, to the English civil wars, to the Europeanizing of North America, to the American Revolution, to our Civil War, to the mercantile and then the industrial revolution. In each of these social revolutions, outcast groups, newly empowered by a sense of presence, found the spirit to stand up against the powers of the world.

Even the Russian Revolution, though it claimed to be atheist, found power in the Marxist belief that the revolution of the proletariat was inevitable. Theirs was not some Sartrean existentialism creating meaning out of nothing. No, they believed in a God they called History. And they firmly believed that they were on the side of history, that ultimately they would win because History was marching inevitably in the direction of world communism. Their God was marching on! Their revolution, like Luther's, was then grounded in a belief in an essential truth, and History was the presence that gave them the courage to fight.

Belief in essence, in presence, however "wrong" theoretically or philosophically or theologically, is thus a necessity for any revolution, however small. Irony cannot empower; only essentialism can. Deconstruction can tear down the old castles, but it cannot build new ones. It can tear down the temple, but it cannot be the basis for a new religion.

The Sixties were an essentialist, Romantic rebellion against the neo-orthodox Fifties, which had emphasized contingency and powerlessness. From Martin Luther King's, traditional appeal to the God of the Protestant tradition, to Norman O. Brown's call to let go of the reality principle and have faith in the possibility of the resurrection of the body, to acid's promise of the revelation of the final I behind the i, the Sixties were fueled by a Romantic faith in presence. This faith gave the rebels a place to stand from which they could then attack the established power. It gave them the faith to leave the comforts of Egypt and boldly go into the wilderness in search of the Promised Land.

III

There is no life in thee, now, except that rocking life imparted by a gently rolling ship; by her, borrowed from the sea; by the sea, from the inscrutable tides of God. But while this sleep, this dream is on ye, move your foot or hand an inch; slip your hold at all; and your identity comes back in horror. Over Descartian vortices you hover. And perhaps, at mid-day, in the fairest weather, with one half-throttled shriek you drop through that transparent air into the summer sea, no more to rise for ever. Heed it well, ye Pantheists!
—Melville, *Moby-Dick*

What September 11, 2001, added was the shock of the real, the cold reminder that to drift too far into relativism and subjective theory is to lose touch with the literal. We may not know or be able to find any reality outside our texts, but somehow Reality has a way of finding us and reducing us once again to "Sinners in the Hands of an Angry God." Manson would say we had won our Helter Skelter. The terror of September 11 can be thought of as the scraping of the keel along some rocks, warning the captain that he had sailed too far off course. Even worse the scraping reminds the passengers and crew that their deconstruction of the captain has had consequences, that no matter how corrupt or illegitimate he may be, we do need someone, or something, some construct, at the helm. Perhaps the neo-orthodox cynics like Didion and Vonnegut were right? Perhaps a false construction, Vonnegut's "foma," is better than none at all? For if the captain is also a sham, then what is left? If even the I at the helm cannot be trusted, then what is left of the voyage? Perhaps we should have stayed in Egypt? Perhaps Cypher was right to return to the Matrix? Perhaps Kesey's puppy should have stayed in its kennel? If there is nothing but wilderness outside of structure, what use has terror but to keep us safely encaged?

From the perspective of more recent critical terminology, the experience encompassed by what once was called the Fear of God is the deconstruction of what Louis Althusser calls ideology. It is the destruction of the entire structure of belief in order to force a return to the primordial experience, to the basis on which all ideology and spirituality began, a return not to some internal sense of presence but to a terrifying experience of absence. What Martin Heidegger called "those primordial experiences in which we achieved our first ways of determining the nature of Being" were experiences not of some essential absolute within the soul; they were experiences of the void. This was not a plural but a singular experience, and only an elect few were destined to face it. The Calvinists called it the Fear of God. Barth called it the "NO" of God's word against man. It was the awakening from mythological conditioning. To find oneself in the bondage of Egypt was to find oneself bound within the web of someone else's ideological mythmaking, the meaning of which was a mystery. What followed this awakening was the flight from Egypt into the wilderness. This was at first an act of faith and hope, but it became a terrifying descent into the void between myths, the black unknowing of demythologized terror. If myths and ideologies and doxa are a lie, then this terror was the Truth. To confront this terror was to face the fear of God. Only out of this experience, went the story, could a new mythos be born and the Promised Land be entered. This confrontation with terror was that primordial experience out of which belief was originally and could be again created: "In the fear of God is the beginning of Wisdom." Michael Herr put it nicely: "A lot of things had to be unlearned before you could learn anything at all."

Thomas Hooker, one of the earliest of the American preachers of hellfire, tried to write of this experience but found himself restricted by the language then available to him. We have for this "no word in our English tongue," he said, "but only a shiverednesse of soule all to pieces." For him, the call to the wilderness, to the crucifixion, was thus also a call to madness, to a sojourn beyond the borders of rational structure and control, to a wilderness of danger made tempting by the mystical promise. The first European Americans were called into this very wilderness in the hope of attaining mystic vision and passing from the corruption of the Old World into the kingdom of liberty.

Terror has its uses, as it did in Puritan preaching. One does have to step back from the corruption and lies of culture when those become too much to bear. But in stepping back from that sham, one eventually comes to the edge of the cliff. When the literal reveals itself a sham, when rationality and common sense are discredited, a dreamlike theory of image and association replaces them. Questions replace answers. Doubt replaces certainty. Everything is "problematized." Meaning is unpeeled, and every problem gets looked at from a score of different possible perspectives. When anything thus becomes possible, then anything can happen, and one steps off the roof of the once so proud and solid world into the void. Then, as Melville warned, "your identity comes back in horror."

To be forced out into that cold sea would be a de-centering of the mind, a destruction of cultural belief, a murder of the father and the fathers, the crashing of our cultural towers. Worse, because our very perception is tied to the web of language and culture, the destruction of that web would destroy perception itself. The world would no longer appear as it does. The walls would melt and the stars rush through us. Edwards noted that a baby reaches out for the moon not yet knowing that the moon is far away, in space, beyond reach. Our sense of the moon and stars as things out there is part of what we are taught through culture. It is not natural, or organic, or essentially true, but socially constructed. Jefferson was an innocent essentialist: nothing is truly "self-evident," as his own holding of other people not as equals but as slaves well proves. We have been conditioned to accept the world as taught, that walls are walls, dogs are dogs, cats are cats, stars are stars, the moon is an object out there, and the World Trade Center cannot fall. But despite the self-evident appearance, the sun does not rise; the earth revolves so that we face it. From birth, all of our training has been to help us function within the context of the particular culture or combine into which we were born. Without it we would be lost. We would go mad.

Much of traditional literature and criticism reinforces the established constructs of culture, but the best literature has always questioned inherited constructs and exposed those visions that hump us through the night. In this spirit, literary criticism today likes to atomize, to deconstruct a text down to the meaninglessness of the sounds we call words. This is done as part of an effort to undermine traditional patterns of meaning, to challenge the social structures of class, race, and gender that are so deeply embedded in our texts and in our minds. If the texts

society respects can be stripped of their fig leaves, then the social structure itself will be left naked and exposed.

Deconstruction is thus a necessary reaction to the lies that classical
culture imposed upon readers and upon society. Today's deconstructionists supply the guns for the defense of liberty in the fight against
structure. They help us break out of the prisons of others' generalities
and categories. Men cannot speak for women, or whites for blacks, or
Christians for Jews, or politicians for any of us. But each of us must try
to tear ourselves free of the old arminian webs and stand free, if only
for a moment. Each of us needs to stand alone to experience Melville's
"mortally intolerable truth; that all deep, earnest thinking is but the intrepid effort of the soul to keep the open independence of her sea; while
the wildest winds of heaven and earth conspire to cast her on the treacherous, slavish shore."

In an interview in the *Paris Review,* Kesey explained that what he
explored in all his work was "wilderness." There is, he said, "something
we are afraid of, but it doesn't have the clear delineation of the terror
the Hurons [a fierce Indian tribe] gave us or the hydrogen bomb in the
cold war. It's fuzzy, and it's fuzzy because the people who are in control
don't want you to draw a bead on the real danger, the real terror in the
country."

What is this terror? asks the interviewer.

It is "a big hollow, the great American wild hollow, that is scarier than
hell, scarier than purgatory or Satan, that empty place inside us all.
That's the wilderness that I've always wanted to explore, and it's connected to the idea of freedom, but it is a terrifying freedom." Derrida
was wrong: there is something outside the text, the terror of the void, a
terror that our ancestors once believed was the means of our transformation. To quote Scripture: "In the Fear of the Lord is the beginning
of wisdom." To quote Melville: "Up from the spray of thy ocean perish-
ing—straight up, leaps thy apotheosis!"

But the alternative to the traditional cultural cages within which we
live may be worse than the cages themselves. Liberation from the security of the cage may result in madness or death. At the very least, when
we reject the established ideology that has sustained us and has been
the medium of our identity, we need to face the lesson of the Sixties that
when we enter psychic freedom, there may await us not some Garden of
Eden but anarchy. Below our structures of meaning, however false
those structures are, may be an abyss. Egypt is the typological symbol
in Scripture of the false structures of the world; but the alternative to
Egypt was the wilderness. The alternative to the idolatry of our socially
constructed selves may also be nothing—no vision, no ideology, no
dogma, no Golden Fleece—only the void. The immediate alternative to

structure may be madness. The self, even the righteous, revolutionary self, may be even at its deepest core a sham. The return to nature may be a sojourn not into a garden but into a howling wilderness. The wolves there may not be the overgrown puppies on the yuppie T-shirts but dangerous red-eyed killers after all.

So the conservative urge to cling to tradition has within it more than a shred of wisdom. The visions that hump us through the night arose for reasons, and the fact that they keep us humping (even if they keep humping us) suggests that they not be rejected lightly; as Scripture warns, "Where there is no vision, the people perish." We reject the wisdom of social evolution at our peril, though question it we must. We need our cages.

But this is no reason to surrender to what Zygmunt Bauman called "our own contingency." We need to free ourselves from as much of the web of cultural structure as we can, if only to see it for a brief moment for what it is. The dilemma is that we cannot live without it. We need a cultural context, an intellectual structure of belief, as much as we need a political and economic structure, as much as we need the web of electric power lines and roads, as much as we need our bodies. To step outside into the wilderness beyond these structures is to step into the void. So the structures that we need in order to live end up controlling us, and we become their slaves without even knowing it. The struggle of consciousness to free itself is the struggle to return to the void at all costs, at least for a moment, to fight back against the power and resist the controls. It is the mad Dionysian impulse that calls us into the wilderness. We must leave Egypt and risk destruction if we are ever to be free. This is the real American Dream.

When in *Cuckoo's Nest* McMurphy makes his last desperate attack on Nurse Ratched, ripping off her starched jacket and revealing her true nature underneath, he opens up for a moment a sight of the truth underneath the constructs. When he throws a party on the ward and brings in booze and girls, the acutes experience the possibility of freedom, of a wild unstructured moment outside the laws, even within the very heart of the combine. For a moment, the poor oppressed acutes can stop trying to be what society wants them to be and can behave according to their original conditioning. They can escape to the deeper layers of personal and cultural conditioning; they can freely be them"*selves.*" That such moments of happy, unconscious freedom cannot last, that the dog will be hit by the car on the highway, is a given. But the point is that the moment of freedom is worth the price. "The thing he was fighting," says the Chief, "you couldn't whip it for good. All you could do was keep on whipping it, till you couldn't come out any more and somebody else had to take your place." In the end of the book, we see the Chief, having killed McMurphy's mindless body, escaping though the window and heading back to his tribal village, to relive his original life in order to "get my mind clear." He is also "heading out in the direction that the dog went." Perhaps the Chief, too, will be hit by the moving machine and crushed by the combine. But he, like the dog, like McMurphy, like the other freed inmates, will have had his moment of freedom.

By his sacrificial death, McMurphy did his Christic duty by pointing to the possibility of a higher state of freedom beyond the structures of the combines that ensnare and encage us all. He didn't stay behind to make the ward a nicer place to live, to improve living conditions within the cage. Instead, with his death, he pointed out the possibility of an escape from Egypt. To escape to freedom, one must first step back from the collective delusion to one's own original personal delusion, to one's own individual contingency, and then step back from that out of the text entirely and break on through to the other side.

Centuries ago, many of our ancestors left the Old World for America because they were no longer willing to accept the arbitrary structures of manmade religions that offered ritual in lieu of reality. Those early Protestants rejected the Mass and all the rich ornamentation of the Catholic Church in the belief that such human constructions offered a false substitute and thus kept people from searching out the real thing. The wafer of the old Catholic Mass, they said, was not the true body of Christ but only a symbol. To accept it as the true presence would be to accept "seemings." They wanted not the pretense offered by ritual and works, not some politically correct hypocrisy, but real love. They came to America, not for material wealth alone, but in search of truth. They came with the faith, naïve though it may have been, that we do not have to accept socially constructed lies but can, facing Truth alone in the wilderness, be ravished by a spirit which is ultimately true, ultimately sincere, and from the heart of the universe. To do this, we need to break out of the cage of lies and illusion and stand alone for a moment in the clear dawn. "Be it life or death" said Thoreau, "we crave only reality."

The great danger was the temptation created by that "old deluder," the Devil, to accept some pleasant substitute, some "seemings," and to fall once again for illusion as Cypher did. This is the reason for opposition to the social constructionists' insistence on the priority of political responsibility for improving living conditions in the cage. To make the illusion more just, more fair, more comfortable for all, may even seduce us into forgetting that this is an illusion, into mistaking this pleasant oasis for the true Kingdom of Freedom. This is why Huck lights out for the wilderness in the end.

Not all who believed that they had sipped of this wine fell for the delusion. Not all who felt they had tasted this grace then tried, like John

Brown or Charlie Manson, to put God's order into the world. There
were those who recognized that their experience had been temporary,
that back in the world and the flesh they still could not trust themselves.
These were the truer saints, the ones of humble heart who remembered
the glimpse of Zion, knew that they no longer had it, and wept.

IV

> *Broken, shattered like an empty cup*
> *And I'm just waiting on the Lord*
> *To rebuild and fill me up.*

—Bob Dylan

To listen to Bob Dylan's 1997 Album *Time out of Mind* is to catch
once again the echoes of Emily Dickinson's apocalyptic expectations of
the return of divine vision to an empty soul once ravished, then left be-
reft, the bride at the altar praying for the return of the bridegroom. On
this echo, we hear too the repeated pattern of American poetry pulsating in waves from the 1600s to the 1860s to Dylan's own signature era
of the 1960s and our own millennial age. For the lost love to which both
these poets pour out their hearts is only symbolically another person. As
it did in the Old Testament, as it did in Puritan poetry, as it often has in
great American literature, the human other stands in for a transcendent
reality, for a truth outside the texts of human culture.

In William Faulkner's "Bear," when McCaslin quotes from "Ode on
a Grecian Urn" the line "Forever wilt thou love and she be fair," Ike
says to him, "He's talking about a girl." McCaslin snaps back, "He had
to talk about something. He was talking about truth. Truth is one, it
doesn't change. It covers all things which touch the heart—honor and
pride and justice and pity and courage and love. Do you see now?" The
point is, as Faulkner says, that humans can "comprehend truth only
through the complexity of passion and lust and hate and fear which
drives the heart."

Even the old Puritans wrote love songs that on the surface were thoroughly sensual, but they were clearly addressed not just to the human
form. In 1685 the New England Puritan minister Edward Taylor wrote
a poem based on *Canticles* 7.3: "Thy two breasts are like two young roes
that are twins." The final stanza goes:

> Lord put these nipples then my mouth into
> And suckle me therewith I humbly pray,
> Then with this milk, they Spiritual babe I'st grow,
> And these two milk pails shall themselves display
> Like to these pretty twins in pairs round neat
> And shall sing forth thy praise over this meat.

Taylor also wrote the first American poem about Christ's heavenly coach that carries the saints all bound for glory. With these and other poems, he confirmed an enduring American tradition in which the poet breaks out of the literal, corrupt, worldly Egypt and dares a long hard trip across the wilderness in the hope of reaching on the other side the Promised Land of transcendent vision. Rock 'n' roll was born out of gospel and the blues, and the most powerful aspect of this music, rock critic Greil Marcus tells us, "did not come from Africa but from the Puritan revival of the Great Awakening, the revival that spread across the American colonies more than 200 years ago. It was an explosion of dread and piety that southern whites passed onto their slaves and that blacks ultimately fashioned into their own religion." It is this tradition that both Dylan and Dickinson use to understand their spiritual experience.

Both Emily Dickinson and Bob Dylan suffered a similar breaking out of the cage of conditioned consciousness to stand for a moment outside of the text, outside of the cause-and-effect relationships of time, to be awakened from the walking sleep of normal consciousness to experience the light of what Dickinson called Eternity. But both lost that vision; the moment passed, leaving them back in the literal world ravished but abandoned, damaged goods unable to return to Egypt but unable to forget their glimpse of the Promised Land. Left alone with an unbearable longing for the return of that vision, both were forced to put back on the human masks with which we all lie our way through the world. "I did not know the wine came once a world," asked Dickinson. "Did you?"

For we who read and listen to their poetry, it is what they made of the "hours of lead," that "quartz contentment," the long ordeal in the spiritual wilderness, that is important. Both of these Americans reacted with the same fierce need to give voice to their longing and their loss—walking, as Dylan sang, "through streets that are dead." And to that, we owe the power of their poetry.

Dickinson's and Dylan's understanding of their similar experiences was shaped by a peculiarly Protestant reading of the Christian Scripture that had been reinforced and that spread in the colonial awakening. Whatever the experience actually was, however interpreted and through whatever analytical tradition, both of these poets chose to interpret their experience in those traditionally American biblical terms. "I had," said Dylan, "a born-again experience. If you want to call it that. It's an overused term, but it's something people can relate to." Both poets also returned to the Song of Solomon, to the love songs of the Old Testament, in which the longing for the divine other is typologically figured as a longing for a lost human love. We read it in Solomon, we read it in the love poetry of that seventeenth-century Puritan mystic Edward Taylor, we read it again in Emily Dickinson; and now Bob Dylan has joined this holy train.

Unfortunately, we have also seen repeated the consternation of critics who do not understand the symbolic consciousness that colors this tradition. Just as there are legions of critics trying to identify the man whom Emily Dickinson must have been writing to (this "Lord" she refers to must have been the judge Otis Lord, they babble), so we have critics who imagine that the lost love Dylan mourns in every cut on this album must be a human woman. Not that there cannot be a human person in either Dickinson's or Dylan's mind. When the real person, Otis Lord, asked for Emily Dickinson's hand in marriage, she rejected him with a clear statement showing her ability to distinguish the merely symbolic nature of human flesh: "You ask the crust but that would doom the bread." The human lover, if there is one, stands as a symbolic representation of the other-worldly experience, which cannot be voiced in its mystical fullness but must be expressed symbolically, dressed in human form. To actually marry a person to achieve this love would be to fall to idolatry and forget the vision of Zion that is truly God.

This is of course to argue that Dylan still lives and writes in the shadow of his 1978 conversion experience, when, he says, he was "broken, shattered like an empty cup / And I'm just waiting on the Lord / To rebuild and fill me up." That experience, whatever it was, had a profound effect upon him, giving him at least temporarily a whole new orientation and identity. Emily Dickinson also had a very specific moment of shattering. For her, the event occurred in 1861, and it blew her away. Much of her poetry refers to this mystical moment of both "madness" and ecstatic vision. It was a moment in which the old self, the old identity, was shattered and a vision suddenly made possible of that which exists outside of the limits of any finite self. In the middle of the 1800s, Dickinson's holy train bound for glory was, like Edward Taylor's, a horse-drawn carriage, and the moment of her revelation was "the Day / I first surmised the Horses' Heads / Were toward Eternity—".

This moment of revelation was a revelation both of the sham of the old self and the "glory" of eternity. It was at once both "vision and veto"; and much of her best poetry combines the images of destruction and revelation: "The wounded deer leaps highest." And she saw the metaphor of Christ on the Cross as the symbol of this combination of the death of the old ego and the resurrection of a new spiritual sense, the attainment of a higher consciousness, what she called a "costumeless consciousness," pure spirit liberated from its "corporeal friend." Of Christ on the Cross, Dickinson asked, "Did he know how conscious consciousness could grow?" Apparently the vision came in waves over a period of several days: "And then—a Day as huge /As Yesterdays in pairs / Unrolled its horror in my face— / Could it be Madness—this?" Her old identity crucified, she believed that she had caught in that moment what the majority call madness, if only like Moses in passing—a glimpse of the divine. This is why she wrote, "Much madness is divinest sense."

So Dylan in his "Time out of Mind" harkens back to a moment of both loss and vision, when, as he says in the first cut, "I spoke as a child / You destroyed me with a smile / While I was sleeping." Awakened from sleep, his old self destroyed, he has fallen into some vision of love. It is a love he wishes he could escape from, that he could be free from—but he cannot escape. "I'm sick of love," he sings, "but I'm in the thick of it. I'm trying to forget you; I'd give anything to be with you."

Emily Dickinson recorded her moment of disintegration as a "funeral in my brain" in which "a service like a drum / Kept beating—beating— till I thought / My Mind was going numb." The drumming in her brain accelerates until it reaches a crescendo and then breaks. After the break, she is spaced out in a kind of cosmic stillness: "As all the heavens were a Bell / And Being but an ear / And I and silence some strange race / Wrecked solitary here." In a similar vein, Dylan recalls, "Yesterday everything was going too fast / Today it's moving too slow." As a result, he "has nothing to go back to now." The line has a double reference, for there is nothing in the world to go back to, only the old sham. Once that has been exposed as an illusion, as a lie, as mere worldliness, nothing of it can ever satisfy again, not even human love. But neither is there any experience of holy vision to return to, for that, too, has withdrawn itself. So Dylan is left, as Dickinson was, like Moses in the wilderness praying to be allowed to enter the Promised Land. "It always seemed to me a wrong," wrote Dickinson, "to that old Moses done / To Let him see the Canaan / Without the entering." Both American poets know, in Dylan's words, that "the mercy of God must be near," but both find themselves "standing in the doorway crying" in what Dylan, using the classic biblical pun, calls "the dark land of the son."

But in no way can Dylan get the vision out of his mind or memory. In this, too, he is like Dickinson, who wrote:

> If I had not seen the sun
> I could have borne the shade,
> But light a newer wilderness,
> My wilderness has made.

Like Dickinson, Dylan has "been praying for some vision / Laying 'round a one-room country shack." But like Dickinson, he is weary of the wait and is growing "tired of talking, trying to explain." He has not yet spoken the dark desire that haunted the earlier poet, the self-destructive wish: "What if I say I shall not wait! / What if I burst the fleshly gate— /And pass escaped to thee!" But as the memory "grows dimmer," he does feel abandoned, "20 miles out of town—cold irons bound." Admitting "I don't know how much longer I can wait," he darkly warns, "It's not dark yet / But I'm getting there."

Nevertheless, for both poets the longing is made somewhat easier by what little still is left of the memory of the love that's been lost. Both seem to claim that, as the old Puritans preached, they are "in the world but not of it." Dickinson could claim that the moment of vision gave her at least a tiny taste of eternity, a glimpse of the reality outside false perceptions of the world. It was, she said, "my being's worth, a single dram of heaven." But that single dram, though it only came once a world, was better than never having seen a glimpse of what is outside the worldly cage. She did have her memory of her vision of Eternity, and at times that was more than enough; it was the promise of election sealed and delivered in that one painful, glorious white flash. It was, she wrote, "Mine—by the right of the white election. Mine long as ages steal." So Dylan ends up his album of longing with the claim, "My heart's in the highland." His body is stuck in the "same old rat race / Life in the same old cage," but his spirit is back there with his lost love. He is in the world with its illusion of flesh and dirt and its lies and deceptions and sham identities, but, he sings in the last two lines of the album, "I'm there in my mind / And that's good enough for now."

All of our ancestors left someplace else, whether voluntarily or dragged onto slave ships or stuffed into steerage. Our first American ancestors left old identities behind, and we have had to renew, generation after generation, that constant turning from the lies of old identity to the hope of a new and better vision. The pattern of American life, repeated in Dylan's own numerous transitions, has been the search for a new and better identity, only to find, eventually, even that new and better identity to be "as hollow as it seems" until the pattern repeats and a new break from the new identity, to find an even better newer one, repeats the cycle. And so we beat on across the wilderness with the vision of the Promised Land somewhere up ahead, over the rainbow, beyond the horizon, breaking out of the old cocoon, born again, decayed again, and reborn, from century to century in a long continuous march toward we don't yet know what.

Our poets sing of this our sojourn. And it is they who remind us as they remind themselves that we are searching not for some new worldly identity, not for a new politics, or economics, or a new gender, or any new worldly form, but for an identity that transcends all the forms of time and space and puts us in touch with Eternity. Many would be more comfortable if the form Dylan chose to express his experience were not so dogmatically Christian. But some such inevitable human forms, of whatever tradition, are part of what we have to overcome. The train we ride may be a "slow train coming," but it is coming; it is moving along its tracks, heading not for a literal worldly destination but for a "time out of mind."

V

"keep this fear alive in my heart"

The comparison of Dylan and Dickinson brings us full circle, back to the orthodoxy and neo-orthodoxy from which the Sixties first rebelled. With this, the cycle is completed, fulfilled, until it begins again.

That the very self at the core of the journey is a sham is thus not a new idea. The idea is as old as Solomon: "Vanity, vanity, all is vanity." The Reformation itself was fought over the debate between absence and presence in the text. The Catholics' claim that the wafer ingested during the Mass literally is the host is a claim to have the essential presence of Christ. The Protestants' denial of that presence symbolized a theology built around a sense of absence. As Calvin said, "All we can conceive concerning God in our own minds is an insipid fiction" because "man's understanding is pierced by a heavy spear when all the thoughts that proceed from him are mocked as stupid, frivolous, insane, and perverse." For these Protestants, knowledge of God was not knowledge of some benevolent presence but of a holy terror. The wafer is only a human symbol; we do not have the real thing. That is the terror of which Kesey spoke, the American terror, that neither the head nor the heart really knows, that we are on our own. As the old blues song has it, "Sometimes I feel like a motherless child, a long long way from my home."

The mind is torn between these two poles, structure and freedom, Egypt and Canaan. But neither of these, the head nor the heart, can be trusted. To believe the socially constructed narratives of society is to be enslaved to the given. It is to be trapped in institutional constructions like segregation that are morally repugnant. It is to accept a codification of the evils of the world. Yet to change the old narrative for a newer one is simply to create a better cage. To reject any cage altogether, and to follow the promptings of the spirit, is to risk death and destruction in the wilderness. This side of some second coming of some revealed truth, these are our only choices, the lies of structure or the terror of the void, Egypt or the wilderness. A conservative clinging to the ways of the past is as dangerous as a radical acceptance of the new and different just because it is new and different. And there is no safe place in the middle; we cannot sail straight up into the wind.

And so we tack back and forth, between the head and the heart, between a panic-stricken clinging to the past and a carefree libertine embrace of the spirit, between a neo-orthodox sense of absence and an essentialist faith in presence. This has been the pattern of American culture since the Reformation. In following this pattern, the Sixties were as American as apple pie.

But this metaphor of tacking back and forth implies some forward motion as well and not just an eternal swinging of the pendulum. Each antinomian moment, followed though it is by a return to structure, leaves us just a little bit more open, a little closer to the truth—which may yet prove itself either a terror or a joy. The heart of American culture, from the Children of Israel to the children of Europe and Asia and Africa, is the hope that in such an opening up, in such a change, a reality can be found, or at least approached. We have left Egypt behind. We may be in the wilderness. But the faith that keeps us going despite everything is the faith that somewhere across this desert, perhaps behind those far mountains, lies a true Promised Land.

We know we are trapped in consciousness. We know we are only playing games. The biggest danger is that we would make out of this fear of our own unknowing an idol that we would worship as if at least our fear of the truth were itself a truth we could embrace and build upon. It isn't. The Puritans were wrong to imagine that their understanding of the Fear of God made them a new Israel and their culture Zion. The nineteenth-century evangelicals were wrong to imagine that the revivals had created the Kingdom of God on Earth. The hippies and radicals of the Sixties were wrong to believe that their counterculture had any more basis than the old culture. And today's postmodernists are wrong to imagine that their nihilistic disparagement of the "meta-narratives" of culture gives them any insight about anything. Neither head nor heart can be trusted. We cannot return to the old structures, but neither do we have a clear alternative. We are in the wilderness between Egypt and Canaan. The human mind remains a factory of idols.

Instead, like the faithful seventeenth-century minister Jonathan Mitchell, who prayed to be undeceived by "seemings," we must remember to cry, "Lord, keep this fear alive in my heart." If we can resist the temptation to succumb to idolatry, we can then, as Scripture says, "stand fast in the liberty in which Christ hath made us free." By so doing, we can keep open the possibility, the true American dream, that this sham shall be replaced by the coming of a true Reality, a vision of

7. Mr. Natural's mysticism confronts Flakey Foot's rationalism. Courtesy of Robert Crumb.

that-which-is. Like Bob Dylan "shattered like an empty cup," we can "wait on the Lord" to rebuild and fill us up. We can hold wide the door to the cage that our ancestors fought open, look to the heavens, and perhaps, like Increase Mather awaiting the Millennium, cry "How long, O Lord, how long, how long, how long?"

Bibliographic Essay

IN KEEPING WITH THE PERSONAL VOICE OF THE BOOK AND THE SIXTIES spirit of Gonzo journalism, I chose not to encumber the text with a dense smattering of footnotes for every section. Instead I have chosen to include a bibliographical essay for each chapter indicating where the material and references came from. Many, however, came from my own experience and memory, and therefore cannot be justifiably footnoted. Others, such as the material on Manson, is largely contained on videotapes I own of his many interviews and not widely available. Anyone who insists upon more exact documentation of every line is a hopeless arminian and won't understand much of this book, or the spirit of the Sixties, anyway.

Some may object that the voice of this book is too subjective, too indebted to a particular discourse, a religious one at that. Such critics need to ask themselves if they have the same objections to books written from a Marxist or postmodernist or gender-grounded viewpoint, and if not, why not? The myth of academic objectivity has long since been discarded. If all discourses are equal, then no one discourse should be exclusively privileged as "more equal" than the others. The religious discourse at the heart of this text may be unfamiliar to many, but it is one of the many varieties of American discourse, indeed one of the oldest and most influential. For that reason, if for no other, it too deserves to be heard.

INTRODUCTION

I

The historical background upon which this section draws can be found in many places. My old advisor William McLoughlin's book *Revivals, Awakenings, and Reform* (University of Chicago Press, 1978) provides an historical outline of the Great Awakening paradigm as an

American phenomenon. David Hall's collection of documents titled *The Antinomian Controversy 1636–1638: A Documentary History* (Wesleyan University Press, 1968) is another important source. For Joseph Campbell's analysis of Darth Vader, see his interview with Bill Moyers, "The Hero's Adventure" (PBS 1968). Gordon Liddy's autobiography *Will* was published by St. Martin's Press, 1980. Cotton Mather's *Magnalia Christi Americana* (Hartford, CT, 1820) is the source of the quote from Jonathan Mitchell, the Puritan minister who dreaded "seemings." It is also (Book VII, Chapter IV) the source of the colorful quote by "Fisher the Quaker." Norman O. Brown's *Love's Body* (University of California Press, 1966) is one of the most important texts of the Sixties and is noted here for the first time. It should be read along with his earlier *Life against Death: A Psychoanalytic Reading of History* (Vintage, 1959). Civil Religion is a theme that has been developed and explored in such works as Catherine Albanese's *Sons of the Fathers* (Philadelphia: Temple University Press, 1974) and Russell Richey and Donald Jones, eds., *American Civil Religion* (Harper and Row, 1974). James Baldwin's essay on Mailer, "The Black Boy Looks at the White Boy," can be found in Esquire's *Smiling Through the Apocalypse* (McCalls, 1969). The quote from Mailer is from the last paragraph of his *Why Are we In Vietnam?* (Holt, Rinehart, Winston, New York, 1967). Joan Didion's essay "On Morality" was published in her essay collection on the Sixties, *Slouching Towards Bethlehem* (Farrar, Straus, Giroux, New York, 1968).

II

The epigraph is taken from John Winthrop's "A Short Story of the Rise, reign, and ruine of the Antinomians, familists, & Libertines" in David Hall's excellent documentary history *The Antinomian Controversy, 1636–1638* (Wesleyan University Press, 1968). The best and most readable book on Martin Luther is still Erik Erikson's *Young Man Luther: A Study in Psychoanalysis and History* (W.W. Norton, 1962). Sacvan Bercovitch's *The Puritan Origins of the American Self* (Yale University Press, 1977) provides a readable introduction to the arguments for Puritanism's impact on American culture then and now. Benjamin Schwartz's essay on "The Diversity Myth" in *The Atlantic Monthly* (May, 1995) contains a compelling defense of the unfortunate reality of WASP hegemony in U.S. history. A good recent study of the similarities between post-modernism and orthodox theology is *Derrida and Negative Theology* (SUNY Press, 1992) which includes an essay on the subject by Derrida himself. Calvin's *Institutes of the Christian Religion* (Westminster Press, 1960) is a crucial text. This famous quote is from his chapter on "Idolatry." Three books that helped shape my understanding of the medieval background are Peter Laslett's *The World we Have Lost* (Scribner's, 1971); *Vexed and Troubled Englishmen, 1590–1642* (Oxford University Press, 1976); and Michael Walzer's *The Revolution of the Saints: A study in the Origins of Radical Politics* (Harvard University Press, 1965). Arthur Lovejoy's *The Great Chain of Being* (Harvard University Press, 1964) has also been very helpful. The quotations concerning Luther and the Reformation are from Will Durant's history of the Reformation. For the peasant revolts and the events of Muenster, I relied upon Kyle Sessions' edited collection *Reformation and Authority: The Meaning of the Peasants' Revolt* (DC Heath, 1968) as well as upon George Williams's *The Radical Reformation* (Truman State University Press, 2000). John Winthrop's Arbella Sermon can be found in almost any anthology of American texts. This quotation is from the Old South Pamphlets edition. The quotes from Jonathan Edwards are from "The Divine and Supernatural Light" and from his "Personal Narrative" both of which can be found in the Yale edition of his works. The quotation from Charles Chauncy is from Perry Miller and Alan Heimert's collection of documents *The Great Awakening* (Bobbs-Merrill, 1967). Quotations from Ralph Waldo Emerson are from his "Self-Reliance" and "Nature," both widely available, as is Henry David Thoreau's "Civil Disobedience." Octavious B Frothingham's quote is from his *Transcendentalism in New England* (Putnam's, New York, 1876). The Emily Dickinson Poem is number 870 in Thomas Johnson's *The Complete Poems of Emily Dickinson*. My own *Wilderness Lost: The American Origins of the American Mind* (Susquehanna University Press, 1987) also includes a close reading of this material as well as a reading of Emily Dickinson's poetry in its original spiritual context.

The occasional quotes from Herman Melville are from *Moby Dick*.

1. FINDING IS THE FIRST ACT—

I

Most of this chapter is based on my reading of Ken Kesey's *One Flew Over the Cuckoo's Nest* (New American Library, 1962). Readers of that book must also read Tom Wolfe's book about Kesey *The Electric Acid Kool-Aid Test* (Bantam, 1969). No study of Kesey is complete with his interview in *Paris Review* (Spring 1994). I was aided by Scott McFarlane's *The Hippy Narrative* (McFarland & Co, 2007) which covers many more texts than mine does. For deconstruction, Jacques Derrida is the principal spokes person. Consider *Of Grammatology* (Johns Hopkins

University Press, 1998) as the basic text. But there are numerous somewhat more readable attempts to explain deconstruction available. *The Social Construction of Nature* by Claus Eder (Sage, 1996) is the book I had in mind here. A good introduction can be found in the anthology of articles titled A *Postmodern Reader* (SUNY Press, 1993) edited by Joseph Natoli and Linda Hutcheon. Wordsworth's poem "Tintern Abbey" is the source of the quote and can be found in any collection of his poetry. Emerson's acceptance of the possibility that he is the child of the Devil is a part of "Self-Reliance."

II

David Morine's *Good Dirt: Confessions of a Conservationist* (Ballantine, 1993) provided me with his quote and some good background on attitudes toward nature in the fifties. But Joan Didion is my favorite writer from that era. Her *Slouching Towards Bethlehem* (op. cit.) and *The White Album* (Simon and Schuster, 1979) are both collections of excellent essays that explain the neo-orthodox mindset from the inside. The Updike quote appeared in "Each Man Was an Island" *Newsweek,* Jan 3, 1994. For the Franklin story about the fish, check out his *Autobiography.* Neo-orthodoxy's leading theologian was Karl Barth. *The Epistle to the Romans* (Oxford University Press, 1933), *The word of God and the Word of man* (Hodder and Stoughton, 1928) are classics and well worth the effort to get into them. Williams Faulkner's "Bear" can be found along with "The Old People" in *Go Down Moses* (Vintage, 1990). Perhaps the best introduction to Perry Miller's work on the Puritans is his influential collection of short essays, *Errand into the Wilderness* (Harper and Row, 1964). The leading American neo-orthodox theologian was Reinhold Niebuhr, whose *Moral Man and Immoral Society* (Scribner's, 1932) and *The Nature and Destiny of Man* (Scribner's, 1964) were quite influential. His brother, H. Richard Niebuhr, who wrote *The Kingdom of God in America* (Harper's, 1959) is also an important historian of the movement. Two other of his works, *Christ and Culture* (Harper, 1956) and *Radical Monotheism and Western Culture* (Harper, 1960) are crucial texts of neo-orthodox thought. Stephen Vincent Benet's portrait of the Christian slaver is in his epic poem *John Brown's Body* (Rinehart, 1928).

III

Martin Luther King's own books are still the best source of his thought. *Stride Toward Freedom* (Harper and Row, 1964) chronicles the Montgomery Bus boycott. *Why We Can't Wait* (N.A.L., 1964) is the story of the Birmingham campaign and is oriented around his magnificent essay "Letter From A Birmingham Jail." Malcolm X's quote can be found in a collection of his speeches titled *Two Speeches by Malcolm X* published by Pioneer Press in 1964. *Black Activism: Racial Revolution in the U.S. 1954–11970,* by Robert Brisbane (Judson 1974) also provided some powerful material. The editorial in SNCC by the *New York Times* appeared on Aug 7, 1966, two days after they published an early version of Stokely Carmichael's position paper on Black Power and whites in the movement. For Richard Rorty, look in *Contingency, Irony, and Solidarity* (Cambridge University Press, 1989).

IV

For a history of the Folk Song revival of the early 60s, check out Ronald Cohen's *Rainbow Quest: The Folk Music Revival and American Society 1940–1970* (University of Massachusetts Press, 2002) or Dick Weissman's *Which Side Are You On?* (Continuum, 2006). The founding document of SNCC and SDS's "Port Huron Statement" can be found is *The Sixties Papers: Documents of a Rebellious Decade (Praeger, 1984).* The quotations from the Berkeley Free Speech movement were all taken from interviews recorded in "Berkeley in the Sixties," a videotape documentary produced by Kitchell Films, 1990. Jerry Rubin's *DO IT!* (Simon and Schuster, 1970) is the source for most of the Rubin material. Norman Mailer's "The White Negro" can be found in his latest collection of essays and stories *The Time of our Time* (Random House, 1998). I am deeply indebted to Todd Gitlin's *The Sixties: Years of Hope, Days of Rage* (Bantam, 1987) from which his comments about the Beats are taken, and Kirkpatrick Sale's political history of SDS, simply titled *SDS,* (Random House, 1973).

2. The Second, Loss

I

This chapter, while lengthy, relies heavily on a few important books, starting with Kesey's *Cuckoo's Nest* (N.A.L., 1962).

II

For the politics of the early Sixties, David Halberstam's *The Best and the Brightest* (Fawcett, 1972) was an important source. For Jonathan

Edwards' analysis of free will, see his famous *The Freedom of the Will* (Yale University Press, 1957) and my essay "Skinner, Edwards, and the Therapy of Conversion" in *Harvard Theological Review* 74:4 1981. Any standard history of the European Enlightenment will provide information on the contributions of Locke and Rousseau on the nature of human consciousness. William Bradford's sneer at the communitarians can be found in any edition of his *History of Plimouth Plantation* in the section titled "End of the Common Course and Condition." B.F. Skinner's most accessible work is his *About Behaviorism* (Vintage, 1976), but those who have not yet read it are urged to begin with his utopian novel *Walden II* (Macmillan, 1948). Emerson's poem "Grace" and Emily Dickinson's poem # 435 can be found in their collected works. The scatalogical quote from Martin Luther is from Erik Erikson's *Young Man Luther: A Study in Psychoanalysis and History* (Norton, 1962). Edwards' quote on the doctrine of Original Sin is from his text, *Original Sin* (Yale, 1957). On the subject of Schizophrenia, I used Thomas Szasz, *The Myth of Mental Illness* (Harper & Row, 1974). The DSM quote is from *Diagnostic and Statistic Manual* volume III.

III

The best book on the political history of the Vietnam war remains Stanley Karnow's *Vietnam* (Viking, 1983). Frederick Goodwin's article on the psychological significance of the Kennedy assassination, "How the Kennedy Killing Drove America Crazy," was published in the *Washington Post,* November 13, 1988. Henry Idema's *Before our Time* was published by the University Press of America (1996).

Most of the material on King, including his comment on JFK's assassination are from *Why We Can't Wait.* Baldwin's portrait of Norman Mailer is from "The Black Boy Looks at the White Boy." "My Dungeon Shook" and "Down at the Cross" are the two essays that comprise Baldwin's *The Fire Next Time* (Vintage, 1993). Robert Crumb's "White Man" originally appeared in Zap Comix. The quotations from Malcolm X are from *Two Speeches by Malcolm X,* a Socialist Labor Party pamphlet I bought for 25¢ in 1966. Stokely Carmichael's "SNCC Speaks for Itself" can be found, along with a goodly collection of primary Sixties material in the collection *The Sixties Papers: Documents of a Rebellious Decade* (Praeger, 1984). The quotes from the *New York Times* are from August 5 and August 7, 1966.

Phil Ochs "Talking Vietnam Blues" was recorded in 1964. Franz Fanon's *Wretched of the Earth* was published by Grove Press, 1963. Most of the material on McNamara is from Karnow's *Vietnam* and from Paul Hendrickson's *The living and the dead : Robert McNamara and five lives of a lost war* (Knopf, 1996). The quotation from Mickey Kraus is from an essay that appeared in *Newsweek* , September 5, 1988. Todd Gitlin's *The Sixties: Days of Rage, Years of Hope* (Bantam, 1987) remains one of the best histories of the decade.

IV

Mark Kitchell's informative video "Berkeley in the Sixties" was produced by First Run Features in 1990. Much of the material in this section can be found there.

V

Richard Alpert tells the story of his transformation in Baba Ram Dass in *Be Here Now* (The Lama Foundation, 1971). Other important sources for the history of the psychedelic movement are Timothy Leary's *High Priest* (New American Library, 1968) and Jay Stevens' *Storming Heaven: LSD and the American Dream* (Atlantic Monthly, 1987). Norman Mailer's *The Deer Park* was published by Putnams Sons, 1954.

3. Third, Expedition for the "Golden Fleece"

I

Much of the material for this chapter has already been noted, but I shall nevertheless repeat it here. Tom Wolfe's *Electric Kool-Aid Acid Test* is perhaps the most extensively used text. Several video recordings were also heavily relied up. These include the PBS series on the History of Rock'n Roll and the movie *Woodstock*. "Granfalloon" is a word popularized in Kurt Vonnegut's *Cat's Cradle* (Laurel, 1988). For the Newport Folk Festival of 1966, I used the PBS "Rock 'n Roll" video recording as well as my older brother Paul Williams' *Performing Artist: The Music of Bob Dylan* (Underwood, 1990). A recent history of this musical era, *Rainbow Quest,* was also helpful.

II

The Henry David Thoreau quotes are from *Walden,* the chapter entitled "Where I lived and what I lived for." Frank Zappa's definitions of "Freak" is from the liner notes of one of his albums.

III

Norman O. Brown's *Life against Death: The Psychoanalytic Meaning of History* (Vintage 1959), *Love's Body* (University of California Press, 1966), and *Apocalypse and/or Metamorphosis* (University of California Press, 1991) are must readings for anyone interested in the intellectual life of America in the twentieth century and its connection to our own religious past. His Phi Beta Kappa speech at Columbia is included in the latter. The importance of the Cuban Missile Crisis in the evolution of Brown's thinking was included in a private letter to the author. Freud's *Civilization and its Discontents* (W. W. Norton, 1961) remains an important text, as does Calvin's *Institutes of the Christian Religion* (Westminster, 1960) from which this famous quote is taken.

IV

Among the underground comics cited, Willy Murphy's "The Big Blow Out in the Do-Nut shop" is in *Flamed Out Funnies*, 1975. Most of Robert Crumb's 1960s comics can be found in his 16 volume *Complete Crumb Comics*, most notably for this book volume 4 "Mr Sixties" (Fantagraphic Books, 1989) which includes "Whiteman" and "Meatball." For his own comments on his work, consult his *Your Vigor for Life Appalls Me: Robert Crumb Letters 1958–1977* (Fantagraphic Books, 1998). The Quote from Kesey is in his interview in *The Realist*, first published 1971, May/June, number 90. Jerry Rubin's *Do it!* was cited earlier Joan Didion's portrait of Comrade Laski in her essay "Comrade Laski, C.P.U.S.A.-M.L." appears in *Slouching Towards Bethlehem* (Simon and Schuster, 1968).

V

The quote on Transcendentalism from Octavius Brooks Frothingham was from *Transcendentalism in New England* (1972) and cited in the author's *Wilderness Lost: The Religious Origins of the American Mind* (Susquehanna University Press, 1987).

VI

The best edition of the *I Ching*, with an introduction by Carl Jung is by Richard Wilhelm (Princeton University Press, 1967). Copies of *The Golden Guide to Hallucinogenic Plants* (Golden Books, 1975) can barely be found, but they can be found on the internet. A great loss to the

Sixties, to journalism, and to literature was the premature death of Don McNeil, whose essays for *The Village Voice* were collected and published under the title *Moving Through Here* (Citadel Press, 1990). His essay "What Died in San Francisco" chronicled the funeral of Hippy in San Francisco in 1967. Ray Mungo's several books can be read together in a collection titled *Mungobus* (Avon Books, 1979). Andrew Kopkind's Woodstock essay "Coming of Age in Aquarius" can be found in *Conversations with the New Reality,* edited by the editors of ramparts Magazine, 1971. Most academic books on religion in the 60s, like Mark Oppenheimer's *Knocking on Heaven's Door* (Yale University Press, 2003) and Robert Ellwood's *The Sixties Spiritual Awakening* (Rutgers University Press, 1994) concentrate on the institutional churches and thus were not very helpful for this analysis. But Wade Roof's *A Generation of Seekers: The Spiritual Journeys of the Baby Boom Generation* (Harper San Francisco, 1994) is an exception.

4. FOURTH—NO DISCOVERY

I

Much of the material of this chapter comes from Kirkpatrick Sale's exhaustive and apologetic history of Students for a Democratic Society simply titled *SDS* (Vintage, 1974). Other texts referenced include Ken Kesey's *Cuckoo's Nest,* Norman Mailer's "The White Negro," and Baldwin's pained response to Mailer, an essay titled "The black boy looks at the White Boy, " which can be found in his *Notes of a Native Son* (Beacon Press, 1984).

II

The essay protesting the treatment of women in SNCC "Women in the Movement" is reproduced in *The Sixties Papers: Documents of a Rebellious Decade* (Praeger, 1984). Taylor Branch's *Parting the Waters* (Simon and Schuster, 1988) and *Pillar of Fire: America in the King Years* (Simon and Schuster, 1998) are also important sources for the Civil Rights movement.

III

The material on the demise of the counter culture in California is largely from Yablonsky's *The Hippie Trip* (Pegasus, 1968) and Joan Didion's collection of essays on the sixties *Slouching Towards Bethlehem* (op. cit.). In addition, Tom Wolfe's *Electric Kool-Aid Acid Test* (op. cit.) is a primary if not altogether reliable text of this phase of the era.

IV

Howard Stern's essay "Altamont: Pearl Harbor to the Woodstock Nation" can be found in *Conversations with the New Reality* (Colophon Books, NY, 1971). The 1970 film *Gimme Shelter* distributed by Maysles Films Inc provides great primary documentation of Altamont. Richard Alpert's comments are from a series of interviews published under the title *LSD* in 1966 by New American Library (p. 26).

V

The material on Bubba Free John come from his own account of his sojourn, "Bubba Free John in India," published in his magazine *The Dawn Horse*, Middletown, Ca, in 1974, vol 1, #2. Also quoted are Kurt Vonnegut's *Cat's Cradle* (op. cit.), Cotton Mather's *Magnalia Christi Americana* (op. cit.) and Gary Snyder's poem "I Went into the Maverick Bar" which is in *Turtle Island* (New Directions Books, 1974).

VI

The Quote from Ralph Waldo Emerson can be found in "The Transcendentalist" published in 1842. And the note from Leary on his escape from prison appeared in *San Francisco Good Times,* September 18, 1970.

5. FIFTH—NO CREW

Rather than attempt what has already been well accomplished, a detailed history of the American involvement in the Vietnam War, I felt it best to concentrate on one representative text, Michael Herr's justly famous *Dispatches* (Knopf, 1977).

Other texts were called upon and used for material, however. Foremost among these were Stanley Karnow's *Vietnam: A History* (op. cit.), David Halberstam's *The Best and the Brightest* (Fawcett, 1972), and Robert Mason's *Chicken Hawk* (Viking, 1983).

The Melville poem is "The March into Virginia" found in *Battlepieces* and widely anthologized. The Quote from SNCC is from their position paper on Vietnam found in *The Sixties Papers: Documents of a Rebellious Decade* (op. cit.). Franz Fanon's *The Wretched of the Earth* (Grove Press, 1963) was an important source of America's introduction to viewpoints outside the combine, viewpoints which showed U.S. foreign policy in an altogether different light. The quotations from Bill Ehrhart as well as from Charles "Tex" Sabatier are from the PBS series *Vietnam: A Television History,* still one of the best presentations of both, or all, sides of the war from the mouths of the combatants themselves, both common soldiers on both sides as well as such luminaries as General Giap who commanded the North Vietnamese forces at both Dien Bien Phu and Khe Sanh. The quotation from General Ky is from *Life Magazine,* July 23, 1965, quoted by Mason in *Chicken Hawk.* Griel Marcus's *Mystery Train,* has little to do with Vietnam but is an excellent guide to the cultural origins of Rock 'n' Roll. For Samuel Sherwood's "The church's Flight into the Wilderness," see the author's *Revolutionary War Sermons* (Scholars Facsimiles and Reprints, 1981). Erik Erikson's *Young Man Luther* (Norton, 1958) and his article "Autobiographical Notes on the Identity Crisis," *Daedalus* 99 (Fall 1970) were useful. Richard Slotkin's *Regeneration Through Violence* was published by Wesleyan University Press in 1973. The quote from the young Al Gore condemning the cold war mentality of America was published in the *Washington Post* ("Gored by His Own Words," 11/21/94). He has regretted it but not denied that he wrote it. Jonathan Edwards "Sinners in the Hands of an Angry God" is the source of the Edwards quote. We've all been there.

6. Finally, no Golden Fleece—

Since Charles Manson has never himself published anything in his own right, the best sources of his words are the many interviews he has conducted since being sent to prison.

A book by Nuel Emmons titled *Manson: In His own Words* (Grove, 1986) is not in Manson's own words at all but in the words of a former cellmate who saw a way to profit off his brief encounter. Tex Watson's *Will You Die For Me?* (Revel, 1978), while full of informative information, needs to be read in the context of its author's attempt to evade his own responsibility. Vincent Bugliosi's *Helter Skelter* (Norton, 1974) remains the definitive text on the Manson trial, written by the prosecutor himself. It is full of information and reliable quotations. When Manson was still on trial, an interview with David Felton appeared in the June, 1970, *Rolling Stone* titled "Year of the Fork; Night of the Hunter." It was later published in a collection titled *The MindFuckers: The Rise of Acid Fascism in America* (Straight Arrow Books, 1972), to which I made a small introductory contribution. It is an excellent sourcebook. Also excellent is Ed Sanders, *The Family,* (EP Dutton, 1971). Edward George's *Taming the Beast: Charles Manson's Life Behind Bars* (St. Martin's, 1998) reveals its sensationalist bias in its title, but it does contain transcripts of Manson's 1970, 1986, and 1992 parole hearings in a lengthy appendix. Much of this material once could be found on the Web site maintained by Manson's confidant St George at http://www .atwa.com. Transcribed lyrics to several of his songs can be found in *The Garbage People* (Omega Press, 1971) by John Gilmore and Ron Kenner.

Among the interviews given by Manson, including his parole interviews, for which I have either VHS videotapes or written transcripts and which I used for this piece are:

1981 "The Tomorrow Show" with Tom Snyder
1985 interview with "Maurie Povich"
1986 "Nightwatch" with Charlie Rose
1989 "Inside story" with Patti Daniels
1981 interview with Geraldo Rivera
1991 Hard Copy Interview "Charlie Manson Today"
1994 Diane Sawyer "Turning Point" Interview "The Manson Women"
Parole Hearings:
1970, 1977, 1982, 1986, 1992, 1997

7. JASON—SHAM—TOO

I

The epigraph is from Thomas Haskell's *Objectivity is Not Neutrality* (Johns Hopkins University Press, 1998). Camille Paglia's *Sexual Personae: Art and Decadence from Nefertiti to Emily Dickinson* (Yale University Press, 1990), especially the first chapter "Sex and violence or nature and Art," was one of the most important books of the 1990s. The Ben Franklin quote is from his *Autobiography.* Scanlon is one of the acutes in Kesey's *Cuckoo's Nest.* Thomas Ricks, military reporter for the *Washington Post,* wrote *Fiasco* (Penguin, 2007), a history of the screw-ups that got us mired in the Iraq war. Julie Stephens *Anti-disciplinary Protest: Sixties Radicalism and Post-modernism* (Cambridge University Press, 1998) makes an attempt to search out the post-modernist aspects of the late Sixties. For Richard Rorty's contribution, his *Contingency, Irony, and Solidarity* (Cambridge University Press, 1989) is the best source.

Books on or about or trying to explain Post-modernism abound but most are almost incomprehensible. I like *A Postmodern Reader* edited by Natoli and Hutcheson for its presentation of a number of different attempts to corral the monster. But Post-modernism is not an ism nor an it and by its practitioners own boasts cannot be defined as a unity or a consistent school of thought. At best, it is a variety of approaches that share some but not all attributes and thus cannot really be defined. Zygmaunt Bauman's "Living with Ambivalence," the lead essay in this collection, offers a good example of the genre and the problem. For Jacques Derrida himself, the late writings on religion are for this reference the most useful. *Religion,* edited by Derrida and Gianni Vattimo (Stanford 1998) contains Derrida's "Faith and Knowledge: the two sources of religion' at the limits of reason alone." See also *Post-Modernism and Christian Philosophy* Edited by Roman Ciapolo (American Maritain Assoc, 1997); *Theology and Social Theory* by John Milbank (Oxford University Press, 1990); and *Essays in Postfoundationalist Theology* by Wentzel and Huyssten (Grand Rapids, 1997). Several books have attempted to link Post-modernism to the Sixties on the lame connection that both are anti-establishment without as much as a nod to the glaring contradiction that the sixties radicalism was based on an essentialist romantic spirit which Post-modernism explicitly rejects. See, for instance, Marianne DeKoven *Utopia Limited* (Duke University Press, 2004). The words of Norman O. Brown can, once again, be found in *Love's Body* (op. cit.). The Merovingian's speech can be found in *The Matrix Reloaded* (Warner Brothers, 2003.)

II

The epigraph is from Daniel Quinn's *Ishmael: An Adventure of the Mind and Spirit* (Bantam 1992) one of the cult books of the nineties beloved by latter-day hippies. Jonathan Edwards essay "The Mind" can be found in the Yale edition of his works titled *Scientific and Philosophical Writings.* The quotes from Martin Luther King are from *Why We can't Wait* (op. cit.).

III

For an explanation of Barth's "NO" of God's word, see *The Word of God and the Word of Man* (London, 1928). The quote from Martin Heidegger is from *Being and Time* (New York, 1962), p. 44. Hooker's sermons "The Soules Humiliation (1637) and "The Soules Preparation for Christ, Or, A Treatise of Contrition" (1632) are useful for anyone open to a post-modern reading of Puritan theology. Ken Kesey's interview in the *Paris Review* can be found in the Spring 1994 edition, number 130. The line from Thoreau is from *Walden,* the chapter titled "Where I Lived and What I lived For."

IV

The section on Bob Dylan and Emily Dickinson was published previously in two places: *Crawdaddy* (#19 Spring 1998) and *On The Tracks* (Spring 1998). The quotes from Dylan are mostly from his 1997 album "Time out of Mind." The quotations from Emily Dickinson are from the Johnson edition of her works. Edward Taylor's poem can be found in Harrison Meserole's *Seventeenth century American Poetry* (Anchor, 1967). Faulkner's quote is from "The Bear" one of the stories in *Go Down Moses* (Vintage, 1990). Greil Marcus in *Mystery Train: Images of America* (Dutton, 1976) demonstrates a powerful feel for the spiritual links that tie our own culture back to the old religion. This quote is from his chapter on Robert Johnson.

V

The quotes from John Calvin are from his *Institutes of the Christian Religion* (op. cit.). Increase Mather's prayer is from "The Mystery of Israel's Salvation" reprinted in *The Puritans in America,* Alan Heimert and Andrew Delbanco, eds. (Harvard University Press, 1985).

Index